CREATING INSECURITY

This book is dedicated to my parents.

Critical Security Series

Series Editors:
Neil Renwick and Nana Poku

Editorial Board:
Richard Bedford, *University of Waikato*
Tony Evans, *University of Southampton*
Tony Mcgrew, *University of Southampton*
Mark Miller, *University of Delaware*
Robert Morrell, *University of Natal*
David Newman, *Ben Gurion University*
Fiona Robinson, *Carleton University*
Peter Vale, *University of Western Cape*

Creating Insecurity
Realism, Constructivism, and US Security Policy

ANTHONY D. LOTT
St. Olaf College

LONDON AND NEW YORK

First published 2004 by Ashgate Publishing

Reissued 2018 by Routledge
2 Park Square, Milton Park, Abingdon, Oxon OX14 4RN
711 Third Avenue, New York, NY 10017, USA

Routledge is an imprint of the Taylor & Francis Group, an informa business

First issued in paperback 2018

© Anthony D. Lott 2004

Anthony D. Lott has asserted his right under the Copyright, Designs and Patents
Act, 1988, to be identified as the author of this work.

All rights reserved. No part of this book may be reprinted or reproduced or
utilised in any form or by any electronic, mechanical, or other means, now
known or hereafter invented, including photocopying and recording, or in any
information storage or retrieval system, without permission in writing from the
publishers.

A Library of Congress record exists under LC control number: 2003065199

Notice:
Product or corporate names may be trademarks or registered trademarks, and are
used only for identification and explanation without intent to infringe.

Publisher's Note
The publisher has gone to great lengths to ensure the quality of this reprint but
points out that some imperfections in the original copies may be apparent.

Disclaimer
The publisher has made every effort to trace copyright holders and welcomes
correspondence from those they have been unable to contact.

ISBN 13: 978-0-815-38827-2 (hbk)
ISBN 13: 978-1-138-62200-5 (pbk)
ISBN 13: 978-1-351-16088-9 (ebk)

Contents

Acknowledgements	*vii*
1 Introduction	1
The Historical Origins of the Current Crisis	3
The Argument that Follows	7
2 Realists on Security	10
Morgenthau	10
Herz	12
Wolfers	14
Waltz	15
Buzan	17
Realism and the Traditional Study of Security	20
The Success and Failure of the Traditional Approach	25
3 Constructivists on Security	27
Writing Security	28
Security, Identity, and Interests	31
The Culture of National Security	35
Security: A New Framework for Analysis	38
Constructivism and the Study of Security	40
The Successes and Failures of Constructivism	46
4 Understanding the Sources of Insecurity	48
Constructivism as Epistemology	51
Interpreting Politics	53
Realism, Cautious Paranoia, and Material Capabilities	54
Political Constructivism, Identity, and Cultural Reflection	56
Balancing Security Considerations	64
5 Creating Insecurity I: Unilateral BMD Development and U.S. Security	68
The History of BMD Development	70
Realism and BMD Development	77
Political Constructivism and BMD Development	87

vi   *Creating Insecurity*

    Enhancing Security   93

6 Creating Insecurity II: U.S. Policy Toward Colombia   98

    Colombian History and U.S. Policy   99
    Realism and the War on Drugs   108
    Political Constructivism and the War on Drugs   112
    Enhancing Security   116

7 Creating Insecurity III: Democracy, Globalization, and Protests
from Below   120

    A History of the Democratic Peace and U.S. Policy   121
    Sophisticated Realism and the Democratic Peace   125
    Political Constructivism and the Concept of Democracy   128
    Enhancing Democratic Security   134

8 Creating Insecurity IV: Regime Change, WMD, and the Invasion
of Iraq   137

    The United States and a *Casus belli* for War with Iraq   138
    A Realist Interpretation of U.S. Policy   142
    A Political Constructivist Interpretation of U.S. Policy   150
    Toward a Balanced Critique of the U.S. Invasion of Iraq   154

9 Conclusion   156

Bibliography   *162*
Index   *175*

Acknowledgements

While I take complete responsibility for the opinions offered and the arguments put forth in this work, I am unable to claim it as my own. The staff at both the Watzek Library at Lewis and Clark College and the Wilson Library at the University of Minnesota provided research assistance and a quiet environment within which to work. Anne Keirby, Kirstin Howgate, Carolyn Court and Maureen Mansell-Ward at Ashgate made the editing and publishing process enjoyable. Through long discussions and feeble early drafts, friends and colleagues challenged me to develop these ideas more completely and push the boundaries of our discipline. Their thoughts are imprinted on the pages that follow. Alan Gilbert pushed me to undertake this work with a gentle hand and a reminder of the need to make this world a better place. Karen Feste provided a detailed and thorough analysis of the arguments as they emerged and challenged me to stick to the task when it seemed daunting. Jack Donnelly required me to defend the weakest of my arguments and strengthen the strongest; much work remains in this regard. Lewis Griffith undertook a thorough reading of this work near the end stage and offered valuable comments and insight. Gary Scott and Craig Carr spent time throughout the process pushing me to think critically about the ideas expressed and cajoling me to keep at it. Gary Scott, Craig Carr, Lisa Simons, Lisa Schunk, Maria Montello, and Skippy carried me through the writing process with necessary distractions beyond the halls of academia. Finally, this work would remain incomplete without the support and assistance of my family. Jennifer and Stephanie Lott coped with the eccentricities of their brother and remained supportive friends as well. My parents, Susie and Nick Lott, to whom this book is dedicated, demanded of their son just one thing: to find something in life he enjoyed that would benefit others in some way. I cannot express in words my gratitude to them for their love, support, and patience. In addition, their work editing and preparing the manuscript resulted in the pages that follow.

Chapter 1

Introduction

What is security? It has long been the dominant issue in international politics. Every successful theoretical approach to the study of the relations between states is prefaced on a commitment to understanding the concept. But while this can be stated with a high level of assurance, it is also the case that the subject of security and the sources of perceived insecurity are varied and problematic. During the Cold War, the concept was linked to the protection of the state and issues were framed as 'national security' concerns. Accordingly, security was associated with territorial integrity and the preservation of sovereignty. The physical base of the state required the vigilance of a *national security apparatus* dedicated to recognizing the capabilities and intentions of others. This version of security further rests on a subjective core that manages perceptions of threat and the enemy. However, the constraints of the Cold War mandated that these perceptions be left unproblematic in order to manage the policy relevant and immediate problems of securing the state.

But as the Cold War came to an end, alternative voices could be heard advocating versions of security that seem to contradict the focus and energy of the Cold War studies. Recognizing that emphasis on the state as the primary referent of security marginalized much of the human condition, more recent works focus on *human* security concerns. These works note the often deleterious effect that a state may have on human welfare.[1] In addition to this negative effect of the state on individual security, founding the concept of security on the state amounts to making a category error. The individual can be the only true referent of security, and the state, simply an instrument for the protection of that primary referent.[2]

These two interpretations of security appear incommensurable. At the same time, neither interpretation invalidates the other. Even before the events of 11 September 2001, the physical integrity of the state remained a central concern for

---

1 See, for instance, the collection of essays in Keith Krause and Michael C. Williams, eds., *Critical Security Studies* (Minneapolis, MN: University of Minnesota Press, 1997); Nana Poku and David T. Graham, eds., *Redefining Security: Population Movements and National Security* (Westport, CT: Praeger Publishers, 1998); Richard Ullman, 'Redefining Security,' *International Security* 8 (Summer 1983), pp. 129-153; Jessica Tuchman Mathews, 'Redefining Security,' *Foreign Affairs* 68 (Spring 1982), pp. 162-177.

2 Bill McSweeney, *Security, Identity and Interests: A Sociology of International Relations* (Cambridge: Cambridge University Press, 1999), p. 33.

2 *Creating Insecurity*

the policy maker and realist scholar. The concept of *national security* still resonates with IR theorists as the state continues to be the primary political unit in world politics. Yet, developments in human rights, global ecology, and economic development strategies, as well as the success of transnational civil society in constructing action networks for the promotion of disparate political issues,[3] make the logic of human security more acceptable to mainstream security scholars. Moreover, the importance of *culture* as a variable in understanding insecurity has emerged from the mainstream box in which it was kept.[4] Recognizing the importance of both approaches to security, however, only returns us to our initial question: *what is security*?

This project is intended to bring together these seemingly contradictory approaches to the study of security. However, it is not my intention to build a meta-theoretical device that can bridge the serious epistemological, ontological, and methodological differences that animate the various approaches. Rather, a more modest attempt will be made to balance a critical form of realism with the political discourses that are emerging out of constructivist writers in Security Studies. Doing so, it is hoped that various insecurities can be seen in a new way. I begin with the premise that there is something fundamentally important about *national* security matters. At this point in human history, the state plays a necessary role in mitigating the uncertainties of international anarchy for its citizens.[5] While this may not hold true for all states in the system, it does hold for citizens living in 'reasonably decent polities.'[6] Where states have accepted the responsibility for protecting their citizens, the security of the state is a prerequisite for the security of the individual. To this interpretation, however, we must inquire as to what those studies that question the emphasis on the state can contribute to our understanding of security. Even if the state can be incorporated into an account of security such that it becomes a tool for the betterment of the human condition, it may also be the case that traditional or mainstream studies of security, rooted in the events of the Cold War, rest on faulty epistemological premises – these studies may not adequately conceptualize security. If this is the case, then it is our responsibility to reflect on the current state of Security Studies and offer an understanding of the sources of

---

3 See, for example, Margaret E. Keck and Kathryn Sikkink, *Activists Beyond Borders: Advocacy Networks in International Politics* (Ithaca, NY: Cornell University Press, 1998); Ronnie D. Lipschutz, ed., *On Security* (New York: Columbia University Press, 1995).

4 Jutta Weldes, Mark Laffey, Hugh Gusterson, and Raymond Duvall, eds., *Cultures of Insecurity: States, Communities, and the Production of Danger* (Minneapolis, MN: University of Minnesota Press, 1999).

5 Barry Buzan, *People, States & Fear: An Agenda for International Security Studies in the Post-Cold War Era*, 2nd edition (Boulder, CO: Lynne Rienner Publishers, 1991), p. 70.

6 Craig Carr uses the term 'reasonably decent polities' in a discussion of fairness and obligation. See, Craig L. Carr, 'Fairness and Political Obligation,' *Social Theory and Practice* 28 (January 2002), pp. 1-28.

Introduction 3

insecurity that reflects both the earlier realist focus on national security and the more recent focus by constructivists on epistemological coherence and cultural influence.

Before turning to an introduction of the chapters that follow, the discussion below explores the historical roots of the security crisis now confronting the field. The growing schism within Security Studies suggests further conceptual thinking is necessary. Traditional studies, often espousing realist principles and consistently empiricist, insist on a military and strategic emphasis. These studies seem wedded to a particular interpretation of international politics and its study. Conversely, studies drawing on a broadly-defined constructivism often eschew state security concerns and focus on problematizing identity constructs in order to render secondary military and strategic matters. Both approaches undermine the development of a more comprehensive study of security. Traditional concerns resting on a faulty epistemology, while focused on the policy-relevant topic of national security, collapse in incoherence and incompleteness. Just the same, constructivist renderings of identity and culture that do not address state policy concerns collapse in irrelevance. As the study of security bridges the divide between theory and policy, it is imperative that a concept of security emerge that is both philosophically coherent and policy relevant. In what follows, the historical origins of the current crisis are explored in an attempt to understand the task that lies before us in the subsequent chapters.

The Historical Origins of the Current Crisis

The origins of IR as a distinct field of study and the pursuit of international peace by scholars and statesmen must be seen as more than mere coincidence. The concurrent desire for both national and international security lies at the heart of the Anglo-American IR community formed at the beginning of the Twentieth Century.[7] Recognizing the limitations of human nature and the constraints of the international system, scholars sought either to mitigate or transcend the sources of insecurity. Historically, these early works pitted idealists who advocated legal and moral mechanisms that would transcend insecurity against realists who sought to mitigate the dangerous excesses of insecurity.

While both approaches desired the same end- *peace and security*- the events of World War II demonstrated the 'ineffective and dangerous policies' advocated by legal and moral idealists.[8] The texts of post-war realists like

---

7 Ken Booth, 'Security and Self: Reflections of a Fallen Realist,' in Krause and Williams, p. 114.

8 For a discussion of the legal and moral idealists, see, Yale H. Ferguson and Richard W. Mansbach, *The Elusive Quest: Theory and International Politics* (Columbia, SC: University of South Carolina Press, 1988), pp. 91-97.

4 *Creating Insecurity*

Carr,[9] Morgenthau,[10] Herz,[11] and Kennan[12] became required material for those attempting to understand international relations and construct a more stable and secure international system. Realism quickly became synonymous with the study of security, and as the politics of the Cold War constrained the actions of states and the theoretical investigation of those actions, an inseparable link between realism and strategic studies was forged.[13] Realism quickly took on an aire of theoretical invulnerability. Its precepts and premises were taken to be governing laws of the behavior between states, and realism was considered a general theory of international relations.[14]

Realism's apparent success at explaining the behavior of states, however, masked two substantive flaws that would later confront both the theory and the field of Security Studies. At a general epistemological level, realism's commitment to empiricism resulted in truth claims about the world that suggested an opportunity to understand the world from an *'objective'* perspective. These claims sought to describe the world as it existed- objectifying threats and reducing the explanatory role of particular cultural constructs.[15] Realism became a strategic science- reducing the likelihood of war by more accurately maintaining a balance between states. A second flaw in the logic of realism followed from the first. Because a close association between realism and strategic studies made high political issues salient, security became synonymous with military matters.[16] Thus, while a close inspection of realist texts finds that security is not explicitly limited to military and strategic concerns,[17] the corpus of security works could not help but be limited to the overriding issues of the Cold War.[18]

The end of hostilities between the U.S. and the U.S.S.R. and the rise of constructivism as an alternative approach to the study of world politics presented a

---

9 Edward Hallett Carr, *The Twenty Years' Crisis, 1919-1939: An Introduction to the Study of International Relations*, 2nd edition (New York: Harper and Row, Publishers, 1964).

10 Hans J. Morgenthau, 'The Mainsprings of American Foreign Policy: The National Interest vs. Moral Abstractions,' *American Political Science Review* 44 (December 1950), pp. 833-854; Hans J. Morgenthau, *Politics Among Nations: The Struggle for Power and Peace*, 5th edition (New York: Alfred A. Knopf, 1972).

11 John H. Herz, *Political Realism and Political Idealism* (Chicago: University of Chicago Press, 1951).

12 George Kennan, *Realities of American Foreign Policy* (Princeton: Princeton University Press, 1954).

13 Buzan, p. 8.

14 Ferguson and Mansbach, p. 96.

15 Barry Buzan, Ole Waever, and Jaap de Wilde, *Security: A New Framework For Analysis* (Boulder, CO: Lynne Rienner Publishers, 1998), p. 204.

16 Buzan, *People, States & Fear*, p. 10.

17 See, for instance, Harold Brown, *Thinking About National Security: Defense and Foreign Policy in a Dangerous World* (Boulder, CO: Westview Press, 1983), p. xii; Amos A Jordan and William J. Taylor, Jr., revised ed, *American National Security: Policy and Process* (Baltimore, MD: The Johns Hopkins University Press, 1984), p. 3.

18 Buzan, *People, States & Fear*, p. 10.

Introduction

5

challenge to the empiricist-dominated field. Following Wittgenstein, it could be argued that the limits of our language were the limits of our world.[19] Language, in other words, allows us to make sense of the world we inhabit. What we take to be threats represent linguistic claims rather than objective facts.[20] This does not mean that theorists become 'security relativists'. However, by claiming that language is the central factor in determining the sources of insecurity, constructivists have uncovered social facts that remained hidden in Cold War studies. The importance of language also represented a new way to view the realism. Instead of describing the world as it is, the post-positivist approach to epistemology explored in this study, and loosely termed *constructivism,* demonstrates that realism is actually a sophisticated interpretation of a particular world-view. Realism's force comes not from understanding it as a theory of international politics but rather its application as a rhetorical tool to influence the policy maker.

The question soon arises, however, that if realism is mere rhetoric, then no matter how sophisticated it is, why should its precepts and premises be judged any more important than those of other approaches? Drawing further on constructivist principles, scholars have re-examined the importance of *identity* and *culture* and demonstrated how entrenched cultural constructs and embedded identities result in specific interpretations of enemies and threats. Moreover, these studies suggest that conscious *reflection* can adjust the ideational construct of the enemy. Therefore, the negative and pessimistic world-view of the realists may be both incomplete and exaggerated. The search for security may lie in a group's collective critique of its own enemy perception rather than its defense by material means. Realism seems to provide only half of the security story.

In addition to the concern for both epistemological coherence and the inclusion of culture and identity, alternative approaches to security studies also demand a re-interpretation of the concept itself in the aftermath of the Cold War. Closer examination of the state's role in protecting citizens and a heightened concern for human (individual) welfare requires that realism answer for its state-centric bias and infrequent discussion of complex welfare issues. Alternative approaches seek to demonstrate how many states in the system represent a hazard to individual security rather than a means for its promotion.[21] In addition, complex

---

19 Ludwig Wittgenstein, *Tractatus Logico-Philosophicus,* trans. D.F. Pears and B.F. McGuiness (London: Routledge and Kegan Paul, 1961), p. 115.

20 Here, Wittgenstein's discussion of logic and the limits of the world is intriguing. 'Logic pervades the world: the limits of the world are also its limits. So we cannot say in logic, 'The world has this in it, and this, but not that.' For that would appear to presuppose that we were excluding certain possibilities, and this cannot be the case, since it would require that logic should go beyond the limits of the world; for only in that way could it view those limits from the other side as well. We cannot think what we cannot think; so what we cannot think we cannot *say* either.' Ibid.

21 See, for instance, Brian L. Job, 'The Insecurity Dilemma: National, Regime, and State Insecurities in the Third World,' in *The Insecurity Dilemma: National Security of Third World States* (Boulder, CO: Lynne Rienner, Publishers, 1992).

6 *Creating Insecurity*

environmental, economic, and societal issues have recently been labeled *security concerns* in an attempt to jettison studies of security from the constraints of the Cold War paradigm.[22]

The effect on national security discourse could not be sharper. A growing schism now appears in the field. Committed to a traditional emphasis on national security issues and a reliance on a negative view of human relations, traditional works dismiss the constructivist challenge as policy-irrelevant and esoteric in principle. Similarly, committed to raising new questions that have been subsumed by realism's dominance, alternative approaches demonstrate the incoherence of realist tenets and the marginalization of pressing welfare matters. Intransigence on both sides leaves the study of security in a rather schizophrenic state.[23] More to the point, the theoretical pursuit of security risks being marginalized by bureaucratic agencies and political actors that consider the concept apolitical, requiring little more than policy implementation.[24]

It is during this moment of crisis that a re-evaluation of the concept of security becomes necessary. There can be little doubt that a limited conceptual understanding of *national* security, accepting the state as the central focus of study, is an attractive feature of realism even as global transformative processes challenge our historical understanding of the importance of the state. When the Low Countries were devastated during the *Blitzkrieg* or the jetliners crashed into the World Trade Towers, it is the physical integrity of the state that has been compromised. At these moments, individual security requires a sufficient national security apparatus for enhancement. This offered, however, it is also the case that the above account of language as representing the limits of our world offers a much more coherent epistemological base than the naked empiricism recurring in realist thought. In addition, what role culture and identity might play in the development of a robust security policy seems to require further study.

To this debate, we must also introduce more practical political problems that require attention. Any useful study of security must not only be theoretically sound, it must be applicable to the relations between states. This commitment to practical political matters was true before 11 September 2001, but now takes on added urgency. If the concept of security is to resonate, then it must be applicable to the political units capable of producing system-wide effects because of their policies. In today's international climate, this means that the concept of security must make sense to and remain cogent for the United States and other powerful actors. Power and influence still matter in an environment defined by the anarchical relations between sovereign states. In sympathy with constructivist concerns for language,

---

22 See Poku and Graham; Ullman; and Tuchman Mathews, supra note 1; and Simon Dalby, *Environmental Security* (Minneapolis, MN: University of Minnesota Press, 2002).

23 Ian Clark, *Globalization and International Relations Theory* (Oxford: Oxford University Press, 1999), p. 125.

24 Ronnie D. Lipschutz, 'Negotiating the Boundaries of Difference and Security at Millennium's End,' in *On Security*, pp. 214-215.

we might recognize the role that the hegemon plays in the articulation and promotion of specific speech-acts. The actions of the U.S. have a profound influence on the way states relate to each other. While other actors will play a (significant) role in the political world that emerges in the future, the extent to which that world is tied to neoliberal economic strategies, multilateral security programs and the principles of international law will be determined primarily by the actions of the United States. The ability to reflect on and interpret U.S. security issues is a necessary addition to a more comprehensive understanding of security. This is more than an argument for disciplinary expediency. The moral requirements of speaking truth to power are ever-present in the construction of a coherent concept of security. In order to speak truth to power, theorists must be engaged critics, meeting the state at a point that is both intellectually honest and policy relevant. The pages that follow seek to find such a meeting point.

The Argument that Follows

In the chapters that follow, I will explore what a sophisticated form of realism and a political form of constructivism have to offer us in our attempt to build a robust understanding of security that can be used to implement successful policy. Chapter two explores the use of realism as a rhetorical tool for understanding the necessities of power and the limitations of moral and legal mechanisms to achieving security ends. I seek to demonstrate that while realism does not succeed as a general theory of international politics, it does provide a necessary understanding of the relationship between national security and human welfare in 'reasonably decent polities.'[25] Moreover, realists have often been considered apologists for the state. This reading of realism, however, articulates a critical side of realist thought that is substantially at odds with the policy making apparatus of the state. This critical undercurrent in realist literature suggests an opportunity to return to the tenets of realism in subsequent chapters when offering a concept of security that remains policy relevant while incorporating the concerns of constructivists.

Chapter three will explore the ways in which constructivism (as an epistemology) can be used in an analysis of security concerns. I will begin this chapter with a discussion of language, interpretation, and the social construction of threats. It is then necessary to outline the success of previous constructivist texts in better conceptualizing security. However, the major drawback for all constructivist studies is their collective lack of a policy-oriented focus which allows the state to implement findings. This shortcoming will be discussed as one of the primary problems confronting Security Studies today. In addition, it suggests the need to move beyond the corpus of constructivist security texts in an attempt to build a more policy-relevant approach.

---

25 Carr, p. 1.

8   *Creating Insecurity*

In chapter four, this attempt to move beyond the limitations of the current constructivist texts will be developed further. By re-introducing realism into the broad epistemological arena offered by constructivists, it becomes possible to re-orient the field and engage in policy-relevant discussions. After demonstrating the importance of an epistemological constructivism, I will bring together a critical form of *realism* that engages in a dialogue with the policy maker and a *political constructivism* that presents the value-laden lens through which the security constructivist often operates. Realism and political constructivism both offer something to the construction of a Security Studies that is theoretically focused and policy relevant. Balancing the concerns of each, it will be demonstrated that both approaches not only complement each other but become necessary for this more comprehensive reading of the sources of insecurity.

Having articulated the theoretical apparatus that moves this study forward, chapters five through eight contain applications of this approach to U.S. security issues. These applications are not intended to stand as comprehensive case studies concerning U.S. security practices; such an endeavor goes beyond the scope of this work and would, I am convinced, require three separate, detailed works of their own. Rather, the applications below demonstrate how an understanding of security that balances the state-centric and policy relevant approach of critical realists with the identity-conscious concerns of the constructivists might be employed to (re)view current U.S. security questions. In chapter five, I will focus on a central security theme that has engaged analysts during and after the Cold War. Debate surrounding a national missile defense system provides an interesting instance of created insecurity. By re-examining the issue in light of the theoretical work discussed below, I seek to demonstrate the hidden sources of insecurity that exist outside the mainstream epistemological boundaries of Security Studies and articulate how realists and political constructivists might be employed together to enhance that understanding of insecurity while simultaneously offering a means to move beyond the current security deficit.

In chapter six, a regional example is explored that further demonstrates the applicability of this approach to U.S. security issues. Studying the current war on drugs in the Andean region (with special attention paid to Colombia) provides another instance of policy development during and after the Cold War. Here again, the point is to examine how the United States may in fact be undermining its security interests and creating its own insecurity. By analyzing how instances of security are interpreted and formed by the language employed, we can develop an understanding of the particular threats envisioned by U.S. policy makers. Balancing the complex sets of issues discussed by realists and political constructivists allows a picture of the drug war to emerge that links the domestic agenda in the U.S. with the foreign policies pursued in the Andean region. It also places a number of issues into the discussion of narcotics security that have been marginalized in many mainstream works.

The seventh chapter explores the relationship between national security and democracy. It has been argued that democracy requires the presence of a stable

Introduction   9

national security apparatus in order to flourish. It has also been argued that the perpetuation of democratic governance and economic globalization around the globe will enhance national and international security. Both arguments avoid meaningful discussion of the concepts they employ. The discussion in chapter seven questions both premises by taking *democracy* and *national security* seriously. Here, too, by balancing the concerns of realists with political constructivists it is demonstrated that a robust form of deliberative democracy is a prerequisite for national security. A democratic society that pursues the common good is quite different from the procedural forms analyzed by democratic peace scholars. The theoretical approach discussed below provides a way into this discussion by advocating the importance of language and identity performances.

The eighth chapter examines the policy rationale for seeking regime change in Iraq. As will be demonstrated, the decision to go to war is a striking example of creating insecurity. While it is too early to provide a thorough historical review of U.S. policy towards the Hussein regime and the WMD programs that existed in the minds of U.S. policy makers, it is clear that the myriad foreign policies of the United States towards Iraq have created a number of instances of insecurity. Returning to the theoretical approach taken here, I seek to outline how realists and political constructivists view U.S. policy toward Iraq. Then, in keeping with the goal of this book, a balanced security analysis that takes into account the material issues of the realists and the ideational concerns of the political constructivists will be outlined.

Chapter 2

Realists on Security

Realism plays a central role in the development of International Relations as a discipline throughout the Twentieth Century. In the sub-field of Security Studies, the influence of realist scholars quietly linked the theoretical disposition to military and strategic matters for decades. This chapter investigates the interpretation of the state and international relations by traditional security scholars. Here the connection between realism and security is made clear. By analyzing the writings of five realist scholars, Morgenthau, Herz, Wolfers, Waltz, and Buzan, we will be able to recognize key features present in each text. In order to recognize these features, each author will be examined using a similar format. First, I will explore each writer's concept of security. While some of the authors below resist defining such a contestable term, each does offer insight into its scope and limits. Then, I will examine how each seeks to advise the policy maker so as to bring about enhanced security. In the remaining sections, I will summarize the similarities and differences that animate these realist texts and then discuss the successes and failures inherent in the current understanding of realism and national security studies. Doing so, it is hoped, we will come to see realism as a *rhetorical* device used to influence the state rather than a general theory of international politics. It also becomes clear that realists often offer a critical assessment of state policies rather than an apology for those policies.

Morgenthau

The writings of Hans Morgenthau engage our first discussion of realism and security. His concern, specifically, is with defense of the national interest and the pursuit and containment of power. Yet in his observations of both the national interest and power, we can make certain inferences concerning his understanding of the importance of security. Indeed, in the past, if realism has been confused with national security studies, it is unlikely that Morgenthau will provide us with a means to differentiate the two issues.

For Morgenthau, the concept of security ultimately rests on a subjective or psychological base. In discussing the requirements of a state to arm itself against others, he writes, '[t]he generally professed and most frequent actual motive for armaments is *fear* of attack; that is, a *feeling of insecurity.*[1] However, Morgenthau is committed to recognizing that a feeling of security results from material conditions that bring about the subsequent psychological condition. Understanding the relationship to material conditions allows us to find a link between Morgenthau's concept of the national interest and his concern with security.[2] Speaking of the United States, Morgenthau writes that it 'pursued a policy seeking to maintain at first its security and very soon its predominance of the Western Hemisphere.'[3] This is the primary (national) interest in U.S. foreign policy during its formative years and remains so into the mid-Twentieth Century. Thus, Morgenthau links the concept of security to physical integrity and sovereignty.

Here we recognize a further component of Morgenthau's understanding of security. The state represents the primary referent. This component to his work is a given and does not require further analysis. In addition, although the concept of security may rest on subjective feelings, it is the collective feelings represented in the state that informs Morgenthau's understanding. To this psychological component, Morgenthau makes clear that no state can survive where there remains an external threat to its integrity, i.e., its physical safety.[4]

These two components make up Morgenthau's elementary understanding of security. *Feeling* secure allows a state to stop arming. From an existential viewpoint, *being* secure means a state is not in physical danger of attack from beyond its borders. Finally, security lies at the heart of the national interest. And, achieving the national interest requires that states counter-balance the pursuit of power with the possibilities of diplomacy. In one attempt to explicate his understanding of the national interest, Morgenthau writes, 'it assumes continuous conflict and threat of war, to be minimized through the continuous adjustment of conflicting interests by diplomatic action.'[5] Leaving aside the problematic nature of Morgenthau's use of this term, it is clear that he centers his concept on the psychological components of security discussed above.

Morgenthau's writings are not dedicated to explaining terms but seem rather to be written as advice to statesmen and the broader polity. Therefore, while Morgenthau's concept of security may lack clarity, his desire to see it achieved through particular policy recommendations expands our understanding of his view of the state and international relations. Two policy recommendations, in particular, seem central to Morgenthau's quest for security. First, like many realists, Morgenthau recognizes the practical limits of goodwill in international politics and

---

1   Hans J. Morgenthau, *Politics Among Nations: The Struggle for Power and Peace*, 5th edition (New York: Alfred A Knopf, Inc., 1972), p. 404. *My italics.*
2   Ibid.
3   Hans J. Morgenthau, *Politics in the Twentieth Century: The Impasse of American Foreign Policy*, volume two (Chicago: University of Chicago Press, 1962), p. 56.
4   Ibid.
5   Hans J. Morgenthau, 'Another "Great Debate": The National Interest of the United States,' *American Political Science Review* 46 (December 1952), p. 978.

12   *Creating Insecurity*

the requirements incumbent on each state actor to ensure a proper defense.[6] Second, the ability to balance power with power represents one of the finer arts of diplomacy and a requirement for good state management.[7]

Minimizing the level of uncertainty (i.e., managing insecurity) represents the logical limit of international politics for Morgenthau. This need to limit uncertainty manifests itself in the requirements for an effective foreign policy.

> To minimize these hazards is the first task of a foreign policy which seeks the defense of the national interest by peaceful means. Its second task is the defense of the national interest, restrictively and rationally defined, against the national interests of other nations which may or may not be thus defined. If they are not, it becomes the task of armed diplomacy to convince the nations concerned that their legitimate interests have nothing to fear from a restrictive and rational foreign policy and that their illegitimate interests have nothing to gain in the face of armed might rationally employed.[8]

Beyond the advocacy of strategies that first seek peaceful solutions and then insist on force, statesmen are also admonished to seek policies that balance against the power of other states. Morgenthau insists on making the balance of power a central part of any foreign policy strategy that attempts to defend the national interest. Speaking of U.S. policy in particular, Morgenthau notes that the creation or restoration of a balance of power in the international system has been at the core of U.S. diplomatic and military strategy since the beginning of the Nineteenth Century.[9] A consistent policy of balancing strengthens the position of the U.S. and enhances national security.

Absolute security appears as a utopian ideal in Morgenthau's writings. But while absolute security cannot be achieved, insecurity can be mitigated through the careful application of strategies that signal to others the power possessed by a state and the intent to defend that state against hostile actions by another state or the accumulation of power by any state in the system.

Herz

While Morgenthau's treatment of security suggests that it is assumed to be a necessary value, John Herz considers the concept central to his understanding of world politics. For Herz, insecurity is an environmental effect of anarchy. 'Wherever such anarchic society has existed... there has arisen what might be called a "security dilemma"'.[10] This condition occurs no matter the nature of

---

6   Ibid.

7   Ibid.

8   Ibid.

9   Morgenthau, *Politics in the Twentieth Century*, p. 57.

10 John H. Herz, 'Idealist Internationalism and the Security Dilemma,' *World Politics* 2 (January 1950), p. 157.

Realists on Security

particular actors. Indeed, social cooperation and pacific feelings only enhance the consequences of anarchy as these elements invigorate particular identities thereby strengthening inter-group competition.[11] At some point, whether it is at the individual, group, or state level, all units living in anarchy confront the requirement of security and the constraints of the security dilemma. Mirroring Morgenthau's concept, it is first a psychological condition (Herz calls it an urge)[12] and second a physical necessity (linked to power defined by capabilities).[13] Founding realism on a preeminent desire to seek security as an ultimate end, Herz finds realism and security fundamentally linked and often indistinguishable. 'Realist thought is determined by an overpowering impact of the security factor.'[14] With the rise of the state system, Herz, again like Morgenthau, is drawn to link power and security to the state and recognize that while other actors participate in world politics, it is the state that becomes the primary referent for the pursuit of security.[15]

But, while the pursuit of security is an inevitable requirement for those existing in anarchy, Herz demands that a successful strategy for achieving national security requires that policy makers go beyond the realist pursuit of power. This is a striking component of Herz's advice to statesmen and parallels Morgenthau's desire to see policies of peace balanced with policies of force.[16] In his advocacy, Herz seeks to balance the inevitable pursuit of power with pacific strategies. He calls his policy advice 'realist liberalism' and grounds it in the following remark by Huxley, which should remain intact for our purposes.

> The practices of that which is ethically best involves a course of conduct which, in all respects, is opposed to that which leads to success in the cosmic struggle for existence. In place of ruthless self-assertion, it demands self-restraint; in place of thrusting aside, or treading down, all competitors, it requires that the individual shall not merely respect, but shall help his fellows; its influence is directed, not so much to the survival of the fittest, as the fitting of as many as possible to survive. It repudiates the gladiatorial theory of existence.... The ethical progress of society depends, not on imitating the cosmic process, still less in running away from it, but in combating it.[17]

The logic of the security dilemma and the need to pursue power strategies remain a central feature for Herz. However, 'in international relations the mitigation, channeling, balancing, or control of power has prevailed perhaps more often than the inevitability of power politics would lead one to believe.'[18] While the

---

11 Ibid., p. 158.
12 Ibid.
13 Ibid.
14 Ibid.
15 Ibid., p. 173.
16 Morgenthau, 'Another 'Great Debate', p. 978.
17 Thomas H. Huxley, *Evolution and Ethics and Other Essays* (New York: Appleton, 1896), p. 81. Cited in Herz, 'Idealist Internationalism,' p. 179.
18 Ibid.

14 *Creating Insecurity*

challenge of balancing these strategies complicates foreign policy making, Herz recognizes it as essential to state survival. This is not an easy task. For Herz, realist liberalism is 'the most difficult of arts, and to formulate its principles the most difficult of sciences. But if successful, Realist Liberalism will prove to be more lastingly rewarding than utopian idealism or crude power-realism.'[19] In relatively simple language, Herz is able to develop a sophisticated understanding of the need for security in the current international environment and outline the general requirements for achieving that end.

Wolfers

The broad strokes of the 'security dilemma' painted by John Herz are further refined by Arnold Wolfers. Noting the connection between the national interest and security, he argues that 'it would be an exaggeration to claim that the symbol of national security is nothing but a stimulus to semantic confusion, although used without specifications it leaves room for more confusion than sound political counsel or scientific usage can afford.'[20] While not specifically mentioning the problems that Morgenthau encounters when defining the national interest, Wolfers seems to require further conceptual thinking on the matter of security. Toward that end, Wolfers is first committed to seeing the normative character of national security policies. Citing Walter Lippmann's early work on the subject, Wolfers demonstrates the connection between a sense (or feeling) of security and the preservation of certain core societal values. '[A] nation is secure to the extent to which it is not in danger of having to sacrifice core values, if it wishes to avoid war, and is able, if challenged, to maintain them by victory in such a war.'[21] This leads Wolfers to argue that security 'in an objective sense measures the absence of threats to acquired values, in a subjective sense, the absence of fear that such values will be attacked.'[22] As with earlier definitions, security is considered both the psychological absence of fear and the existential lack of physical danger.

The assumption that security is best considered in relation to the state is clear when we look to Wolfers's advice to statesmen. He begins with a rhetorical question. 'Is not insecurity of any kind an evil from which the rational policy-maker would want to rescue his country?'[23] Wolfers offers two compelling reasons why the state should moderate its (necessary) thirst for security. First, 'every increment of security must be paid for by additional sacrifices of other values usually of a

---

19 Ibid.

20 Arnold Wolfers, 'National Security as an Ambiguous Symbol,' in *Discord and Collaboration: Essays on International Politics* (Baltimore, MD: The Johns Hopkins Press, 1962), p. 149.

21 Ibid., p. 150.

22 Ibid.

23 Ibid., p. 158.

kind more exacting than the mere expenditure of precious time... by something of a law of diminishing returns, the gain in security no longer compensates for the added costs of attaining it.'[24]

Second, in a further explication of Herz's security dilemma, Wolfers argues that, 'national security policies when based on the accumulation of power have a way of defeating themselves if the target level is set too high because "power of resistance" cannot be unmistakably distinguished from "power of aggression"'.[25] Therefore, '[what] a country does to bolster its own security through power can be interpreted by others... as a threat to their security.'[26] Security, then, requires that a state balance between the need for an adequate defense and the appearance of moderation in that defense. Wolfers's comments on the ideal security policy speak to this delicate strategy.

> It should be kept in mind that the ideal security policy is one that would lead to a distribution of values so satisfactory to all nations that the intention to attack and with it the problem of security would be minimized. While this is a utopian goal, policy-makers and particularly peace-makers would do well to remember that there are occasions when greater approximation to such a goal can be effected.[27]

Here we see Wolfers echoing the argument of Morgenthau and Herz. A balanced foreign policy that tempers the accumulation of power with pacific intentions leads to a more secure environment than would a policy based on brute power accumulation. However, Wolfers also recognizes the complexities of such a strategy. In noting the near 'utopian goal' of pursuing a balanced strategy, Wolfers accepts the constraints of international life.

Waltz

Kenneth Waltz continues many of the themes put forth by the realists above in an attempt to build a *scientific* theory of international politics. Beginning with the state as the primary locus for security considerations, Waltz articulates what security entails. The condition of anarchy means that a general atmosphere of insecurity exists for all states in the system. Waltz claims that, 'states... do not enjoy even an imperfect guarantee of their security unless they set out to provide it for

---

24 Ibid.
25 Ibid.
26 Ibid.
27 Ibid., p. 161.

16 *Creating Insecurity*

themselves.'[28] At the heart of this argument is Waltz's claim that all states wish for survival,[29] making the pursuit of survival and that of security synonymous.

If security requires that states engage in self-help tactics in order to survive, then what can Waltz offer the policy maker by way of practical advice? First, we need to look to his general theory of international politics. Beyond the primary requirement of maintaining adequate military capabilities, the logic of balance-of-power represents the most important strategy for ensuring the security of the state. Assuming a competitive system, Waltz finds that the logic of balance of power is reproduced over and over again. As long as states seek survival, then we need not assume rationality or constancy of will in order to see the presence of balance of power tendencies.[30] While the tendency to seek a balance in international politics does not ensure survival, Waltz is insistent that it is a consistent remedy to the potential destruction of the state system. 'Safety for all states... depends on the maintenance of a balance among them.'[31]

Second, although Waltz insists that IR theory is not foreign policy,[32] the logic of balance of power does provide the security manager with specific policy consequences. This understanding is most important for the policy consequences of the United States. Following the balancing logic articulated in *Theory of International Politics*, Waltz argues that the current unipolar moment will not last.[33] The United States will be unable to maintain its unchallenged position in world politics into the indefinite future. This is a rather standard (neorealist) treatment of power and balancing in international relations and provides a study of security very little in the way of prescriptive direction. The claim, however, becomes interesting when Waltz begins to explore how unilateral activities on the part of the United States will hasten the end of unipolarity and initiate great power balancing. 'In international politics, overwhelming power repels and leads others to try to balance against it. With benign intent, the United States has behaved and, until its power is brought into balance, will continue to behave in ways that sometimes frighten others.'[34] Thus, it is the *behavior* of the United States that causes others to seek balancing and not simply the material capabilities of the hegemon (the United States). Waltz's disdain for unreflective American unilateralism demonstrates a need to examine the earlier warnings of Morgenthau, Herz, and Wolfers. Speaking to a need to balance power considerations with

---

28 Kenneth N. Waltz, *Man, the State and War: A Theoretical Analysis* (New York: Columbia University Press, 1959), p. 201.

29 Kenneth N. Waltz, *Theory of International Politics* (New York: Random House, 1979), pp. 91-92.

30 Waltz, *Man, the State, and War*, p. 203.

31 Waltz, *Theory of International Politics*, p. 132.

32 Kenneth N. Waltz, 'International Politics is Not Foreign Policy,' *Security Studies* 6 (Autumn 1996), pp. 54-57.

33 Kenneth Waltz, 'Structural Realism After the Cold War,' *International Security* 25 (Summer 2000), p. 27.

34 Ibid., p. 28.

Realists on Security 17

cooperative ones, Waltz argues that, '[r]ather than learning from history, The United States is repeating past errors by extending its influence over what used to be the province of the vanquished. This alienates Russia and nudges it toward China instead of drawing it toward Europe and the United States.'[35] It appears that it might be possible, even recognizing Wolfers's claim to the most difficult of arts, to draw a potential balancer into alignment with a hegemon. U.S. foreign policy would seem to have a powerful effect on the direction that Russia (and China) takes in the future. In a telling reading of the U.S. propensity to create insecurity, Waltz cogently argues that to

> alienate Russia by expanding NATO, and to alienate China by lecturing its leaders on how to rule their country, are policies that only an overwhelmingly powerful country could afford, and only a foolish one be tempted, to follow. The United States cannot prevent a new balance of power from forming. It can hasten its coming as it has been earnestly doing.[36]

Although Waltz is committed to differentiating between theories of international politics and those of foreign policy, his desire to understand 'balancing tendencies' informs both areas of study. For our purposes, it is clear from much of his later work that a thoughtful security manager can draw policy-relevant conclusions from Waltz's theoretical approach to international politics.

Buzan

Barry Buzan's *People, States, and Fear* represents a further explication of realism with specific attention paid to matters of security. As with the earlier realists, the issue of the state is central to Buzan's work. 'As a form of political organization, the state has transcended, and often crushed, all other political units to the extent that it has become the universal standard of political legitimacy.'[37] Buzan continues, arguing that in theory, 'the state dominates both in terms of political allegiance and authority, and in terms of its command over instruments of force, particularly the major military machines required for modern warfare.'[38] In language that demonstrates some affinity with Waltz's structural realism, Buzan further elaborates his understanding of world politics: '[this] theory is close to reality in a large minority of states, and enables the biggest and best organized of

---

35 Ibid., p. 37.

36 Ibid., p. 38.

37 Barry Buzan, *People, States and Fear: An Agenda for International Security Studies in the Post-Cold War Era*, 2nd edition (Boulder, CO: Lynne Rienner, Publishers, 1991), 58. For a cogent discussion of the rise of the nation-state and its transcendence over other political forms, see, Hendrik Spruyt, *The Sovereign State and Its Competitors* (Princeton, NJ: Princeton University Press, 1994).

38 Buzan, p. 58.

18   *Creating Insecurity*

them to exert powerful system-wide influence.'[39] Moreover, 'the protection of territory and population must count as fundamental security concerns' because 'the state ultimately rests on its physical base.'[40] Buzan seeks to link security with the physical safety of the state.

This understanding of the concept of security revolves around how we come to understand two distinct terms – *threat* and *vulnerability*. In a discussion of these terms, Barry Buzan offers a moderate realist version of international affairs. Agreeing with the writers above, he argues that state insecurity 'reflects a combination of threats and vulnerabilities.'[41] These threats and vulnerabilities possess a material component. Threats require a vigilant state apparatus. Because threats are external to the state, they may be 'impossible to measure, may not be perceived' or their perception 'may not have much substantive reality.'[42] Moreover, it may be difficult to distinguish 'threats serious enough to constitute a threat to national security, from those that arise as normal day-to-day consequences of life in a competitive international environment.'[43]

Recognizing the material base of external threats leads Buzan to construct an interesting analogy. He writes that '[each] state exists, in a sense, at the hub of a whole universe of threats.'[44] Adding that, 'because international threats are so ambiguous, and because knowledge of them is limited, national security policy-making is necessarily a highly imperfect art,' Buzan demonstrates that states are required to engage in 'constant monitoring and assessment, and the development of criteria for deciding when threats become of sufficient intensity to warrant action.'[45] It is important to note the material component of threats as they are acknowledged by Buzan. If the state is the hub, then threats exist 'out there' on the rim of the international relations wheel. This picture of international life is a demonstrably negative vision where all other states are potential enemies. These threats are calculated in terms of the physical capabilities that might be harnessed in an attack on the state. The mere uncertainty of international life creates a threatening environment for the state.

Vulnerabilities, on the other hand, are internal problems (but nonetheless material) that demonstrate a deficiency in the capability of a state to manage its security affairs. Buzan argues that vulnerabilities 'can be reduced by increasing self-reliance, or by building up countervailing forces to deal with specific threats.'[46] Such a rendering of both *threat* and *vulnerability* can be interpreted by the state policy establishment and used to construct monitoring and information assessment

---

39 Ibid.
40 Ibid., p. 95.
41 Ibid., p. 112.
42 Ibid., p. 114.
43 Ibid., p. 115.
44 Ibid., p. 141.
45 Ibid.
46 Ibid., p. 331.

that allows for a calculation concerning the relative level of state security. Intelligence gathering and processing becomes integral to the maintenance of state security.[47] It follows, since security is tied to both physical capabilities (Wolfers's objective clause) and the interpretation of those capabilities (Wolfers's subjective clause), that it is possible to *measure* the level of 'security' one possesses relative to another. Weapons systems, both offensive and defensive, can be quantified and measured against the systems of other states.

Finally, Buzan argues that anarchy tends to impose three conditions on our understanding of security.[48] First, as discussed above, states are 'the principal referent object of security because they are both the framework of order and the highest source of governing authority.'[49] For this reason it is entirely appropriate to confine discussions of security to matters of national importance and speak of a specific (and narrow) security problematique. But focusing simply on the state does not tell us much about the international consequences of insecurity.

Anarchy's second condition suggests an answer to this problem. Buzan notes that, 'the dynamics of national security are highly relational and interdependent between states.'[50] For this reason, '[i]ndividual national securities can only be fully understood when considered in relation both to each other and to larger patterns of relations in the system as a whole.'[51] In language that appears to foreshadow the argument of his later collaborative effort, *The Logic of Anarchy*, Buzan recognizes that international security issues are best understood in systemic terms in that they have powerful effects on how secure individual states feel.[52] Incorporating the critical school's concern for the 'insecurity dilemma',[53] Buzan writes that while domestic insecurities may remain an issue for some states, attention needs to be paid to external threats, as these 'will almost always comprise a major element of the national security problem.'[54] Mirroring the classic security dilemma, anarchy mandates that insecurity is an environmental condition that must be managed by states through signaling, posturing, and the appropriation of capabilities, but can never be overcome.

---

47 For a traditional discussion that links intelligence to greater security, see, Roy Godson, 'Intelligence and National Security,' in Richard Shultz, Roy Godson, and Ted Greenwood, eds. *Security Studies for the 1990s* (Washington, D.C.: Brassey's 1993), pp. 211-235.

48 Buzan, pp. 22-23.

49 Ibid., p. 22.

50 Ibid.

51 Ibid.

52 See, Barry Buzan, Charles Jones, and Richard Little, *The Logic of Anarchy: Neorealism to Structural Realism* (New York: Columbia University Press, 1993), pp. 132-154.

53 Brian L. Job, 'The Insecurity Dilemma: National, Regime, and State Securities in the Third World,' in *The Insecurity Dilemma: National Security of Third World States* (Boulder, CO: Lynne Rienner, Publishers, 1992), p. 18.

54 Buzan, *People, States and Fear*, p. 22.

20   *Creating Insecurity*

Finally, the third condition demonstrates that anarchy is a necessary condition for understanding security matters and that its enduring nature severely constrains what states can do. Here, Buzan articulates a position quite close to that of Wendt, noting that 'the practical meaning of security can only be constructed sensibly if it can be made operational within an environment in which competitive relations are inescapable.'[55] When considered so, security becomes a relative condition. Only if anarchy ceases to be the defining structural attribute of international politics will our understanding of security be re-considered.

Realism and the Traditional Study of Security

The writers discussed above are self-defined realists. They work in a tradition that situates the state in a hostile environment and mandates that the search for security is central to their theoretical endeavor. In doing so, realist principles and national security policies become strikingly similar. Exactly what this means for the development of a more robust concept of security is unclear. While it is exceedingly difficult, if not impossible, to locate an essential core of realist thought running through each of the writers above,[56] we are able to recognize a certain family resemblance that makes the study of security similar among them. Realism and national security studies became synonymous during the Cold War and recognizing their principle components will allow us to undertake a critique of traditional security studies in the final section of this chapter.

Three issues in particular animate the realist concern for security. First, the state plays a (the) central role in mitigating insecurity on behalf of the individual. Second, power is inextricably linked to national security. Third, due to the condition of anarchy, security is always relative and requires consistent re-evaluation due to the shifting fortunes brought about by attempts to balance power. Therefore the mitigation of insecurity rather than its transcendence is the appropriate focus of realist thought. Each of these issues might be discussed in further detail.

First, the assumption of state preeminence in world affairs quite often means that its investigation is not undertaken but rather assumed. This is true for each of the realists above who recognize the importance of the state in matters of security but assume its relevance rather than explicating it. While Buzan is most explicit in recognizing that the primary referent for security must remain the individual,[57] all of the writers suggest the state is the necessary locus of political investigation as the state represents the political unit charged with protecting that individual. That the state is necessary for individual security does not mean that the state is a *given* in

---

55 Ibid., p. 23.
56 Jack Donnelly, *Realism and International Relations* (Cambridge: Cambridge University Press, 2000), p. 13.
57 Buzan, *People, States and Fear*, p. 35.

international politics. It is quite possible that other political forms could manage the uncertainties of global politics for the individual. However, it is often recognized that the state has been and will continue to be that indispensable institution charged with specific duties in the security realm.

Upon investigation, however, the realist placement of the state at the center of the security problematique does not rely solely on existential consideration of its dominance in world politics. There is a second, ethical component that animates the critical realist reading of the state. The state, it should be remembered, *incurs the obligation* to manage international uncertainty on behalf of its citizenry.[58] States, in the words of Scott and Carr, are 'organizations to which people look to perform functions of the first importance that they cannot perform for themselves.'[59] In the realm of security, Kal Holsti summarizes the importance of this function, 'in the implicit contract between individuals and the state... the most fundamental service purchased... is security.'[60] This contract is taken seriously by both state and citizen alike. The citizen grants a measure of authority to the state in exchange for the obligation incurred by the state to protect and defend.[61] The implication, then, for the traditional approach is that the state might be taken *as if* it were a given in international relations for the purposes of security studies. This understanding of the state and its role in international politics is further outlined by Scott and Carr.

> Let us characterize the responsibility the state owes to its citizenry as the obligation to manage international uncertainty in the best interest of the citizenry. The obligation, of course, is owed to the state's citizenry, but it gives purpose and direction to the state's foreign policy. It seems appropriate, then, to describe the state as the advocate of its citizen's interests in the international world. Inter-state relationships correspondingly should be regarded as relationships between advocates charged with pursuing the interests of their respective clients; their citizenry.[62]

The obligation argument is continued in the work of Robert Jackson, who notes that the '[s]ecurity provided by independent governments to their citizens within the confines of international borders is the basic (although by no means the only) point of the state. Indeed,... the security afforded by the state is the essential means

---

58 Gary L. Scott and Craig L. Carr, 'Are States Moral Agents?,' *Social Theory and Practice* 12 (Spring 1986), p. 83.

59 Ibid., p. 84.

60 Kal J. Holsti, *The State, War, and the State of War* (Cambridge: Cambridge University Press, 1996), p. 108.

61 While the events of 11 September 2001 would seem to have strengthened this relationship, recent scholarship seems to be questioning this historic contract, see, for example, Daniel Deudney, 'Political Fission: State Structure, Civil Society, and Nuclear Security Politics in the United States,' in Ronnie Lipschutz, ed., *On Security* (New York: Columbia University Press, 1995), pp. 87-123.

62 Scott and Carr, p. 79.

22 *Creating Insecurity*

for developing the good life.'[63] Matters of security do not rest with a discussion of the sources of insecurity but require consideration of the position of the state in mitigating whatever sources of insecurity are thought to exist.

Whether explicit or not, each of the realists above centers the study of security around the state and considers *national security* a limiting factor in the scope of issues that present themselves to the theorist. At their core, issues of security rest on the physical integrity of the state. This statement, however, requires more than a strategic or military emphasis. While the particularities of the Cold War often linked security with military or strategic matters, few of the security definitions used during the Cold War limit security considerations to military strategy.[64] Moreover, this limiting factor, when considered in relation to the second and third issues, suggests both the success and failure of the traditional approach to security studies.

A fascination with power, its central place in a study of international politics, represents a second issue shared by the realists above. For each, power seems to be a prerequisite for security. Morgenthau, Herz, and Wolfers consider power the necessary complement to pacific intentions. Waltz and Buzan (committed to a scientific approach to international politics) equate power with military capabilities and suggest their fundamental role in the protection of the state. State capabilities can be measured against one another and the relative level of security for each state in the system can be calculated.[65] While any discussion of power in realist thought tends to become problematic, it is useful to recognize the rhetorical force of their claim more than the accuracy of their concept. The overriding concern with power points to a view of the world as imperfect and dangerous, one that may require force as a tool of state. In a frank discussion of its necessity, John Mearsheimer provides a concise example of this realist concern. 'Uncertainty is unavoidable when assessing intentions, which simply means that states can never be sure that other states do not have offensive intentions to go to war with their offensive military capabilities.'[66] This 'offensive capability' is something that each state must consider when assessing other states in the system. Again, Mearsheimer presents a standard realist response to concern with offensive capabilities: 'states inherently possess some offensive military capability, which gives them the wherewithal to hurt and possibly to destroy each other. States are potentially dangerous to each other.'[67] Continuing, he argues, '[a] state's military power is usually identified with

---

63 Robert Jackson, 'The Security Dilemma in Africa,' in Brian L. Job, ed. *The Insecurity Dilemma*, p. 84.

64 See, for instance, the discussion by Barry Buzan, *People, States and Fear*, pp. 16-17.

65 Waltz, *Theory of International Politics*, p. 131.

66 John J. Mearsheimer, 'The False Promise of International Institutions,' in Michael Brown, Sean M. Lynn-Jones, and Steven E. Miller, eds. *The Perils of Anarchy: Contemporary Realism and International Security* (Cambridge, MA: The MIT Press, 1995), p. 337.

67 Ibid.

the particular weaponry at its disposal, although even if there were no weapons, the individuals of a state could still use their feet and hands to attack the population of another state.'[68] In language more direct than the realists above, Mearsheimer articulates a common theme to each. As Donnelly notes, 'realists are unanimous in holding that human nature contains an ineradicable core of egoistic passions; that these passions define the central problem of politics; and that statesmanship is dominated by the need to control this side of human nature.'[69] It is in the need to control the dark side of human nature that power becomes a requirement for the state.

What makes power a tool of such importance for the realist is also what makes it such a problem. For, while the realist insists that states are required to possess power in order to survive, each also realizes that unbalanced power signals to others a danger that must be overcome. This places the state in an environment that requires it to balance its own power with that of others. As each of the realists discussed above makes clear, this is a dangerous game of equilibrium, but one that must be played in order to ensure national security. In an interesting variation on this theme, Charles Glaser expands on the writings of the security dilemma and the need to choose between strategies of conflict and those of cooperation.

> A security-seeking state that is comparing competition and cooperation must confront two fundamental questions. First, which will contribute more to its military capabilities for deterring attack, and for defending if deterrence fails? Second, appreciating the pressure created by anarchy and insecurity, the state should ask which approach is best for avoiding capabilities that threaten others' abilities to defend and deter, while not undermining its military capabilities? The tension that can exist between these two objectives lies at the core of the security dilemma.[70]

Glaser articulates a consistent theme in realist thought and one that is often overlooked by its detractors. Power, for realists, is a necessary but insufficient component to an overall security plan. States cannot rely solely on power to enhance security, but each state must possess a certain level in the event that it becomes necessary for maintaining security. In addition, Glaser's comments on the security dilemma point to the third issue to be discussed. His remarks are paradigmatic of realist thought in not seeking to transcend the presence of insecurity in international relations, but in attempting to manage it.

This mitigation of insecurity rather than its transcendence represents a third key feature of realism. The historical writings of Morgenthau, Herz, Kennan, Wolfers, Carr, and others, are as much a critique of inter-war legalism and moralism that

---

68 Ibid.
69 Donnelly, p. 10.
70 Charles L. Glaser, 'Realists as Optimists: Cooperation as Self-Help,' in Brown, Lynn-Jones, and Miller, eds. *The Perils of Anarchy*, p. 387.

24 *Creating Insecurity*

sought transcendence over conflict[71] as they are explanations of world affairs. These inter-war idealists sought to transcend violence, war, and conflict. In the aftermath of the First World War, idealists attempted to construct legal norms against the use of war.[72] It was argued that individual national securities could be guaranteed if all states entered into collective security arrangements and outlawed war as an institution for deciding political disagreements.[73] This approach reaches its apogee, perhaps, in the Kellogg-Briand Pact renouncing the use of war.[74]

Jaded by a darker sense of history and a pessimistic vision of human potential, realists responded by arguing the futility and naiveté of the idealist approach to international peace and security. When attempting to provide an answer for the horrors of war, realists argue that legal mechanisms cannot eliminate its potential and might very likely exacerbate national insecurity. States are required to demonstrate their potential for waging an effective war in order to deter the potential aggression of others. In this way, states can minimize the use of war as a policy instrument and achieve a modicum of national security. Their collective message, if one were to attempt to locate a common theoretical focus in these disparate works, is a rhetorical attack on 'utopian idealism, with its chiliastic approach and its failure in practice.'[75] Morgenthau, in a rather frank discussion of idealist interpretations of history, is perhaps a spokesperson for the realist cause.

> If anybody should be bold enough to write a history of world politics with so uncritical a method he would easily and well-nigh inevitably be driven to the conclusion that from Timur to Hitler and Stalin the foreign policies of all nations were inspired by the ideals of humanitarianism and pacifism. The absurdity of the result is commensurable with the defects of the method.[76]

The concept of world peace through world law[77] seems imprudent to realist scholars interested in what they see as an imperfect and *imperfectable* international system. And, while utopian liberalism no longer plays a major role in theoretical

---

71 Consider, for instance, Joel H. Rosenthal, *Righteous Realists: Political Realism, Responsible Power, and American Culture in the Nuclear Age* (Baton Rouge, LA: Louisiana State University, 1991), pp. 1-36.

72 Woodrow Wilson, 'The Fourteen Points,' from an address to Congress, January 8, 1918 reprinted in John A. Vasquez, ed. *Classics of International Relations* (Englewood Cliffs, NJ: Prentice-Hall, 1986), p. 18.

73 The best example of this philosophy might be the post-WWII work by Grenville Clark and Louis B. Sohn, *World Peace through World Law* (Cambridge, MA: Harvard University Press, 1960).

74 The official name of the 1928 Kellogg-Briand Pact is, of course, the *General Treaty for the Renunciation of War*. For a discussion concerning the treaty, see, Seyom Brown, *The Causes and Prevention of War*, 2nd edition (New York: St. Martin's Press, 1994), pp. 170-171.

75 Herz, 'Idealist Internationalism,' p. 177.

76 Morgenthau, 'Another "Great Debate",' p. 966.

77 Clark and Sohn, supra note 73.

discussions of international politics, later realists like Waltz, Mearsheimer, Buzan, and Glaser demonstrate a similar tendency to counter the thinking of interdependence writers of the 1970s[78] and democratic peace scholars of the 1980s.[79] Waltz, for instance, consistently claims that anarchy reduces the possibility of cooperation because self-help systems require states to act to ensure that their survival is not dependent on the survival of others.

Security for the realist is quite different from that for the idealist. Summing up the focus of realist security concerns, Donnelly argues, '[s]ecurity' thus means a somewhat less dangerous and less violent world, rather than a safe, just, or peaceful one. Statesmanship involves mitigating and managing, not eliminating, conflict.'[80] The management of conflict, rather than its transcendence, becomes the obligation of each state in the system.

The Success and Failure of the Traditional Approach

The realist tradition has had some success in understanding the problems of national security and advocating policy proposals for its enhancement.[81] Perhaps most importantly, realism presents the negative or pessimistic side of interstate relations to state actors. (Herbert Butterfield was said to have remarked that realism is more a boast than a political philosophy.[82] Such a claim fits our attempt to envision realism as a rhetorical device that presents the dangerous environment in which states operate rather than a general theory of international politics.) Even when pacific relations dominate the interactions between states, the potential for interstate violence requires that states manage Herz's dilemma. For this, the state needs the input of a particular approach to politics that presents the view of the 'cautious paranoid'. In a world of potential dangers and unseen threats, realists advocate a strategy of low-risk. In the words of Morgenthau, Herz, and Wolfers, this means balancing the 'power of resistance' with that of the 'power of aggression'. For Waltz, this means a consistent desire to promote survival through the enhancement of capabilities while seeking to dissuade others from similar enhancements. For Glaser, this appears as a series of contingencies between policies of conflict and those of cooperation. But no matter how the topic is put, a similar pessimism bordering on paranoia engages the realist.

---

78 Robert O. Keohane and Joseph S. Nye, Jr. *Power and Interdependence: World Politics in Transition* (Boston: Little, Brown, 1977).

79 See, for instance, Michael W. Doyle, 'Liberalism and World Politics,' *The American Political Science Review* 80 (December 1986), pp. 1151-1169; and Bruce Russett, et. al. 'The Democratic Peace,' *International Security* 19 (Spring 1995), pp. 164-184.

80 Donnelly, p. 10.

81 Rosenthal, p. 151.

82 Herbert Butterfield, cited in Jeffrey W. Legro and Andrew Moravcsik, 'Faux Realism,' *Foreign Policy* (July/August 2001), p. 81.

26   *Creating Insecurity*

In addition to providing the state a negative view of the world, realism also offers an approach to politics that does not problematize the very assumptions upon which the state exists. Security becomes something that capable actors can manage by paying close attention to: (1) the activities of other states, (2) the cooperative schemes being considered at any given time, and (3) the logical constraints on those cooperative schemes because of our intersubjective understanding of anarchy. Choices concerning specific policy options can be understood in terms of a rationality assumption present in realist thought.[83] Assuming self-interest, there is a standard argument to be made concerning why particular options have been chosen over others.

By attempting to solve the problems that the state sees, realists enter the policy debate at a point that the state can accept. Once threats have been sufficiently demarcated, there can be little doubt that emphasis on rational actors and balancing behavior coheres well with the bureaucratic policies of the modern state.[84] In the words of Ferguson and Mansbach, realism represents a clear example of the 'Zeitgeist of their age,' commensurable with and complementary to the world view of the national security state.[85]

But herein lies the problem with realism. Only after threats have been sufficiently understood can realism participate in the policy debate to overcome those threats. This, however, begs the question, *how does a state come to recognize a threat?* What consideration is made prior to something being labeled a threat in order for that label to apply? If realism is to function in the security calculus, then answers to these questions should be forthcoming. Yet realism seems incapable of understanding how threats are constructed.

Dangers in international relations take on importance as security considerations only when they have been interpreted as threats. It is the particular (social) world in which actors live that is a necessary component of this security calculus. It is the social world that lends meaning to danger and threat. This represents a marked departure from the general tenets of realist philosophy. The social world is contingent and discursively constituted, it changes and will continue to do so through time. Words and social practices take on different meanings and we need to recognize this in our attempt to understand the construction of security threats.

In the following chapter we will examine how security considerations are informed by language, interpretation, and the social construction of threats. Recent work in the field of Security Studies demonstrates the influence and importance of *constructivism* in an effort to understand how insecurity is imagined. Scholars in the constructivist tradition seek answers to those questions left unanswered by the realists of this chapter.

---

83 Ferguson and Mansbach, pp. 143-160.
84 Barry Buzan, Ole Waever, and Jaap de Wilde, *Security: A New Framework for Analysis* (Boulder, CO: Lynne Rienner, 1998), p. 206.
85 Ferguson and Mansbach, p. 217.

Chapter 3

Constructivists on Security

Against the traditional approach to security with its empiricist emphasis, a complex and broad challenge has recently emerged. This challenge to the study of national security does not lend itself to a simply label. Furthermore, unlike realism, this alternative approach does not espouse to be a theory of international politics. Rather, *constructivism* is a philosophical approach to making sense of the world. Speaking to the philosophical foundations of human understanding, those employing constructivism present those interested in matters of national security with an altogether different interpretation of the sources of insecurity as well as the means to overcome them. Beginning with those important 'first questions' left unanswered by realists, constructivists ask how threats are recognized, how enemies are labeled, and how groups come to imagine danger. The resulting shift in the issues to be studied could not be sharper. In a telling example of this re-direction, Bartelson argues against the traditional focus. 'Security is not primarily an object of foreign policy; before security can be brought to function as such, it requires a prior differentiation of what is alien, other or simply outside the state and therefore threatens it.'[1]

In the following discussion, four leading constructivist security texts will be analyzed. While the term *constructivism* is employed differently in each text, recognition of the fact that language and human discourse define the world is a similar feature among them. Rather than attempting to transcend the political world and look back upon it as '*objective*' scientists, the constructivists below are insistent that the scholar must remain within the world in order to understand it. Invoking Wittgenstein, constructivists will argue that the limits of our language represent the limits of our world.[2]

The discussion below follows the pattern set by our discussion of realism in the previous chapter. First, I will examine how each work characterizes security. Second, I will discuss how constructivism is employed to understand this version of security. Again, the term constructivism is used by a variety of scholars in a number

---

1 Jens Bartelson, *A Genealogy of Sovereignty* (Cambridge: Cambridge University Press, 1995), p. 164. This agrees with Bartelson's concern that 'the ultimate subject of security is sovereignty, whether personalized in the sovereign, or in the abstract and naturalized sense of the state as a whole, but its precise signification varies with the point of reference.' (p. 163).

2 Ludwig Wittgenstein, *Tractatus Logico-Philosophicus*, trans. D.F. Pears and B.F. McGuiness (London: Routledge and Kegan Paul, 1961), p. 115.

28   *Creating Insecurity*

of different and often competing ways. Third, I will explore what a study of security looks like according to the author(s) of the specific work in question. This section is intended to emphasize the general approach to the idea of security. After analyzing each of the texts, the subsequent section summarizes the similarities and differences in these constructivist security texts. In the remaining section, I attempt to outline the successes and failures of these alternative approaches to the study of security loosely grouped under the rubric 'constructivism.'

Writing Security

The post-modern version of constructivism exemplified in Campbell's work, *Writing Security*, seeks to deconstruct traditional security texts and raise anew the foundations upon which political discourse functions. At the heart of Campbell's work is a need to understand how identity is constituted in relation to difference and then how that difference engenders insecurity which maintains and perpetuates identity.[3] A version of the state as a stable, fixed entity that requires a policy of national security in order to minimize external threats is eschewed for a reflexive approach which sees the state as a manifestation of identity performances, 'and their inescapable indebtedness to difference, through which politics occurs.'[4] The change in both the questions being asked and the understanding of the state has a profound influence on what security is taken to be.

Rather than providing a fixed definition, Campbell insists that we look to how security is used within a particular discourse at a particular moment in time. Security cannot be provided a fixed definition because it is a process rather than an end. The process of securing citizens is something that the state does by drawing boundaries around that which is considered foreign. According to Campbell, national security policies are not simply about protecting the physical integrity of the state. The process of securing the citizen against external dangers is also a means to legitimizing the state project and perpetuating particular identities. Security becomes a way to mark 'the ethical boundaries of identity rather than the territorial borders of the state.'[5] Compared to the external focus on insecurity emphasized in traditional texts, Campbell articulates an understanding of security that is as much concerned about providing meaning to identity at home as understanding difference abroad.

> The need to discipline and contain the ambiguity and contingency of the 'domestic' realm is a vital source of the externalization and totalization of threats to that realm through the discourses of danger. But the achievements of foreign policy for the state

---

3 David Campbell, *Writing Security: United States Foreign Policy and the Politics of Identity*, revised edition (Minneapolis, MN: University of Minnesota Press, 1998).

4 Ibid., p. 227.

5 Ibid., p. 156.

Constructivists on Security

are not due to any inherent characteristic of the state existing in an endangered world. The effectiveness of foreign policy as one political practice among many that serves to discipline ambiguity and construct identity is made possible because it is one instance of a series of cultural practices central to modernity operating within its own specific domain.[6]

This alternative understanding of security and its importance for the state comes from embracing a post-structural epistemology. By not committing the epistemological errors common to the realist tradition, where 'facts' and 'truth' are taken to be independently verifiable, Campbell focuses on how a specific discursive setting establishes what are taken to be 'facts' and 'truth'.[7] Access to a position where independent insight into the world exists is eschewed for an interpretive version of contingent human discourse. 'What is denied is not that... objects exist externally to thought, but the rather different assertion that they could constitute themselves as objects outside of any discursive condition of emergence.'[8] Placing importance on specific speech-acts, Campbell asserts, 'these events and not others have to be interpreted as threats, and the process of interpretation through which they are figured as threats employs some modes of representation and not others.'[9]

How a culture constructs certain threats through repeated acts of expression is what drives Campbell's study forward. Note that these questions are the 'first questions,' the questions that come before policies can be implemented to counter imagined threats. These concerns mark a divide for Campbell between an *ethos of political criticism* and the *rigors of social science*. Those 'pursuing the ethos of political criticism are not much troubled by where their research leaves them in relation to the site of international relations.'[10] Against this ethos, Campbell sees traditional security studies (rooted in the social sciences) as 'constantly concerned about positioning their argument in such a way as to maximize their disciplinary audience and impact.'[11] For Campbell, the policy-making apparatus of the social scientific endeavor ignores the reflective moments of the interpretive approach which considers how insecurity is a creation of discursive practices that reflect the construction of boundaries around particular identity. The contribution of *Writing Security*, 'is to recognize the way such limits establish both the possibility and the insufficiency of particular policy resolutions, to appreciate that despite such

---

6 Ibid., pp. 64-65.

7 Ibid., pp. 20-21.

8 Ernesto Laclau and Chantal Mouffe, *Hegemony and Socialist Strategy: Towards a Radical Democratic Politics*, translated by Winston Moore and Paul Cammack (London: Verso Books, 1985), p. 108. Cited in Campbell, p. 6.

9 Ibid.

10 Ibid., p. 226.

11 Ibid.

30   *Creating Insecurity*

deficiencies decisions must be taken only to be simultaneously criticized and taken again.'[12]

Since we have previously sought to argue that the academic study of security bridges the divide between theoretical undertakings and state policy making, we need to inquire as to how Campbell would envision a study of security. How, using Campbell's approach to security, might we construct a study of security to assist a state in overcoming insecurity? The answer to this question requires that we investigate cultural practices that give rise to identity constructs. It is through a constant process of critique and re-examination that insecurity can be mitigated.[13] Often evasive in providing an answer to the policy relevance of his study, Campbell seems most clear when critiquing practices that label certain concerns 'domestic' and others, 'foreign'. It is during the process whereby borders are drawn and re-drawn that Campbell finds his study useful to the state/society. '[The] central theme of *Writing Security* concerns the needs to rethink those practices and their representations so as to appreciate the role they play in bringing into being the very domains of inside/outside and domestic/foreign, with their associated figurations.'[14] It is in the process of *re-thinking* the boundaries that are created and perpetuated that Campbell seeks to engage the policy community. Accordingly, his approach does not 'advocate one fixed position.'[15] Rather, through constant critique, a polity might better come to understand how their own identity is tied to their sense of security.

> Its contribution is to recognize the way such limits establish both the possibility and the insufficiency of particular policy resolutions, to appreciate that despite such deficiencies decisions must be taken only to be simultaneously criticized and taken again, and to enact the Enlightenment attitude by a persistent and relentless questioning in specific contexts of the identity performances, and their inescapable indebtedness to difference, through which politics occurs... only by pursuing the agonism between closure and disturbance, naturalization and denaturalization, can a democratic ethos be lived.[16]

As these remarks make clear, Campbell's approach requires that the state policy apparatus radically alter the questions it asks and the policy assumptions it makes. Rather than accepting the premise that a security apparatus of the state should contemplate an existential issue of insecurity and find the means to overcome it, Campbell requires the state to contemplate how the initial issue of insecurity was formulated and recognize how such an instance is intimately tied to the equation of identity and difference through which the state operates. A similar approach to the study of security is formulated in *Security, Identity and Interests*.

---

12 Ibid., p. 227.
13 Ibid., p. 12.
14 Ibid., p. 208.
15 Ibid., p. 227.
16 Ibid.

Security, Identity, and Interests

In *Security, Identity and Interests*, Bill McSweeney offers a reflexive model of social order in an attempt to understand the human need for security.[17] By doing so, his work mirrors many of the concerns raised by Campbell. As another alternative approach to traditional security texts, his first move, like that of Campbell, is to separate his approach from realism. As McSweeney puts it, 'how actors construct their relations and theorizing is chronically implicated in creating and recreating the world which theorists observe. Security and insecurity are a relational quality, not a material distribution of capabilities, threats and vulnerabilities independent of such relations.'[18] Security cannot be defined independent of the social milieu of which it is a part. Putting it succinctly, he argues, '[we] learn to know the meaning of security through the practices which embody a particular interpretation of it.'[19] This understanding of security recognizes its 'common 'soft' meaning, referring to intersubjective relations and covering a bewildering array of values which acquire a degree of authenticity and imperviousness to challenge, similar to that associated with the concept of identity.'[20] In this way, security 'embraces all the areas of personal relations in everyday life which are subject to anxiety.'[21] The theorist is challenged to consider how a deeper understanding of security incorporates issues relating to our particular identities and interests. 'Identity, interests and moral choice... appear to be inseparably linked in any adequate account of security and security policy.'[22]

Key to understanding McSweeney's concern with security is recognizing its implications for the human in question rather than the state. 'Ontologically, the state is an instrument of security, and human individuals are its subjects.'[23] This shift in the focus of security studies is striking.

> In the alternative ontology..., the state is not the subject. It is an instrument, as are military forces, weapons, bank vaults, guard dogs and alarm systems. They cannot be considered a primary referent, or subject, or security. Their significance, and our assessment of their ranking in a hierarchy of security instruments, rests on a moral judgment in respect of the human individual, who is the proper focus, and can be the only subject, of security policy.[24]

---

17 Bill McSweeney, *Security, Identity and Interests: A Sociology of International Relations* (Cambridge: Cambridge University Press, 1999).
18 Ibid., p. 3.
19 Ibid., p. 22.
20 Ibid., pp. 81-82.
21 Ibid., p. 82.
22 Ibid., p. 198.
23 Ibid., p. 85.
24 Ibid., p. 87.

32   *Creating Insecurity*

While McSweeney does not leave the state out of his analysis, he recognizes that it cannot be the focus of study either. This is why an appropriate study of security requires ontological consideration. 'The idea of "ontological security" or existential trust is grounded in the secure or trusting relationships which respond to the fundamental want or interest from which other needs – such as the need for sociability – are derived.'[25] In this reading, interest in security 'arises from unconscious, organic, needs.'[26] It is common to all humans and manifests itself in complex social relations. Understanding the organic nature of security, it then follows that the basic unit of security is the individual. However, recognizing the human-centered nature of security requires more than a methodological reductionism from the collective (state) to the individual level of analysis. 'A human security policy... cannot be derived by aggregating individual needs, on the one hand or by attributing such needs to the state *a priori*, on the other.'[27] As simply an instrument for the enhancement of human security, the state plays a limited role in the study of security. Drawing on a variety of sociological literature,[28] his concern is with a proper epistemological account of social order that gives rise to an understanding of the complexities of achieving security at any given time. McSweeney's argument becomes more transparent when he analyzes the shortcomings of the Cold War approach to security.

> [A] definition of security which restricts its meaning to the management of external threats to the state ignores much that is relevant to a policy designed to achieve security. Much of the concern driving the criticism of the narrow definition in the 'national security' tradition, stems from moral opposition to the policy prescriptions derived from it, as much as intellectual disagreement with the contents of the concept. A concept which dictated nuclear deterrence, arms escalation, the subordination of individual and collective rights to the needs of the state, and which gave primacy to the allocation of resources to the management of interstate rivalry during the Cold War, must be redefined in terms yielding more acceptable policy implications.[29]

Those, like McSweeney, who are interested in re-defining the term, are frustrated at the traditional, narrow focus on military and strategic matters. But, McSweeney is not simply concerned with widening the definition.[30] His concern is more fundamental. Following his 'ontological' understanding of security, it is clear

---

25 Ibid., pp. 154-155.

26 Ibid., p. 154.

27 Ibid., p. 208.

28 McSweeney is drawn to Peter Winch, *The Idea of a Social Science* (London: Routledge Books, 1958); Harold Garfinkel, *Studies in Ethnomethodology* (Newark, NJ: Prentice Hall, 1967); Anthony Giddens, *Sociology* (Cambridge: Cambridge University Press, 1989); as well as the work of Emile Durkheim.

29 McSweeney, p. 91.

30 See, for instance, the discussion at Ibid., p. 100.

Constructivists on Security 33

that McSweeney is interested in basic human needs that exist at the most organic level.

> This is a normative argument, implying that security is a choice we make, which is contingent upon a moral judgment about human *needs*, not just human fears; it is not simply an intellectual discovery based on objective observation of facts. Human needs encompass more than physical survival and the threats to it, and they raise the question of the positive dimension of security and security policy.[31]

McSweeney's declaration that security is a choice we make points to an alternative epistemological focus. His reflexive model of social order suggests a particular use of constructivism that shares much in common with other constructivists while maintaining some intellectual distance from many that fall in the constructivist camp.

At times in his assessment of the security literature, McSweeney is as antagonistic to fellow constructivists as he is to traditional security scholars. Understanding how he positions his study in relation to other constructivist critiques of traditional texts enables us to make sense of his reflexive model of social order. McSweeney explains his model by outlining his differences with both traditional security studies (neorealism in this instance) and neo-liberal constructivism (a term employed by McSweeney to describe those replacing a cultural or ideational structure for a material one).

> What is entailed in a reflexive model of the social order can be summarized as follows in propositional form. Identity and interests are mutually constituted by knowledgeable agents, monitoring, managing, and manipulating the narrative of one in respect to the other. To say that both are chosen by human individuals is, firstly, to make a claim – with constructivism, but against neorealism – that the behaviour of states is an effect of cognitive *and* material structures, of the distribution of power informed by ideas. Secondly, the choice is made in context of interaction with other states in the international arena, and with sub-state groups within the domestic. Thirdly – and against constructivism – states choices are not only constrained by structure; they effect the progressive transformation of structure within a reflexive structure-agent relationship which can never be dissolved in favour of the deterministic role of the actor or of the structure of action. This implies, fourthly, that the concept of structure and the conception of causality in the social sciences must be radically distinguished from the ideas applicable to our understanding of the natural order. To affirm the co-constitution of behaviour by agent and structure is to affirm causality in the social order, but it is not to affirm what we mean by 'cause' in respect to the natural order. In the real world, in contrast to that conjured as such by mainstream security analysts, there is no objective structural entity which can function as an independent cause of social relations. There is nothing out there in social behaviour which can stand as an effect of conditions which are independent of the human agent. This is simply a different kind of world.[32]

---

31 Ibid., pp. 91-92.
32 Ibid., pp. 210-211.

34   *Creating Insecurity*

Put simply, humans construct their worlds. Our language, a point we shall return to below, represents the limits of these worlds. And, the language that we use is part of the environment that humans reflect on and react to. As McSweeney argues, 'human beings could not communicate at all except in the context of common meanings and practices structured by repetitive action and routinely reaffirmed norms and rules.'[33] However, it is a mistake to see these normative routines and common meanings as independent structures imposing themselves on human actors. It is equally incorrect to view these structures as *causing* human action. Of the distinction between causal laws and generalizations, McSweeney writes,

> *generalizations are not laws*; they are resources which actors draw upon to make action possible, to give reasons for action, and thus to appropriate as an element of action itself. Generalizations circulate through the framework of the social order, from observer to agent, from agent-as-observer to behaviour, making it impossible to conceive of a social law which functions for social action like the law of gravity.[34]

Accordingly, McSweeney is able to make a generalization about human social order from the analysis he undertakes in *Security, Identity, and Interests*. Namely, 'we choose who we are and who we want to be.'[35] Repeating a familiar refrain, McSweeney argues that neither the competitive and universal structure of anarchy as defined by neorealists, nor the cooperative and particular structure of a peace process put forth by the international community, determine the result for individuals and local communities.[36] Structures, whether material or ideational, influence but do not determine, behavior. But, to this common understanding, we need to add one further point in order to appreciate McSweeney's argument. Recourse to structural investigations leaves something out of a comprehensive security analysis. Security is both a negative and a positive good. Traditional studies, and constructivists who merely replace an ideational structure for a material one, focus on issues involving *negative* security. They worry about the need to be secure *from* something or someone. It is equally important to consider the positive aspect of security – those issues that give meaning to the human experience. Order and stability are positive requirements of human existence and allow us to speak of a secure condition in which to live.

If we accept McSweeney's requirements for the proper investigation of security, the question becomes what does a study of security look like using his approach? Not surprisingly, the twin issues of identity and interest play the central part in individual and collective security. Since identity and interest are 'analytically

---

33 Ibid., p. 211.
34 Ibid.
35 Ibid., p. 196.
36 Ibid.

Constructivists on Security 35

separate elements of all collective action,'[37] it is possible to manipulate both in the creation and maintenance of a successful security programme. The process by which this is done represents the *practice* of security. Specifically, the conscious manipulation of material interests represents a *seductive* activity that brings about a subsequent shift in identity constructs. When this occurs, the practice of security can be enhanced. Alternatively, the conscious shift in identity constructs might bring about a re-calculation of desired interests.

The Culture of National Security

The relationship between state and security needs not be problematized by constructivists. Concerned with epistemological coherence, constructivists are in a position to provide numerous readings of security within their broad approach. As the reading of McSweeney makes clear, it is often the case that some loosely-defined constructivists have more in common with non-constructivists than with fellow constructivists. The remaining constructivist approaches discussed here depart from the readings above in that they do not challenge the state-centered approach to security studies emphasized in traditional scholarship. Accepting the distinct character of the security problematique as discussed by realists, Jepperson, Wendt, and Katzenstein work within a 'traditional, narrow definition of security studies.'[38] While these scholars appear willing to accept the traditional definition of security, they also recognize the need to problematize the 'sources and content of national security interests that states and governments pursue.'[39] This points to a return to those 'first questions' that consistently engage constructivists. As Katzenstein makes clear, '[the] state is a social actor. It is embedded in social rules and conventions that constitute its identity and the reasons for the interests that motivate actors.'[40] A coherent understanding of security, then, requires that we look to the social structures in which states find themselves embedded. Investigating the social environment allows the theorist to understand why particular issues are labeled 'security issues.' Emphasis on the social structures (rather than the realist emphasis on material structures) represents a common concern for those contributors to *The Culture of National Security*. In language that clearly summarizes the perceived shortcomings of mainstream thinking on security matters, Katzenstein states,

---

37 Ibid., p. 179.
38 Peter J. Katzenstein, 'Introduction: Alternative Perspectives on National Security,' in *The Culture of National Security: Norms and Identity in World Politics* (New York: Columbia University Press, 1996), p. 10.
39 Ibid., p. 32.
40 Ibid., p. 24.

36 *Creating Insecurity*

Neorealist and neoliberal theories adhere to relatively sparse views of the international system. Neorealism assumes that the international system has virtually no normative content. The international system constrains national security policies directly without affecting conceptions of state interest. Neoliberalism takes as given actor identities and views ideas and beliefs as intervening variables between assumed interests and behavioral outcomes. In this view states operate in environments that create constraints and opportunities.[41]

What Jepperson, Wendt, and Katzenstein seem most concerned about when critiquing traditional approaches is the tendency to remove what is most interesting and informative (namely, social structures) from an analysis of national security. Offering a brief assessment of this tendency, they write, '[m]aterialists need not ignore cultural factors altogether. But they treat them as epiphenomenal or at least secondary, as a 'superstructure' determined in the last instance by a material 'base'.'[42] '[C]ulture and identity are, at best, derivative of the distribution of capabilities and have no independent explanatory power.'[43] However, these concepts are key to the vision of security studies outlined by these constructivists. In order to develop a more robust understanding of security, Jepperson, Wendt, and Katzenstein insist on treating 'norms, rules, and institutions' as more than mere 'process'.[44] 'We require an approach to security that does not assume that actors deploy culture and identity strategically, like any other resource, simply to further their own self-interests.'[45] Interests are treated as contingent upon the social environments from which they derive meaning. The study of security requires that we look to these interests through the cultural lens. To achieve this, the authors insist that 'security environments in which states are embedded are in important part cultural and institutional, rather than just material.'[46]

How can we characterize the meaning of security that emerges in this work? Katzenstein is frank in his analysis as to why the authors have chosen to accept the narrow definition of security that focuses on material capabilities and the use and control of military force by states. His answer is grounded in 'a healthy respect for the sociology of knowledge.'[47] While new security issues (including the human security emphasized above) represent important topics for consideration, the authors of *The Culture of National Security* insist that widening the meaning of security would only result in a charge of 'skirting the hard task of addressing the

---

41 Ibid., p. 25.
42 Ronald L. Jepperson, Alexander Wendt, and Peter J. Katzenstein, 'Norms, Identity, and Culture in National Security,' in Katzenstein, ed. *The Culture of National Security*, p. 38.
43 Katzenstein, p. 17.
44 Jepperson, Wendt, and Katzenstein, p. 38.
45 Katzenstein, p. 17.
46 Jepperson, Wendt, and Katzenstein, p. 33.
47 Katzenstein, p. 11.

Constructivists on Security 37

tough political issues in traditional security studies.'[48] Instead, these authors are concerned with grafting a constructivist understanding of security onto the traditional parameters of security studies. They represent a structural approach to security studies – but seek to develop their structural approach by recourse to culture and identity. An ideational structure replaces the neorealist structure defined by material issues.

In an attempt to provide some coherence to the myriad studies that make up the volume, Jepperson, Wendt, and Katzenstein argue that they are building

> an orienting framework that highlights a set of effects and mechanisms that have been neglected in mainstream security studies. As such, this framework tells us about as much about the substance of world politics as does a materialist view of the international system or a choice theoretic assumption of exogenous interests. It offers a partial perspective, but one important for orienting our thinking about more specific phenomena.[49]

This 'orienting framework' requires that we take the issues of culture and identity as central to any study of security. In the words of Katzenstein, the authors seek 'to incorporate into the analysis of national security both the cultural-institutional context of the political environment and the political construction of identity.'[50] Attempting to bring together the disparate empirical studies that make up their work, Jepperson, Wendt, and Katzenstein contend there are five main lines of argument that result from the collection. First, 'cultural or institutional elements of states' environments... shape the national security interests or (directly) the security policies of states.'[51] Second, 'cultural or institutional elements of states' global or domestic environments... shape state identity.'[52] These propositions suggest an ideational structure is necessary in order to understand the security considerations of states. Culture and identity constrain behavior and give meaning to interests. Third, 'variation in state identity, or changes in state identity, affect the national security interests or policies of states.'[53] Fourth, 'configurations of state identity affect interstate normative structures, such as regimes or security communities.'[54] These propositions suggest that material conditions may have little to do with the issue of security. Fifth, 'state policies both reproduce and reconstruct cultural and institutional structure.'[55] This fifth proposition argues, with Wendt, that

---

48 Ibid.
49 Jepperson, Wendt, and Katzenstein, p. 36.
50 Katzenstein, p. 26.
51 Jepperson, Wendt, and Katzenstein, p. 54.
52 Ibid., p. 58.
53 Ibid., p. 60.
54 Ibid., p. 62.
55 Ibid., p. 63.

38 *Creating Insecurity*

anarchy is what states make of it.[56] The actions of states are both a reaction to ideational constraints and a reproduction of these structures.

While the emphasis on identity and interests suggests these authors have little in common with traditional security studies, the issues discussed and their approach to the study demonstrates some common ground between the contributors to *The Culture of National Security* and the studies of the previous chapter. Beyond a similar, narrow definition of security, both approaches suggest that we can use empirical techniques to guide a study of security. What is deemed important, however, is quite different. While traditional scholars are interested in the material capabilities of states, these studies 'illuminate how empirical analysis of cultural content and constructed identities can contribute to the study of national security.'[57]

Security: A New Framework for Analysis

A similar approach to understanding national insecurity is explored by Buzan, Wæver, and de Wilde in *Security: A New Framework for Analysis*. Accepting the traditional, narrow definition of security offered by realist texts, these authors argue that national security studies require the analyst to 'reject reductionism (giving priority to the individual as the ultimate referent object of security) as an unsound approach to international security.'[58] In language that sounds similar to subsequent versions of Waltzian neorealism, Buzan, Wæver, and de Wilde note that this rejection of the individual is required, because in terms of national security, the individual plays at best a marginal role. As with traditional studies, these constructivists recognize the specific nature of international security as meaning the 'relations between collective units and how those are reflected upward into the system.'[59]

Although the meaning of security employed here may look similar to traditional texts, the authors' use of a constructivist epistemology suggests deep divisions with mainstream approaches. *Securitizing* some event in international politics 'is essentially an intersubjective process. The senses of threat, vulnerability, and (in)security are socially constructed rather than objectively present or absent.'[60] The very idea of what it is that we study in national security studies requires interpretation. As Buzan, Wæver, and de Wilde suggest, 'security is a quality actors inject into issues by securitizing them.'[61] Theorists learn to 'underline the

---

56 Alexander Wendt, 'Anarchy is What States Make of It: the Social Construction of Power Politics,' *International Organization* 46 (Spring 1992), pp. 391-425.

57 Jepperson, Wendt, and Katzenstein, p. 53.

58 Barry Buzan, Ole Wæver, and Jaap de Wilde, *Security: A New Framework for Analysis* (Boulder, CO: Lynne Rienner, Publishers, 1998), p. 208.

59 Ibid.

60 Ibid., p. 57.

61 Ibid., p. 204.

Constructivists on Security 39

responsibility of talking security, the responsibility of actors as well as of analysts who choose to frame an issue as a security issue.'[62]

Of course, it does not follow that anything becomes a security issue simply by uttering the relevant words. Security actors must have legitimate standing and be accepted by the broader polity. Language is an intersubjective phenomenon; it is not possible for a single actor to give voice to a particular security problem without the participation of multiple actors. Buzan, Wæver, and de Wilde offer a telling reading of the scope and dimension of constructed security threats.

> Securitization is intersubjective and socially constructed: Does a referent object hold legitimacy as something that should survive, which entails that actors can make reference to it, point to something as a threat, and thereby get others to follow or at least tolerate actions not otherwise legitimate? This quality is not held in subjective and isolated minds; it is a social quality, a part of a discursive, socially constituted, intersubjective realm. For individuals or groups to speak security does not guarantee success. Successful securitization is not decided by the securitizer but by the audience of the security speech act: Does the audience accept that something is an existential threat to a shared value? Thus, security (as with all politics) ultimately rests neither with the objects nor with the subjects but among the subjects.[63]

While the social construction of security demonstrates little in common with traditional studies, the focus of the study that emerges looks very much like earlier realist works. The similarities between traditional scholarship and conventional constructivism can be understood by the fact that conventional constructivists see social relations, while discursively constituted, as petrified, inert, and sedimented.[64] Even when state agents are granted constitutive roles in the development of the discourse of international relations, language can be found to be as constraining as objective structures. Language is an *intersubjective* practice and actors are unable to promote change without the consent and acceptance of others.

Explicating conventional constructivism, Buzan, Wæver, and de Wilde demonstrate its similarities with traditional security studies as well as its differences.

> Our approach links itself more closely to existing actors, tries to understand their modus operandi, and assumes that future management of security will have to include handling these actors – as, for instance, in strategies aimed at mitigating security dilemmas and fostering mutual awareness in security complexes. Although our philosophical position is in some sense more radically constructivist in holding security to be a political construction and not something the analyst can describe as it 'really' is, in our purposes we are closer to traditional security studies, which at its best attempted to grasp security constellations and thereby steer them into benign interactions.[65]

---

62 Ibid., p. 34.
63 Ibid., p. 31.
64 Ibid., p. 205.
65 Ibid., p. 35.

40 *Creating Insecurity*

In an examination of existential factors in the military sector, Buzan, Wæver, and de Wilde recognize that in the process of securitization, '[it] is more likely that one can conjure a security threat if certain objects can be referred to that are generally held to be threatening – be they tanks, hostile sentiments, or polluted waters.'[66] This approach to security studies suggests how material factors play an intervening role in the construction of a security issue; 'objects never make for necessary securitization, but they are definitely facilitating conditions.'[67] This version of constructivism demonstrates a desire to recognize and accept the security problems that the state and its policy makers find central.

As the discussion of securitization turns to the requirements of state policy makers in times of international uncertainty, the relationship between ideational and material factors do not warrant a re-assessment of the policy making apparatus. Consider, for instance, how these authors examine international situations requiring state involvement: '[w]hen securitization is focused on external threats, military security is primarily about the two-level interplay between the actual armed offensive and defensive capabilities of states on the one hand and their perceptions of each other's capabilities and intentions on the other.'[68] Once securitization has occurred, the traditional approach is recognized as necessary to the successful management of security.

In the construction of pertinent security policies, states begin to examine issues in fairly standard ways. In a rather common interpretation of the security dilemma, Buzan, Wæver, and de Wilde require of the state sufficient perceptive qualities and rational cognitive functions necessary to perform a security calculus. In a more representative example, the authors demonstrate their concession to traditional studies once the initial construction of a security threat has been made. '[Other] things being equal, historical and material facilitating conditions affect processes of securitization and desecuritization in a fairly systematic way.'[69] This acknowledgment recognizes not only the near constancy of international social relations but the enduring quality of the 'security dilemma' story as told by the realists. Continuing, they write, '[once] military securitization has occurred, issues such as balance and technology development take a more autonomous role.'[70]

Constructivism and the Study of Security

The studies of security examined in this chapter are more diverse in both their theoretical assumptions and policy recommendations. Unlike the traditional

---

66 Ibid., p. 33.
67 Ibid.
68 Ibid., p. 51.
69 Ibid., p. 58.
70 Ibid., p. 57.

security texts of the previous chapter, these authors do not enter the study of security espousing a particular theoretical focus. Constructivism is best understood, initially, as an epistemological approach. Those working within its general parameters need not envision the *practice* of politics in a similar way. As Jorgensen correctly notes, 'constructivism is empty as far as assumptions, propositions, or hypotheses about international relations are concerned.'[71] On the issue of security, the disparate concerns that are manifested in the studies above point to the variety of policies that might follow from adherence to epistemological constructivism. These disparate concerns suggest a number of similarities and differences in the studies discussed in this chapter. In particular, the authors above converge around: (1) a challenge to the positivist approach to the study of world politics and (2) a concern for the importance of identity and culture in the investigation of the sources of insecurity. However, on two issues, the authors are substantially divided. For example, while Campbell and McSweeney make post-structural analysis central to their studies, the authors of *The Culture of National Security* emphasize their structural allegiance. Similarly, as to whether security should be studied using its traditional, narrow definition or should be widened to incorporate issues previously subsumed by security studies, these authors are divided. These differences influence whether the scholars advocate engagement with the state in its conceptualization of security or whether a more detached attitude should be thought appropriate.

Beginning with their similarities, each of the constructivists above is committed to challenging the materialist ontology and empiricist epistemology common to realism. Each recognizes the limits of our language as the limits of our world. Unlike many in the social science tradition, there is no attempt to transcend the 'existing' world and achieve a measure of 'objectivity' with which one can evaluate policy and explain political phenomena. The positivist need to generalize and regularize political life comes from a belief that the theorist can construct an empirical social science capable of explaining the activities of actors in international politics.[72] 'To explain', in this sense, implies the construction of causal models. At their core, such theories employ a *correspondence* theory of truth

---

71 Knud Erik Jorgensen, 'Four Levels and a Discipline,' in Karin M. Fierke and Knud Erik Jorgensen, eds. *Constructing International Relations: The Next Generation* (Armonk, NY: M.E. Sharpe, 2001), p. 41.

72 To complicate this brief description, it is important to note that a challenge to strict positivism (defined as adherence to a materialist ontology and an empiricist epistemology) does not make one a post-positivist. Wendt's more recent work as well as *The Culture of National Security* represent two positivist approaches to constructivism that challenge a materialist ontology but otherwise maintain a desire to construct a social scientific theory of political action. See, Alexander Wendt, *Social Theory of International Politics* (Cambridge: Cambridge University Press, 1999); and Katzenstein, ed., *The Culture of National Security.*

42   *Creating Insecurity*

that envisions an external reality to that of social actors.[73] Prior to Wittgenstein, it
was common to consider how words referred to things in the extra-linguistic world.
The philosopher's job was to match words to these things as they existed.
Prevailing theories of language stressed 'reference, correspondence,
representation.'[74] Theorists seeking correspondence could make sense of attempts
to objectify social relations and 'see' threats existing in the material world.[75]

Against this approach, the constructivists above re-introduce the importance of
the intersubjective world. As David Copeland writes, while attempting to draw the
disparate groupings of constructivism together, 'global politics is said to be guided
by the intersubjectively shared ideas, norms, and values held by actors.'[76] With
particular attention paid to national security, these concerns must be interpreted at
particular moments in history within a social milieu open to change and re-
interpretation. This version of social study is not interested in objectively
explaining behavior and modeling state activities. Rather, constructivists are
involved in interpreting specific actions within a particular social discourse. In lieu
of correspondence to truth, constructivists are involved in analyzing the coherence
of specific speech-acts. A great deal of what follows from the constructivist use of
language is a recognition that words do not stand for things in an external world but
are a part of a complex social fabric that provides the rules for the use of that
language. Hanna Pitkin gives voice to this approach, '[in] mastering a language, we
take on a culture; our native language becomes a part of ourselves, of the very
structure of the self.'[77] When taken seriously, we recognize quickly that
Wittgenstein offers something of profound import when he claims that 'the limits of
language... signify the limits of my world.'[78] If language is considered to represent
the limits of the world, then we cannot make a metaphysical claim about 'objective

---

73 For a concise explication of correspondence theories of truth, see, Mark Neufeld,
   'Reflexivity and International Relations Theory,' *Millennium: Journal of International
   Studies* 22 (Spring 1993), pp. 54-61.

74 Hanna Fenichel Pitkin, *Wittgenstein and Justice: On the Significance of Ludwig
   Wittgenstein for Social and Political Thought* (Berkeley, CA: University of California
   Press, 1972), p. 3.

75 In a discussion concerning how philosophical concepts are brought into the social
   sciences, Hanna Pitkin argues, 'For most of us who work in political and social studies,
   the inherited, unexamined fragments of philosophy we bring to our work derive from
   some form of positivism, and thus from a model of the physical sciences developed by
   philosophers in the 1920s. These fragments are likely to include certain assumptions
   about what constitutes "the real world," such as that it is "out there" rather than "in
   here." They are likely to include the assumption that the world consists exclusively of
   facts, about which we make descriptive statements, and of values, about which we make
   normative statements. They are likely to favor the abstract and general over the concrete
   and specific; objectivity over the self; rationality over affect.' Ibid.

76 Dale Copeland, 'The Constructivist Challenge to Structural Realism,' *International
   Security* 25 (Fall 2000), p. 189.

77 Pitkin, p. 3.

78 Wittgenstein, p. 115.

Constructivists on Security 43

threats.' There is no position at which one can rise above social discourse in order to look back at the discursive world and match it up with an external reality. Here, then, positivist influences on traditional security studies become a common problem requiring attention by each of our constructivists.[79]

The constructivist requirement that we emphasize the intersubjective world translates further into a similar need to recognize the importance of identity and culture on interests. While there are differences in how much to emphasize the issues of culture and identity, it is clear that the cultural milieu in which identities are perpetuated and challenged is a necessary component to a robust understanding of the sources of insecurity. For example, consider how *identity* and *interest* are understood to matter in the work of Martha Finnemore, '[we] cannot understand what states want without understanding the international social structure of which they are a part.'[80] Similarly, Hopf argues that the 'identity of a state implies its preferences and consequent actions.'[81] Therefore, what counts as a security concern (and a reasoned policy option to manage that concern) is intimately tied to a state's sense of self. This is a matter of historical contingency and requires we examine specific cultural identities. Returning to Finnemore, 'the international system can change what states want. It is constitutive and generative, creating new interests and values for actors.'[82] Each of the constructivists above recognizes the importance placed on identity and culture in understanding security.

On two issues, however, constructivists are engaged in serious debate. Campbell and McSweeney are committed to a post-structural analysis. Their works demonstrate as much hostility to the 'ideational structures' of certain constructivists as the 'materialist structures' of neorealists. Structures cannot *cause* behavior. As

---

79 It is crucial to recognize the limits of this 'post-positivist' similarity. The recent writings by Wendt, as well as other 'conservative constructivists' (a term employed by Ralph Pettman) suggests that these constructivists are, in fact, positivists. Increasingly, Wendt has objectified the social world in order to do 'scientific research'. While I am sympathetic to Pettman's concerns, it would appear that some distance still exists between the positivism employed by traditional security texts and Wendt's positivism. Much of this distance is the result of the dissimilar ontological positions of these scholars. Wendt's acceptance of ideational structures and ideas as 'facts' just the same as material structures and physical entities, allows him to employ positivist techniques in the investigation of international politics. However, this does not necessarily mean the Wendt is a thorough-going positivist. As Maja Zehfuss notes, Wendt's most recent writings are an attempt to bridge rationalist and reflexive studies. See, Maja Zehfuss, 'Constructivism in International Relations: Wendt, Onuf, and Kratochwil,' in Fierke and Jorgensen, p. 56. For a deeper discussion that involves an alternative view to that offered above, see, Ralph Pettman, 'Commonsense Constructivism and Foreign Policy: A Critique of Rule-Oriented Constructivism,' in Vendulka Kubalkova, ed. *Foreign Policy in a Constructed World* (Armonk, NY: M.E. Sharpe, 2001), pp. 249-265.

80 Martha Finnemore, *National Interests in International Society* (Ithaca, NY: Cornell University Press, 1996), p. 2.

81 Hopf, p. 175.

82 Finnemore, pp. 5-6.

44   *Creating Insecurity*

McSweeney writes, '[in] the real world... there is no objective structural entity which can function as an independent cause of social relations.'[83] For this reason, McSweeney is drawn to Wendt's earlier work on the agent structure debate[84] but finds his more recent work to reflect philosophical affinity with rationalism. McSweeney's concern with the focus of Wendt's later work represents a paradigmatic example of the ongoing debate between post-structural constructivism and neo-liberal constructivism. As he suggests,

> Wendt appears to have abandoned the recursiveness of the agent-structure relationship which earlier characterized his break with the mainstream approach, in favour of a social constructionist one permitting causal explanation of social events according to the model of natural science. 'Neo-liberal constructivism' is a more accurate label for a school which has far more in common with the liberal-rationalist emphasis on transnational cooperation, institutions and norms, and on the unproblematic primacy of the state than with a research agenda based on reflexivist principles of the continuity of the collective and individual actor and of the co-constitution of agency and structure.[85]

McSweeney wishes to distinguish between a more radical form of constructivism that re-conceptualizes agency, structure, and causality in the social sciences and a neo-liberal constructivism that suggests 'an eirenic endeavor capable of bringing intellectual harmony to a discipline threatened by dissident critics of its positivist mainstream.'[86]

Similarly, we see a need for Campbell to separate his work from the same 'neo-liberal constructivists' that haunt McSweeney. His strongest criticism is saved for the contributors to *The Culture of National Security*. He argues that in their work, culture and identity become essentialist variables that are 'inserted into already existing theoretical commitments.'[87] These theoretical commitments, of course, rest on the positivist principles that Campbell finds suspect. Campbell sees in the effort of *The Culture of National Security* a similar need to treat culture and identity as variables in a causal model of actor behavior. Substituting these variables for the material capabilities of traditional texts, the contributors simply locate the policy maker 'outside the domain of constitution'[88] and able to manipulate these new variables. We see in Campbell's criticism a need to distinguish between an earlier Wendt that recognized mutual constitution and co-determination and a later Wendt that finds much in common with the rationalist research agenda.[89]

---

83 McSweeney, p. 210.
84 Alexander Wendt, 'The Agent-Structure Problem in International Relations Theory,' *International Organization* 41 (Summer 1987), pp. 335-370.
85 McSweeney, p. 207. For a further discussion of the differences between McSweeney and Wendt, see, pp. 122-125.
86 Ibid., p. 203.
87 Campbell, p. 218.
88 Ibid., p. 219.
89 Ibid., p. 220.

The post-structural emphasis by McSweeney and Campbell is tempered in both *The Culture of National Security* and *Security: A New Framework for Analysis*. While the above critique suggests the position of the former, Buzan, Wæver, and de Wilde require more attention. These authors '*do* take identities as socially constituted but not radically moreso than other social structures.'[90] More specifically, these authors recognize how an investigation of identity can be performed in standard ways.

Identities as other social constructions can petrify and become relatively constant elements to be reckoned with. At specific points, this 'inert constructivism' enables modes of analysis very close to objectivist – for example, Waltzian neorealism, as long as one remembers that in the final instance the ontology is not Waltz's naturalism and atomism but some form of constructivism or even, in line with classical realism, rhetorical foundations.[91]

Although Buzan, Wæver, and de Wilde emphasize how 'radically constructivist'[92] their approach is, it is the attempt to implement an objectivist mode-of-analysis that concerns writers like McSweeney and Campbell. This places the state (as an unproblematic unit) at the center of a research agenda that attempts to manage relations between like units.[93] Furthermore, the divide that begins at a meta-theoretical level between Campbell/McSweeney and the writers of *The Culture of National Security* and *Security: A New Framework for Analysis* extends to their theoretical positions.

The traditional, narrow definition of security is employed by Katzenstein, et. al., and Buzan, Wæver, and de Wilde. These authors recognize a need to understand the *particular* security issues envisioned by actors involved in shaping state policy. Their goal is not a refutation of current security programmes but rather a deeper understanding of these issues. Contrary to this approach, Campbell and McSweeney seek to problematize the very issues that are labeled as national *security* concerns. Campbell sees such a need arising from the requirements of fulfilling a *democratic ethos*. McSweeney articulates a new form of security studies arising from the ontological requirements of individual human needs.

As chapter four will discuss, this divide in the constructivist literature points to a distinct political stance arising out of the post-structural constructivism espoused by Campbell and McSweeney. Their commitment to improving the human condition through investigation and reflection of security problems speaks to a desire to transcend the sources of insecurity envisioned by traditional security studies and those working in what McSweeney calls the tradition of 'neo-liberal constructivism'. Before we turn to a discussion of the sources of insecurity and how

---

90 Ibid., p. 205.
91 Buzan, Weaver, and de Wilde, p. 205.
92 Ibid., p. 206.
93 Ibid., p. 206.

46   *Creating Insecurity*

to understand them, the following section considers the successes and failures of the overall constructivist project.

The Successes and Failures of Constructivism

Writers employing some form of constructivism in an attempt to more deeply understand matters of security demonstrate a concern for both a coherent epistemology and an interest in the use of language. Concerned by the limitations inherent in realism's attempt to provide a general theory of international politics, each of the contributors to constructivist security studies challenges the focus and foundation of traditional works. Recognizing how traditional studies often make truth-claims that cannot withstand critical investigation, these constructivists more accurately demonstrate how traditional security studies are particular interpretations of world politics rather than universally-applicable theories of generalized behavior. It is the alternative epistemological account of human understanding exemplified in constructivism that allows us to more accurately characterize realism as a rhetorical tool rather than general theory.

Of course, the knowledge claims useful to constructivists rest on their coherence. It is a reliance on language and its use in making sense of the world that lies at the heart of the constructivist project. Yet language plays a more specific role than as general epistemological tool. Most clearly expressed by Buzan, Wæver, and de Wilde, how specific situations are *securitized*[94] tells us much about the social milieu in which specific actors maneuver. The label *security* is an important one. It differentiates average events in international life from those deemed so important to relevant actors that they require extra-ordinary political decisions. Even where constructivists may disagree as to the use of the term *security*, there is agreement that once that specific speech-act is made, the political stakes have been raised and a highly specialized discourse has been entered into.

But the constructivist project has not been without its problems. Specifically, constructivism has been considered policy-irrelevant. It offers us a way to understand and reflect on our world but does nothing to tell us how to navigate that world. As a policy tool, constructivism would require a moral component. The ability to construct a coherent understanding of world politics requires moral teachings that assist in making political choices from that understanding. While some constructivists have demonstrated how reflection and critique can be used to influence the political process, constructivism seems to complicate the policy making process rather than assist it. As noted, security studies bridges the divide between theoretical investigation and policy relevance. In order to offer something useful to the state, studies must accept many of the assumptions upon which the state exists. The inability to provide policy direction makes the constructivist

---

94 Ibid., pp. 33-35.

project as incomplete an approach to security studies as realist thought, albeit for remarkably different reasons.

In the following chapter, I seek to engage both realists and constructivists in a more rigorous discussion of national security studies. While neither realism nor constructivism presents a comprehensive approach to national security studies, I hope to demonstrate that both are necessary components of a more sophisticated understanding of the sources of insecurity.

Chapter 4

Understanding the Sources of Insecurity

Traditional security studies, drawing on realist premises, insist on a link to military and strategic concerns. These studies present a decidedly negative vision of international politics. Conversely, studies drawing on a broadly-defined constructivism often eschew pressing state security concerns and instead focus on problematizing identity constructs in order to investigate alternative political issues. In their current condition, both approaches undermine the potential for a more successful study of security. Neither approach is a complete rendering of the security problematique. Traditional concerns resting on positivist principles, while focused on the policy-relevant topic of *national* security, collapse in epistemological incoherence while attempting to articulate *real* security threats. When these studies succeed in demonstrating the importance of a particular security issue, their one-sided view of world politics hinders a complete security analysis. However, alternative approaches rarely offer a complete picture either. Those constructivist works emphasizing constant critique of identity and culture neglect state policy concerns and collapse in irrelevance. Unwilling or unable to engage the state at a point necessary for practical policy debate, reflexive scholars become marginalized when needed most. What is necessary is an approach to security that is both philosophically coherent and policy relevant. Toward that end, this chapter brings together conceptual thinking from both approaches in an attempt to construct a more comprehensive concept of security and address the pressing concerns of world politics.

In what will initially appear somewhat controversial, I propose we come to understand constructivism by differentiating two aspects of the approach. First, we might consider a general *constructivist* epistemology as a necessary prerequisite to a coherent analysis of security. This portion of the security process has been suggested to us in the framework outlined by Buzan, Wæver, and de Wilde. Their understanding of constructivism suggests its role in recognizing how language defines the world in which actors live. Accepting this point, we can envision a 'constructivist umbrella' over the discussion that follows. It is important to recognize how this epistemological constructivism challenges our ability to understand security issues. Unlike realists, we are unable to speak of *real* security threats. Securitization is a practice that brings about broad recognition of a threat. The specific act of labeling something a threat makes it real- but we have no 'god's eye' position as analysts, to critique the existential merit of that specific speech-act. Taken to the extreme, this would lead to security relativism. But Buzan, Wæver, and de Wilde insist that such a position need not be taken. The concept of security, like all concepts, is intersubjective in nature. Simply because one actor demands we see a particular act as relating to security does not mean that it is securitized. Speech-acts require the implicit or explicit acceptance of a host of actors to be deemed plausible. Further, specific actions might be 'security' threats even when prominent actors refuse to label them so. The rise of Hitler's Germany presents a classic example. At what point is Hitler a threat to Europe: in 1936 when he reoccupies the Rhineland, in 1938 when he creates the *Anschluss*, in 1939 with the invasion of Poland, or at another point in between his rise and the beginning of the War? While a debate would seem inevitable, realists are content with recognizing that Hitler is a *real* security threat. Whether he is labeled so or not, Hitler's Germany represents an existential threat to international peace and security – a claim that on the face of it would seem to undermine the 'securitization' argument and the form of epistemological constructivism advocated here. However, as will be demonstrated below, constructivists do not deny the phenomenal world. What is at stake at the epistemological level is not *what* constitutes a security threat but *how* that threat becomes known to actors.

Within this epistemological constructivism, two rhetorical visions of politics currently play opposing roles in the investigation of insecurity. We might consider these visions as competing positions along a continuum. These positions are not the logical limits of thought on security politics. Rather, they are best understood as the most prevalent political positions engaged in discourse at this time.[1] The first perspective, realism, acts as a rhetorical device to influence state policy makers. It presents a grossly negative vision of international politics – maintaining that dangers (threats) exist outside the state in the international environment. Management of conflict and the mitigation of insecurity are the rational limits of a realist foreign policy. Realism's policy proposals are best articulated by the 'cautious paranoid' seeking to secure the state against a potential enemy. They are reticent to trust other actors in the system and consistently examine the direst possible consequences of policy options.

The second rhetorical perspective suggests the possibility of overcoming this negative vision and improving the human condition. Adherents suggest it is theoretically possible to transcend the current condition of insecurity. However, this political perspective should not be confused as the philosophical progeny of inter-war political idealism. Early forms of idealism recognized the power of the humanist spirit and sought to transcend insecurity by proposing peace through law, collective security arrangements, democratization, trade, and the success of international peace movements. The rhetorical perspective that is of interest to this study represents a practical (political) application of post-structural constructivism. *Political constructivism* requires policy makers, analysts, and other actors to reflect

---

1   This idea is most clear in Yale H. Ferguson and Richard W. Mansbach, *The Elusive Quest: Theory and International Relations* (Columbia, SC: University of South Carolina Press, 1988), pp. 212-222.

50 *Creating Insecurity*

on and consistently critique their pre-given assumptions concerning identities and interests. A deep investigation of culture is a required component in the process of overcoming insecurity. Political constructivists are a sub-set of the larger community of epistemological constructivists. While all constructivists recognize the importance of general epistemological points, not all constructivists adhere to the reflexive critiques engaged in by political constructivists. Moreover, as discussed below, it is not necessarily the case that constructivism leads to the set of political values emphasized in this chapter. But, there are significant reasons to recognize a distinct community of scholars engaged in understanding the importance of reflection and constant criticism in an effort to transcend the sources of insecurity.

The divergent political visions and policy proposals that confront us when examining the realist and political constructivist world views is striking. If realists are inclined to ask whether the relative difference in material capabilities (power) favors the state in question, political constructivists are inclined to ask how cultural constraints and identity performances reproduce the interests and security dynamics of that state. These divergent perspectives can be set against each other in the analysis of national security. Representing the competing security perspectives largely responsible for the growing schism in the field, each perspective has been treated as a larger theoretical enterprise capable of understanding insecurity and prescribing policy to counter it.[2] In this chapter, I argue that both are necessary components of a deeper process that requires further analysis in order to offer the state a comprehensive and robust security analysis.

As rhetorical devices for understanding international politics, realism and political constructivism are not the last step in the security framework but the first. Insight from both must be filtered through subsequent analytic processes. For instance, after a security issue has been articulated by both perspectives, a security dialogue can further refine the specific understanding of the threat. Because neither realism nor political constructivism seems capable of providing the state with a comprehensive vision of threats and the means to overcome them, this subsequent analysis is necessary in order to construct policy options that balance the requirements of both perspectives. Rather than seeking commensurability or truth from the opposing political visions, this subsequent security calculus attempts to balance the tension between the two. Realism and political constructivism are complementary forces that ask different questions and elicit different answers. Each provides a partial response to the state's concern with insecurity.

In the discussion that follows, I outline each of the components of this approach to analyzing insecurity. Beginning with constructivism as an epistemology, I will

---

2 This is, perhaps, best demonstrated by looking to various scholarly journals. 'Traditional' security studies journals, like *International Security* and *Survival* emphasize the importance of realism and its variants. Journals such as *Millennium* and *Alternatives* have increasingly published articles by security 'wideners' and post-structural security theorists.

Understanding the Sources of Insecurity   51

proceed through a description of each rhetorical vision of politics, and conclude with a vision of security that brings together a realist perspective and a political constructivist perspective.

Constructivism as Epistemology

At the most general level of a security analysis it is necessary to recognize the role that language plays in the process of threat construction and the collective feelings of insecurity. The 'objectivist' features of traditional security studies rest on shaky epistemological foundations. The materialist ontology and empiricist epistemology that pervade neorealism seek to understand *real* threats and dangers that exist in an extra-linguistic universe. Against this approach, we can agree with Buzan, Wæver, and de Wilde that security issues are made so 'by acts of securitization.'[3] While the language they employ is somewhat difficult, their understanding of the importance of 'speech-acts' is central to the development of a coherent security analysis. Emphasizing the constructed nature of our world, these authors do much to influence the direction of security studies. They articulate an understanding of security threats that recognizes the central role played by human interpretation in their creation.

> We do not try to peek behind this to decide whether it is *really* a threat (which would reduce the entire securitization approach to a theory of perceptions and misperceptions). Security is a quality actors inject into issues by securitizing them, which means to stage them on the political arena... and then to have them accepted by a sufficient audience to sanction extraordinary defensive moves.[4]

Here, we can be even more direct. It is not simply that we do not *try* to peek behind particular threats to decide whether they warrant such a label, it is the impossibility of such an endeavor that sets for us the parameters of our security framework. Here, Nicholas Onuf is most clear: '[we] are always within our constructions, even as we choose to stand apart from them, condemn them, reconstruct them.'[5] Similarly, Karin Fierke writes, 'we cannot get behind our language to compare it with that which it describes.'[6] In a very real and meaningful way the limits of our language define the limits of our threats. Threats do not 'exist'

---

3   Barry Buzan, Ole Wæver, and Jaap de Wilde, *Security: A New Framework for Analysis* (Boulder, CO: Lynne Rienner Publishers, 1998), p. 204. See also, pp. 23-26.

4   Ibid., p. 204.

5   Nicholas G. Onuf, *World of Our Making: Rules and Rule in Social Theory and International Relations* (Columbia, SC: University of South Carolina Press, 1989), p. 43.

6   Karin M. Fierke, 'Critical Methodology and Constructivism,' in *Constructing International Relations: The Nest Generation*, Karin M. Fierke and Knud Erik Jorgensen (Armonk, NY: M.E. Sharpe, 2001), p. 118.

52 *Creating Insecurity*

in any objective and measurable sense beyond the speech-acts that create them. In Milliken's words, 'things do not mean (the material world does not convey meaning); rather, people construct the meaning of things.'[7] Therefore, there is no access to a pre-discursive world because such a world cannot be envisioned without using language. 'Our interpretations are based on a shared system of codes and symbols, of languages, life-worlds, social practices. The knowledge of reality is socially constructed.'[8] This is an important point that often causes a great deal of confusion in the philosophy of social science.[9] The form of epistemological constructivism advocated here is not involved in the ongoing philosophical debate between (philosophical) realists and anti-realists. Indeed, it is quite possible to envision a 'constructive realism,' 'according to which the agent has an epistemic but not an ontological influence, that is, knowledge is constructive in nature, but the existence of the world does not depend on the existence of the agent.'[10] Guzzini makes this point.

> Constructivism does not deny the existence of a phenomenal world, external to thought. This is the world of brute (mainly natural) facts. It does oppose, and this is something different, that phenomena can constitute themselves as objects of knowledge independently of discursive practices. It does not challenge the possible thought-independent existence of (in particular natural) phenomena, but it challenges their language-independent observation. What counts as a socially meaningful object or event is always the result of an interpretive construction of the world out there.[11]

Returning to writings on national security, Buzan, Wæver, and de Wilde recognize how material factors contribute to the process of securitization. 'It is more likely that one can conjure a security threat if certain objects can be referred to that are generally held to be threatening – be they tanks, hostile sentiments, or polluted waters.'[12] Continuing, they argue, 'these objects never make for necessary securitization, but they are facilitating conditions.'[13] Constructivism, as a general epistemological approach, demonstrates how language defines the world in which we live. This understanding of constructivism might be differentiated from the

---

7   Jennifer Milliken, 'Discourse Study: Bringing Rigor to Critical Theory,' in *Constructing International Relations*, p. 138.

8   Stefano Guzzini, 'A Reconstruction of Constructivism in International Relations,' *European Journal of International Relations* 6, 2 (2000), pp. 159-160.

9   Jonathan Potter, *Representing Reality: Discourse, Rhetoric, and Social Construction* (London: Sage Publications, 1996), p. 7.

10 Aaron Ben-Ze'ev, 'Is There a Problem in Explaining Cognitive Process?' in *Rethinking Knowledge: Reflections Across the Disciplines*, eds. Robert F. Goodman and Walter R. Fisher (Albany, NY: State University of New York Press, 1995), p. 50. Cited in Knud Erik Jorgensen, 'Four Levels and a Discipline,' in *Constructing International Relations*, p. 39.

11 Guzzini, p. 159.

12 Buzan, Wæver, and de Wilde, p. 33.

13 Ibid.

political constructivism that seeks political change through a consistent, reflexive critique of cultural constructs and identity performances (to be discussed in the following section). Conscious recognition of these parameters allows us to place the rhetorical visions of politics (elevated to the status of general theories of international relations by earlier writers) within a broadly constructivist rendition of international relations so as to more accurately and rigorously analyze the sources of state insecurity.

But we should be clear as to exactly what a constructivist epistemology does and does not do for the study of security. By advocating a constructivist epistemology we have removed the tendency to see threats to security as existing in the material or phenomenal world without the requirement of actor interpretation. Threats become important when relevant actors label them so. Accepting this position, Buzan, Wæver, and de Wilde 'abstain from attempts to talk about what 'real security' would be for people, what are 'actual' security problems larger than those propagated by elites.'[14]

Adopting this epistemological approach does nothing to change the focus of security studies. It remains possible to locate the state at the center of analysis and limit discussions to *national* security issues. Material capabilities, once securitized, are still an important locus of concern for the analyst and policy maker. But, an epistemological constructivism does not confine discussions of security to material factors. The positivist influence on realism required that security analysis be limited to material issues amenable to empirical research. Our constructivist umbrella accepts these issues in an analysis of security, yet remains open to the possibility of exploring further the socially constituted, and therefore socially alterable, world. Karin Fierke puts it nicely. 'The point of departure for constructivism is that the world is changeable, that the past, present, and future are constructed through our practices and interactions with others.'[15] Taking this point of departure seriously, we are able to envelop multiple political visions within a constructivist epistemology that treats language as central to the theoretical endeavor.

We might consider two different visions of politics – realism and political constructivism – within our constructivist epistemology. Unlike previous security texts, I take these visions as partial answers to questions concerning the sources of insecurity. In the following section, I demonstrate how both political visions are required in order to more fully understand security threats.

Interpreting Politics

If we accept the constructivist epistemology outlined above, we are able to subsume a critical form of realism and political form of constructivism into our

---

14 Buzan, Wæver, and de Wilde, p. 35.
15 Fierke, p. 129.

54   *Creating Insecurity*

security analysis. Once subsumed, both are treated as rhetorical devices rather than general theories of international politics. Below, I will examine how each political vision informs a discussion of security. Both discussions will proceed in a similar manner. First, I will explore why each interpretation is better understood as a rhetorical device rather than a general theory. Second, I will explore what each offers a study of security. Third, I will discuss specifically how we can use the interpretation in a robust security analysis.

Realism, Cautious Paranoia, and Material Capabilities

As our discussion in chapter two suggests, realism is best understood as a rhetorical tool for influencing the policy maker rather than a general theory of international politics. Understanding the normative core of realism is necessary in that it allows us to recognize a particular vision of world politics that emphasizes the dangerous side of relations between states. Michael C. Williams articulates the realist attempt to 'objectify' politics by implementing a materialist ontology and empiricist epistemology. He argues that instead of using these ontological and empirical positions to study security issues, neorealists were more likely to have been engaged in *constructing* 'a material and objective foundation for political practice.'[16] Williams insists that we view neorealism as a form of politics seeking to convince others of the merits of treating security issues in a material way. By so doing, he argues that recent attempts to contrast realist and constructivist security studies are misleading. 'These debates should not ... be structured as a contrast between objectivist or "positivist" theoretical foundations [and constructivist foundations], but as historically located disputes about the politics of theorizing security and the practical implications of doing so in different ways.'[17] This is an important contribution to moving the study of security forward. Williams recognizes the rhetorical quality of both realist and constructivist security studies. Moreover, he offers us a way to employ realism in a critical interpretation of state policy. If scholars recognize realism's rhetorical quality and dismiss attempts to view realism as a general theory of international politics, it becomes much easier to establish intellectual space between realist thought and the politics of the state.

Speaking to the realist programme in general, Ferguson and Mansbach demonstrate how the ascendance of realism after WWII perpetuated a consideration of realism as a scientific theory of international politics.

> In successfully setting the agenda, realists also succeeded in perpetuating a false dichotomy; that is, that they were hard-headed empiricists – in contrast to their quixotic adversaries – whose close reading of history enabled them to discern general laws of politics by means of induction. In fact, the general laws that realists propounded were

---

16 Michael C. Williams, 'Identity and the Politics of Security,' *European Journal of International Relations* 4, 2 (1998), p. 206.

17 Ibid.

Understanding the Sources of Insecurity   55

value-laden assumptions buttressed by a ransacking of history. And those assumptions reflect normative commitments antithetical to the beliefs of idealists.[18]

It is necessary to re-orient thinking on this matter in order to employ realism as an important interpretation of international politics. Realism 'is not the heir to a neutral, non-political orientation toward the world, but the (frequently unconscious) result of an attempt to transform theory in order to transform practice.'[19] It represents the voice of the cautious paranoid, the individual wary of acting in any manner that might cause harm or potentially endanger the state. It gains force from investigating and calling attention to potential sources of insecurity. Threats based on the material capabilities of others must be seen as such because of their linguistic claim rather than their existential presence. Material capabilities alone do not make the threat; it is the political imagination that constructs a scenario whereby a threat is said to exist. Realism's reliance on material considerations and empirical research to understand those considerations presents the analyst with a particular set of threat potentials. Recourse to a constructivist epistemology allows us to analyze the security claims made by political actors employing a realist understanding of international politics.

A current example might help articulate this point. At present, the United States national security apparatus is attempting to root out international *terrorists* in a host of countries because it is believed that they represent a threat to U.S. interests. Potentially hostile actors exist 'out there.' 'Reality, on this basis, is a world of tangible, palpable, perceptible things or objects.... It is material and concrete.'[20] Accordingly, empirical evidence is required in order to counter the potential threats posed by terrorists abroad. 'Valid knowledge claims must refer to materially existing, observable objects.'[21] In this way, U.S. security agencies can point to weapons systems, hide-outs, e-mails, and bank accounts as palpable clues in the investigation of state insecurity. This contribution to national security policy making should not be underestimated. Pragmatic responses to the perception of immediate dangers are a necessary component of an effective state. As Williams notes, 'materialism and empiricism can be considered epistemic ethical practices, justified not only in terms of knowledge but also in terms of their practical contributions and consequences.'[22] One of the advantages to realism as an approach to understanding national security issues is that it coheres well with the technical and bureaucratic orientation of the state.

However, we need to recognize exactly what this means for a comprehensive approach to security. In our example above, it is necessary to ask whether the state

---

18 Ferguson and Mansbach, p. 96.
19 Williams, pp. 216-217.
20 Williams, p. 208. Williams is citing the work of Jim George, *Discourses of Global Politics* (Boulder, CO: Lynne Rienner Publishers, 1994), p. 11.
21 Williams, p. 208.
22 Ibid., p. 213.

56 *Creating Insecurity*

security apparatus has discovered a source of insecurity by locating empirical evidence. More generally, do security threats exist 'out there' waiting to be discovered by analysts and state actors? This can only be answered in the affirmative if we accept that a process of securitization has occurred prior to or as a result of the discovery of evidence. Potential sources of existential danger can be discovered to be in existence at any given time. What makes them sources of insecurity, *i.e.* threats to national security, is the specific speech-act by pertinent actors within the state. It is the construction of just how such a 'threat' will endanger the state that makes an existential object a national security concern. Realism's importance in the security calculus comes not from its reliance on positivist principles or its claim to being a general theory but from its persuasive force in articulating the potential dangers resulting from a specific set of concerns – *exemplified by material objects*. Yet a comprehensive understanding of the sources of insecurity would be incomplete if we relied only on realism's material emphasis. We would be left without an answer to those 'first questions.' Our constructivist epistemology allows us to recognize other sources of insecurity as well.

Political Constructivism, Identity, and Cultural Reflection

In *The Elusive Quest*, Ferguson and Mansbach suggest that 'ideas emerge and compete in international relations scholarship in ... response to... the normative temper of the times. Schools of thought in international relations reflect the Zeitgeist of their age as much as do ideas in art and literature.'[23] If their assertion is correct, and there is good reason to believe it is, then what is competing with realism during this particular period of history? If realism provides our study with a negative vision of international relations, is there a political interpretation that outlines a potentially positive vision?

In retrospect, the ascendance of realism during the Cold War seems appropriate. Its negative view of inter-state relations and its emphasis on hostile intent and material capabilities was well-suited for a discussion of the relations between two superpowers possessing large nuclear arsenals and competing ideological postures. It only seems natural, then, that in the aftermath of the Cold War we should see a challenge to realism that is better suited to a different normative temper. In an age increasingly defined by post-modern art, architecture, literature, and performance, the current challenge might best be expressed in post-modern/post-structural terms. Or, drawing on developments in critical studies, this challenge might be expressed as a need to challenge dominant power structures in the work place, at home, and in national and international politics. We might speak of a critical constructivist approach that challenges dominant realist tenets.[24] In what follows, I will outline a

---

23 Ferguson and Mansbach, p. 217.

24 For a discussion of critical security studies, see, Keith Krause and Michael C. Williams, eds. *Critical Security Studies* (Minneapolis, MN: University of Minnesota Press, 1997).

Understanding the Sources of Insecurity 57

version of political constructivism that draws on the post-structural variant of constructivism outlined in chapter three as well as constructivist scholars drawn to critique and reconstitution in an attempt to understand political phenomena. Here, we are interested in the *politics* of a particular set of constructivist scholars rather than the epistemological practices that engage their work. As such, we can locate a *political constructivism* that offers quite a different interpretation of politics from that of realism.[25]

Political constructivism seeks to investigate how identity performances and cultural boundaries define the sources of insecurity by differentiating self and other.[26] In these instances, the other is 'threatening', 'dangerous', and 'destructive' of the self which is defined in opposing terms. It is the image of the other that creates the sense of insecurity. Cultural ideas rather than material capabilities represent the sources of insecurity.

Before a full investigation of this form of constructivism is undertaken, however, it is necessary to consider why political constructivism is appropriately juxtaposed to realism as the most promising alternative to the negative vision of international politics. This discussion revolves around the debate as to where realism and political constructivism are located on the general political continuum. Returning to a standard view of IR theory, it is often noted that realism and neoliberalism represent the two main contending theoretical approaches in the discipline. Furthermore, realism is recognized to reside 'on the right side of the general political spectrum.'[27] 'Adding concerns over human welfare and dignity to the agenda, liberal institutionalists stand to the left of realists.'[28] When the debate

---

25 This idea has been explored by Pauline Rosenau, 'Once Again Into the Fray: International Relations Confronts the Humanities,' *Millenium: Journal of International Studies* 19 (Spring 1990), pp. 83-110. See, also, Yosef Lapid, 'The Third Debate: On the Prospect of International Theory in a Post-Positivist Era,' *International Studies Quarterly* 33, 3 (1989), pp. 235-254.

26 In a recent essay, Yale Ferguson and Richard Mansbach offer a telling reading of the current battle between realism and their version of a contender. For our purposes, it is interesting how their contending approach that might replace realism emphasizes identity and culture (and therefore demonstrates some affinity with the political constructivism outlined here). 'Surely we must discard and replace theory that fails to shed light on issues that any reader of today's headlines knows are most important. But replace it with what? In our view, we should conceive of global politics as involving a world of "polities" rather than states and focus on the relationships among authority, identities, and ideology. Central questions are: In particular times and places, who or what controls which persons with regard to which issues, and why? How and why do old political affiliations evolve or die and new ones emerge?' See, Yale H. Ferguson and Richard W. Mansbach, 'The Past as Prelude to the Future?: Identities and Loyalties in Global Politics,' in *The Return of Culture and Identity in IR Theory* Yosef Lapid and Friedrich Kratochwil, eds. (Boulder, CO: Lynne Rienner, Inc., 1996), p. 21.

27 Nicholas G. Onuf, 'The Politics of Constructivism,' in *Constructing International Relations*, p. 253.

28 Ibid.

58   *Creating Insecurity*

between realism and neoliberalism achieved a rapprochement of sorts in the early 1990s, '[b]eleaguered liberal institutionalists found a fresh voice in constructivism.'[29] Moreover, as work in constructivism grew; other left-leaning scholars not associated with neoliberal institutionalism were drawn to constructivism. 'Scholars from across the left turned to constructivism, finding in it renewed hope for social understanding, a framework for programs of social and political reconstruction, or a critical instrument for political emancipation.'[30]

As our discussion above suggests, a particular political stance does not logically follow from constructivism's epistemological and ontological positions. Yet, scholars studying the political aspects of constructivist literature were quick to make the neoliberal-constructivist link. Mearsheimer, for instance, argues that constructivists are really 'naïve political utopians.'[31] Their works suggest that constructivism is merely a cover for traditional (and according to Mearsheimer, discredited) liberal values. Steve Smith goes so far as to say that 'social constructivism... is very close to the neoliberalist wing of the rationalist paradigm.'[32] Walt, more generally, considers three theoretical approaches involved in current debates within IR – realism, liberalism, and constructivism.[33] He, too, notes the connection between liberal values and constructivism.

The question, however, is *why*? While it may be a curious 'sociology of science fact that for some reason liberal scholars have been more active than realists or globalists in promoting the constructivist turn,'[34] there is no *a priori* reason why conservative political principles could not be espoused by constructivists.[35] If the world is as we make it, then why have conservative scholars not demanded a return to conditions more suitable to their political values? While a full investigation of these questions takes us beyond the scope of the current discussion, it is important to consider what a number of left or liberal scholars have procured from constructivism in order to develop a not insignificant set of political works that demand a reconsideration of the concept of security. In order to do so, it is necessary to differentiate an epistemological constructivism from a sub-set of

---

29 Ibid.

30 Ibid.

31 Discussed in Fierke and Jorgensen, 'Introduction,' in Constructing International Relations, p. 6. This follows the discussion in John J. Mearsheimer, 'The False Promise of International Institutions,' *International Security* 19, 3 (1995), pp. 5-49.

32 Steve Smith, 'Foreign Policy is What States Make of it: Social Construction and International Relations Theory,' in *Foreign Policy in a Constructed World* Vendulka Kubalkova, ed. (Armonk, NY: M.E. Sharpe, 2001), p. 44.

33 Stephen Walt, 'International Relations: One World, Many Theories,' *Foreign Policy* 110 (1998), p. 38.

34 Knud Erik Jorgensen, 'Four Levels and a Discipline,' in *Constructing International Relations*, p. 47.

35 For a compelling discussion of this issue at a deeper, philosophical level, see, Steve Fuller, 'The Reflexive Politics of Constructivism,' *History of the Human Sciences* 7, 1 (1994), pp. 87-93.

Understanding the Sources of Insecurity 59

constructivist scholars that use reflection and critique to challenge the traditional (dominant) view of security issues.

If the realist approach seeks to remove security issues from the political arena so that they can be analyzed in the light of positivist social science, political constructivists are involved in the act of hyper-politicization. Huysmans provides a succinct understanding of this view when arguing that specific security policies are 'neither innocent nor neutral nor inevitable, and therefore [they are] political.'[36] In a more general discussion of the potential for constructivists to engage in political critique, Ralph Pettman outlines what he terms 'commonsense constructivism'. He argues for scholars to not only get close in order to understand the issues they investigate, but also to take part in the political process. 'Commonsense constructivists stand back and look, stand close and listen, take part, then stand back and look again. They objectify, subjectify in the most radical way possible, then objectify again.'[37]

This approach to constructivism places Pettman somewhere between the rule-oriented constructivists like Onuf and the Miami group and the ideas of postmodern constructivists like Campbell. In agreement with rule-oriented constructivists, Pettman argues that a moderate form of rule-oriented rationalism is an appropriate tool for investigating social phenomena, but he does not endorse a positivist epistemology. Also like rule-oriented constructivists, commonsense constructivists recognize the importance of 'getting close' to their objects of study. Against the rule-oriented scholars, however, Pettman claims that it is also necessary to take part in the political world. In the case of foreign or security policy making, this 'means learning to speak the language used in the foreign policy making process itself, the better to take part.'[38] While Pettman finds many postmodern constructivists to be too radical in their anti-rational zeal, he argues that they provide a valuable addition to scholarship. Because postmodernists question the validity of claims made by modernists, they 'provide thinking and speaking spaces for those who get put on modernity's margins, and those who must suffer the injustices that modernity creates.'[39]

Understanding Pettman's concerns, we can begin to recognize: (1) why political constructivists have tended to come from the left and (2) how the issue of security as it is investigated by political constructivists is opposed to the negative interpretation of politics offered by realists. The participation of the scholar in a

---

36 Jef Huysmans, 'Security! What Do You Mean? From Concept to Thick Signifier,' *European Journal of International Relations* 4, 2 (1998), p. 245.

37 Ralph Pettman, 'Commonsense Constructivism and Foreign Policy: A Critique of Rule-Oriented Constructivism,' in *Foreign Policy in a Constructed World*, p. 259.

38 Ibid., p. 261.

39 Ibid., p. 258.

60 *Creating Insecurity*

'deeply reflexive'[40] understanding of national security radically alters the form and content of the study that follows. In addition, the constant presence of criticism as a theoretical tool and political activity runs counter to the universal (foundational) claims of many conservative writers. What is left to be conserved if everything is open to reflection and reconstitution? If critique has no end-point, then is it possible to build a coherent version of conservative international politics?

Politics and scholarly investigation are an inseparable duo for the political constructivist. This challenges the traditional perspective of realism and its policy-oriented study of security. In an attempt to explicate a 'thick signifier' approach to security studies, Huysmans argues that

> interpreting security as a thick signifier also moves the research agenda away from its techno-instrumental or managerial orientation. The main question is not to help the political administration in its job of identifying and explaining threats in the hope of improving formulation of effective counter-measures. Rather, the purpose of the thick signifier approach is to lay bare the political work of the signifier security, that is, what it does, how it determines social relations.[41]

Huysmans's 'thick signifier' account of security necessarily changes the analytic focus of the study. Contrasting his account of security with more mainstream 'conceptual' accounts, Huysmans writes, '[while] conceptual analyses of security in IR assume an external reality to which security refers – an (in)security condition – in a thick signifier approach "security" becomes self-referential.'[42] This is an important component to what I have termed political constructivism and it follows from the epistemological turn that we have made above. But, it is important to note the political implications of this turn. Continuing, Huysmans writes '[it] does not refer to an external, objective reality but establishes a security situation by itself.'[43] The manner by which political constructivism might be differentiated from its epistemological focus is really one of degree rather than kind. The political constructivist takes seriously the *political* content of specific speech-acts. Instead of limiting the discussion of specific utterances to epistemologically significant 'knowledge claims', political constructivists maintain an interest in understanding the larger consequences of these utterances. Again, Huysmans articulates a way to differentiate the two forms of constructivism. 'Why do we call this political? Is this not epistemology? Yes, it is the epistemology of security but this epistemology is political in the sense that it embodies a specific ethico-political position.'[44]

In addition, and this is the point I wish to emphasize, the post-structurally inspired thick signifier approach 'reintroduces ontological insecurity into International Relations, not as an obstacle to be overcome but as a positive force

---

40 Ibid., p. 257.
41 Huysmans, p. 233.
42 Ibid., p. 232.
43 Ibid.
44 Ibid., p. 245.

Understanding the Sources of Insecurity 61

making it possible to re-articulate world politics, to move away from the status quo.'[45] Understanding the sources of insecurity and the means to overcome them requires that policy makers (and larger social groups) reflect on identity constructs in an effort to re-interpret what is foreign, other, and dangerous. 'It is a (plea for the) search for new life strategies... It looks for a way of life which recognizes that accumulating security with the hope of postponing insecurity is doomed to fail.'[46] The questions asked by political constructivists allow for an 'on going activity of representing, reminding, remembering, revising, reciprocating, recycling, reversing, recuperating, regouping, recollecting, returning – that is, a politics of reviving whatever is deadened by the machinery of modernity.'[47]

The question that often plagues scholars employing post-positivist techniques is how can an emphasis on reflection and revision be applied to policy relevant topics like national security? How is political constructivism brought into the policy-side of the security problematique? In order to begin answering these questions, I will return to our example above. To repeat, U.S. security agencies are currently engaged in rooting out *terrorists* in other countries because it is believed these terrorists threaten U.S. national security. While realist scholars accepted the state interpretation of outside 'dangers' and proceeded to ask what material evidence there was for this insecurity, a different set of questions will be asked by the political constructivists. Specifically, how has the state come to interpret certain groups as terrorist threats? Although an answer to this question might seem obvious in light of the events of 11 September 2001, a comprehensive critique of identity performances suggests how both American and Foreign cultural practices are inculcated in the ideational sources of insecurity.

This argument suggests that insecurity is a result of self/other dynamics that play out at the boundaries of identities. How have U.S. foreign policy practices influenced and threatened other groups? How have other groups influenced and threatened the United States? How is the 'terrorist' label an American device to provide purpose and direction for a wide-ranging foreign policy espousing 'liberal-democratic' considerations,[48] market-oriented economies,[49] and hegemonic

---

45 Ibid., p. 247.

46 Ibid., p. 248.

47 Henry Kariel, 'Bringing Postmodernism into Being,' paper delivered at the American Political Science Association's Annual Meeting, Washington, DC, 1988, p. 10. Cited in Pauline Rosenau, 'Once Again into the Fray,' p. 100.

48 A cursory of review of recent texts on American promotion of 'democracy' will demonstrate how the term has been mis-applied to much of the U.S. effort. See, in particular, Alan Gilbert, *Must Global Politics Constrain Democracy?: Great-Power Realism, Democratic Peace, and Democratic Internationalism* (Princeton, NJ: Princeton University Press, 1999); and William I. Robinson, *Promoting Polyarchy: Globalization, US Intervention, and Hegemony* (Cambridge: Cambridge University Press, 1996).

49 A brief discussion of U.S. promotion is supplied by Duncan Green, *Silent Revolution: the Rise of Market Economics in Latin America* (London: Cassell LAB, 1995).

62 *Creating Insecurity*

leadership? How does the terrorist label function to re-produce its own logic in the groups so labeled? These questions move the study of insecurity in a different ontological direction from that of the realists. But, this direction is no less important than the questions asked and the studies performed by traditional security scholars. Critiquing the once 'unencumbered self', an investigation of these questions points to a radically different understanding of the sources of insecurity. Rather than locating threats in the material collection of weapons, bank accounts, terrorist networks, etc., political constructivists argue that insecurity is a result of cultural practices that create enemies. In a very real way, states (or perhaps better, social groups) create their own insecurity.

This discussion should not be read as an attempt to do away with particular identities. Such identities are necessary components to the ability of any social group – and its individual members – to make sense of the world. Badredine Arfi provides a recent understanding of this condition. 'Social identity endows interactions with predictability around a set of expectations, a necessary ingredient to sustain social life.'[50] In the context of our example, the identity performances that perpetuate an image of a terrorist-other threatening the U.S., sustain and give direction to American social life. The question that concerns the political constructivist is whether Antagonistic-Other constructs are required for a sustainable U.S. political culture. Ted Hopf articulates an understanding of the self/other dynamic that points a way through this problem.

> Actors develop their relations with, and understanding of, others through the media of norms and practices. In the absence of norms, exercises of power, or actions, would be devoid of meaning. Constitutive norms define an identity by specifying the actions that will cause Others to recognize that identity and respond to it appropriately.[51]

Using the political constructivist approach to interpret security issues, the problem that concerns us is what the 'appropriate response' by the other is when confronted by a self-identity that treats that other as hostile or threatening. If the conscious interpretation and re-interpretation of the self – defined in opposition to the other – insists on treating the other as a *security* threat, then political constructivists seem to have located a source of insecurity inaccessible to those involved in traditional security studies. What is at stake here should be made clear. There is no doubt about the requirements of identity constructs for the perpetuation of the 'self' concept and a specific (particular) way of life. The argument being put forth is not a suggestion that the social construction of a specifically American 'self' should be eliminated. Arfi, Hopf, and others, recognize the necessity of identity constructs in making life meaningful and providing direction to individual

---

50 Badredine Arfi, 'Ethnic Fear: The Social Construction of Insecurity,' *Security Studies* 8 (Autumn 1998), p. 152.

51 Ted Hopf, 'The Promise of Constructivism in International Relations Theory,' *International Security* 23 (Summer 1998), p. 173.

Understanding the Sources of Insecurity 63

lives.[52] The question that concerns us is whether it is necessary to define the other as a source of insecurity. While the divide between self and other may be necessary, it does not follow that this differentiation need be defined in (*in*)security terms. More to the point, when assessing the issue from a political constructivist understanding, if such a differentiation is made on security grounds, it is ultimately alterable. The fact that we construct our worlds allows us to investigate, critique, and re-construct any security construct. While it may be difficult to alter embedded identity practices, it is at least possible and this allows for an emancipatory praxis to take place.

Returning to the post-structural works of Campbell, McSweeney, and others, it is possible to demonstrate how a reflexive critique of state identity performances can assist in the construction of a more comprehensive security analysis. In much of Campbell's work, including his discussion of U.S. foreign policy during the Cold War, the Gulf War, and U.S. intervention in the Balkans, he is involved in illuminating 'the political consequences that follow from the officially scripted version, and how [this version] legitimizes and produces the conditions of its own acceptance and thus the justification and enactment of war itself.'[53] Reflecting on state activity thus challenges the issues of security that are defined by state actors. But more importantly, recognizing the intersubjective nature of human relations, it is possible to alter state considerations of insecurity by engaging in a consistent critique of identity performances. When *reflective* actions are taken, the process whereby identity constructs are altered is set in motion. Here, then, we come to understand Campbell's claim that his form of inquiry 'embodies an ethos that considers critique to be a form of intervention.'[54] In addition, we come to understand the interpretive vision that is put forth by political constructivists. The world is contingent and malleable. Most importantly, the structures and constraints envisioned by realists and other traditional security scholars are simply manifestations of power-politics that discipline and dissuade actors from recognizing this malleable and contingent nature. Change is not only theoretically possible; it is an active component of the reflective process. The necessarily

---

52 David Campbell, for instance, writes, 'Were there no borders, there would be no danger, but such a condition is at odds with the logic of identity, for the condition of possibility for experience entails (at least to some extent) the disciplining of ambiguity, the containment of contingency, and the delineation of border.' David Campbell, *Writing Security: United States Foreign Policy and the Politics of Identity*, revised edition (Minneapolis, MN: University of Minnesota Press, 1998), p. 81. See, also, Glenn Chafetz, Michael Sprirtas, and Benjamin Frankel, 'Introduction: Tracing the Influence of Identity on Foreign Policy,' *Security Studies* 8 (Winter 1998/9 - Spring 1999), pp. vii-xxii.

53 Richard Price and Christian Reus-Smit, 'Dangerous Liaisons? Critical International Theory and Constructivism,' *European Journal of International Relations* 4, 3 (1998), p. 273.

54 Campbell, p. 227.

64 *Creating Insecurity*

negative vision of international politics emphasized by realists is eschewed for an approach recognizing the possibility for positive change.

Balancing Security Considerations

The differing interpretations of international politics discussed above lead us to consider two types of questions when analyzing any security issue. First, in response to the realist concern with aspects of material power and the constancy of the security dilemma, how do the capabilities of a state enhance or diminish its overall security? Second, in response to the concerns of the political constructivists, how are cultural constructs and identity performances reproduced in the security interests of a state? Both questions require answers if we are to better understand the sources of insecurity that influence state conduct. However, as I hope to have made clear, the focus of each interpretation is quite different. Each provides a partial answer for the presence of insecurity. In order to provide a more comprehensive understanding, it remains for us to discuss both approaches within the context of a single security calculus.

In a variety of ways, this single security calculus has been alluded to by earlier security scholars but has never been examined directly. Herz's attempt to balance realist and idealist principles and create 'realist liberalism' is one such example. Yet, Herz does so by embracing a materialist understanding of existential threats. Similarly, Wolfers balances an 'objective' approach to security (the absence of existential threats) with a 'subjective' approach to security (the absence of fear).[55] However, he, too, remains wedded to materialism and treats the latter as mere feelings and perceptions and the former as an environmental constant. Alternatively, Campbell articulates a post-structural approach that examines the 'texts' of foreign policy discourse while maintaining the possibility that existential threats may indeed harm the state.[56]

Each of these writers recognizes the tension between existential danger and the construction of threat. Understanding the sources of insecurity requires that we

---

55 Arnold Wolfers, 'National Security as an Ambiguous Symbol,' in *Discord and Collaboration: Essays on International Politics* (Baltimore, MD: The Johns Hopkins Press, 1962), p. 150.

56 Campbell's analysis of the Soviet threat during the Cold War represents a case in point. For the U.S., Soviet otherness created 'the basis for an interpretive framework that constitutes the Soviet Union as a danger independent of any military capacity.' (p. 139). In order to complete his analysis of the Cold War, Campbell offers this caveat, 'This is not to suggest that the USSR's military was either insignificant or benevolent.' (p. 139). But does not this beg the question? Even after accounting for the role that identity plays in the construction of a threat, there remains a residual form of insecurity on account of the fact that we cannot know whether the Soviet Union is 'insignificant' or 'benevolent'. Can we assume that the material capabilities of the Soviet Union represent an existential danger that also involves a measure of insecurity?

balance ideational considerations with material or existential ones. However, this tension remains unresolved because each treats its 'rhetorical tools' as something more. In the case of Herz and Wolfers, realism is regarded as a general theory of international relations requiring that *idealist* and *subjective* factors be incorporated into its framework of understanding. For Campbell, existential threats are caveats in a larger post-structural textual analysis of identity constructs.

In this section, I take realism and political constructivism to be two interpretations of international politics capable of providing partial answers to an investigation of the sources of insecurity. Under an epistemological constructivist umbrella, we can treat each interpretation as a rhetorical device that attempts to give meaning to the social world. Each interpretation examines and emphasizes a specific part of this social world. Realism's negative vision and its focus on material aspects of power speak to the 'cautious paranoid' and demand that state actors consider the dangerous consequences of their actions. Political constructivism's intersubjective emphasis recognizes the possibility of ideational changes in constructed threats and enemy images. The reflexive posture present in political constructivism recognizes the potential for embracing a richer and more ethical political framework.

In this security calculus, both approaches are deemed necessary in order to develop a more comprehensive understanding of security. This discussion examines how a simultaneous investigation of material capabilities and identity performances might proceed. The purpose is not to demonstrate how one approach is more useful in the analysis of a particular security issue but rather to examine how both positions might co-exist beneath a constructivist umbrella in the development of a policy-relevant *and* theoretically rigorous account of national security studies.

By way of example, we might return to our earlier example concerning the current U.S. war against terrorism. Our discussion above suggests that realists and political constructivists develop quite different interpretations of this war. The question that concerns us is whether it is possible to balance the interpretations that each approach provides in the hope of offering a more robust analysis of this particular security issue. To begin, Paul Kowert notes correctly that 'constructivists intent on demonstrating the proposition that the world can be constructed in different ways have been loathe to explore material constraints on its construction.'[57] Clearly, the events of 11 September 2001 demonstrated significant material constraints on the U.S. construction of its security. Returning to a realist critique of these events, an external enemy had inflicted physical harm on the state. Responding to this danger, realists demonstrate how the capabilities of the United States can be brought to bear not only on those responsible, but on those that might harness similar resources for a future attack. In the assessment of threat, realists take seriously the requirements of the obligation owed by the state to its citizens. Protection from physical danger is a requirement for individual pursuit of the good

---

57 Paul Kowert, 'Toward a Constructivist Theory of Foreign Policy,' in *Foreign Policy in a Constructed World*, p. 276.

66   *Creating Insecurity*

life. Of course, political constructivists take this discussion as yet another example of the fact that 'the very idea of "national security" (which scholars help transmit, after all) serves state interests.'[58] No doubt, but realists are drawn to the fact that basic ontological security remains a prerequisite for the success of daily life. If this notion holds prior to the terrorist attacks on New York and Washington, DC, the ability to conceive of 'national security' issues makes its construction all the more important after that date. Constructing national security matters within a realist vision of international politics demonstrates the central position of the state in securing individual security. And, it does not follow that a realist interpretation of politics that centralizes the state necessarily apologizes for the state. Critical realists have attacked state policies on a number of issues as the applications below demonstrate. Moreover, and this is a point which needs to be emphasized, when analyzing security issues from within our constructivist epistemology, '[there] is nothing inherently "un-constructivist" in believing... that some constructions make more sense in a given environment than do others.'[59] The realist construction of and repetitive emphasis on the classic security dilemma, the importance of self-help, and the presence of external threats, continues to make a great deal of sense in the present international context.

However, these realist constructs do not provide us with a complete picture of this particular security matter. The simple assertion that absolute security is a chimera places limits on what realists can offer to the state. A security program based on an ever-increasing number of material capabilities in a continuously expanding field of security is both impractical and dangerous. Founding a security policy on the eradication of material capabilities existing outside the state does not demonstrate a terribly sophisticated understanding of the sources of insecurity. Simultaneous to a realist picture of the global terrorist threat, we need to investigate the issue as it is understood by scholars working within the political constructivist tradition. An investigation of identity performances (those of the United States and the perceived 'other') can be undertaken in an effort to more accurately assess the success of the realist interpretation.

The critique provided by political constructivists is not simply a negative critique offering a deconstruction of the realist interpretation. Political construc-tivists are also involved in reflection, reconstruction, reconceptualization. 'Among other things, reconceptualization implies that well known, neglected, or apparently irrelevant materials can be looked at from a different perspective and sometimes gain new relevance for our attempts at making sense of world politics.'[60] As Campbell makes clear, 'the deconstruction of identity widens the domain of the

---

58 Ibid.
59 Ibid.
60 Jorgensen, 'Four Levels and a Discipline,' p. 48.

political to include the ways in which identity is constituted and contains an affirmative moment through which existing identity formations are denaturalized and alternative articulations of identity and the political are made possible.'[61] For instance, when Edward Said undertook an examination of the social construction of 'orientalism' in the west, 'he also managed to reduce the power of the socially constructed image of orientalism, thus having an impact on one world of our making.'[62] When political constructivists challenge socially constructed images of 'others,' they are challenging the political policies that result from those constructed images. As this occurs, actors involved in the political process are induced to reconsider those policies in order to render them more coherent.

In the context of the U.S. fight against international terrorism, political constructivists might investigate two related issues. First, how are U.S. cultural constructs and identity performances reproduced in the tactics to eradicate terrorist organizations? Second, how are U.S. cultural constructs and identity performances of the 'other' interpreted by this 'other'? If the first question examines how the international politics of U.S. hegemony are a reflection of a particular American understanding of self, the second question examines how others react to and interpret America's sense of self in their own construction of security themes. A sophisticated study that interrogates both questions affects the realist interpretation of material capabilities. When material capabilities are claimed by realists to enhance or detract from a state's security and these capabilities are demonstrated by political constructivists to be out of line with or antagonize self/other images, a degree of imbalance has appeared in the study of national security. This imbalance requires further analysis – it requires reflection, reconceptualization, and reconstruction if Wolfers' ideal security policy is to be approached.

In the following chapters, the security approach outlined in this chapter will be applied to pressing U.S. security concerns. I seek to demonstrate that a robust and coherent security strategy can only be developed by incorporating and balancing the concerns of realists and political constructivists beneath an epistemological constructivist umbrella. The current development of a national missile defense system, the war on drugs in the Andean region, the construction of procedural democratic regimes around the globe, and U.S. efforts to foment regime change in Iraq provide intriguing examples of how the United States might be creating its own insecurity while attempting to manage national and international concerns.

---

61 Campbell, p. 223.
62 Jorgensen, p. 40.

Chapter 5

Creating Insecurity I: Unilateral BMD Development and U.S. Security

The theoretical discussion above suggests the need to balance between the negative vision of realism and the positive vision of political constructivism in order to provide a more robust understanding of national security. Such a balance allows analysts to recognize the sources of insecurity in material dangers as well as in cultural boundaries. In the following chapters, our focus moves from the theoretical underpinnings of security to a series of applications employing the above approach. The theoretical endeavor above is intended to offer a new way to cut into pressing security concerns. The remaining chapters offer evidence as to the usefulness of this form of security analysis. However, each of the four applications cannot be read as a complete case study of the issue at hand. Instead, the applications below represent the practical use of a concept of security that is neither wedded to a negative realist vision of international politics nor a reflexive constructivist view but attempts to balance both approaches in order to offer a stronger security analysis. The unilateral creation of a ballistic missile defense system has been a U.S. policy consideration since the early days of the Cold War. Basic systems were devised and constructed only to be shut-down and dismantled. More elaborate systems have been theorized but have been beyond the technological capabilities and political will of the country. The idea of a 'missile shield' defending the United States resonates with an important segment of decision makers in Washington and has re-emerged during successive administrations in one form or another.

The George W. Bush administration has made 'national missile defense' a cornerstone of its 'new strategic vision'. However, this policy could have deleterious effects on U.S. national security, undermining the post-Cold War rapprochement with Russia, souring relations with China, and hastening an international political climate detrimental to U.S. interests. Far from enhancing security, the unilateral research and development of a national missile defense shield, or a more modest forward-based boost-phase system, might actually create insecurity.

In this chapter, I examine the ballistic missile defense (BMD)[1] debate. First, I will explore the historic development of BMD systems. This discussion details the policy debate during various periods of the Cold War as military technology improved and strategic thinking on the meaning of nuclear arsenals developed. Of particular importance, this discussion focuses on the re-emergence of the BMD debate in the post-Cold War. The re-emergence of the debate surrounding BMD after the Cold War suggests reasons to include political constructivism in a subsequent policy analysis. Second, a realist interpretation of BMD will be examined. The purpose of this section is to analyze the issue from the position of the 'cautious paranoid'. Because the BMD issue involves a 'high politics' military/strategic matter, realism is well-suited to providing a theoretical understanding of the potential international implications of BMD. What makes this issue of interest to our discussion, however, is the skeptical view of BMD taken by many realists. Their interpretation of its costs and benefits suggests reasons why state policy makers might wish to re-consider BMD development. The third section, a political constructivist interpretation of the BMD debate, offers compelling answers to why state policy makers have forged ahead with BMD plans in spite of realists' concerns. As we would expect, the questions asked and the analysis offered by political constructivists are of a different nature from those of the realists. Pointing to how American identity affects U.S. interests, political constructivists challenge the official state rationale for a BMD system. The answer to why U.S. policy makers have continually returned to the idea of insulating America from attack might have less to with ballistic dangers that lurk beyond the borders of the United States and more to do with the 'idea' of an insulated America. Even when realists point out how ineffective BMD systems will be to attacks arising from alternative delivery mechanisms, it is the political constructivists that seem to offer the best explanation for state development of such systems. Finally, in an attempt to be more policy relevant than previous constructivist studies, balancing realism and political constructivism will demonstrate that alternative strategies for enhancing national security might evolve from the (policy-oriented) realist critique of BMD and the ideational considerations of political constructivists. In the final section, I attempt to balance the interpretations put forth by realists and political constructivists in an effort to provide the state a more comprehensive analysis of BMD and nuclear security.

---

1 Debates concerning BMD are often complicated by multiple and competing system designs and what these designs are intended to do. Wherever possibile, I shall use 'BMD' (ballistic missile defense) to refer to the general set of systems designed to defend against a nuclear missile attack. At times in the following discussion, the use of the terms 'ABM' (anti-ballistic missile) and 'NMD' (national missile defense) will become necessary.

70 *Creating Insecurity*

The History of BMD Development

The idea of BMD emerged soon after the twin developments of the missile and the atom bomb. While an exact date for the idea cannot be given, research into defending against a missile attack had begun within months of the September 1944 German V-2 rocket attack on a suburb of Paris.[2] As early as 1945, U.S. officials recognized the need to defend against the possibility of missiles carrying atomic weapons.[3] By the early 1950s, private industry, universities, and the U.S. military were developing systems to detect and destroy incoming missiles.[4] Even before the construction and successful launch of the first ICBM, theorists had envisioned the need to defend against these weapons and, as early as 1952, had considered the possibility of a missile interceptor rocket paired with early-warning radar systems.[5] Much of the available anti-aircraft technology, it was theorized, could be adapted to ensure rudimentary defenses against incoming ballistic missiles.[6] 'In November 1955 serious efforts at developing a missile defense system began when Bell Telephone Laboratories (BTL) undertook a feasibility study for the Army (even before the first ICBM ever flew) on the problems and practicality of missile defense.'[7] As a consensus emerged in the United States that rapid advances in missile technology would make ICBMs a major delivery system for nuclear devices, and with the successful Soviet test of an ICBM in August of 1957, followed by a successful U.S. test later that year, full-scale development of the Army's NIKE-ZEUS system was authorized.

The technological problems and deployment controversy that plagued the NIKE-ZEUS project, ultimately leading to its demise, provide an early lesson in U.S. Cold War nuclear strategy. First, it was recognized early in ICBM development that decoys and penetration aids could be developed and integrated into the terminal stage of an ICBM's trajectory. Even though the Soviets had yet to develop such decoys, their theoretical possibility made the NIKE-ZEUS system less attractive. Second, nuclear strategists also recognized that an increase in offensive capabilities could always overwhelm a ballistic missile defense system. Third, and a related point, the United States was moving to a nuclear strategy that favored the overwhelming potential of offensive weapons. These weapons cost less to build and maintain than BMD and any money spent on defense would mean less

---

2   Benson D. Adams, *Ballistic Missile Defense* (New York: American Elsevier Publishing Company, 1971), p. 17.

3   Ibid., p. 19.

4   Ibid., p. 17-19.

5   Ibid., p. 20.

6   The U.S. Army's first ABM, the 'NIKE-ZEUS', is actually the third generation antiaircraft missile. The first two missiles, 'NIKE-AJAX' and 'NIKE-HERCULES' were the first air-to-surface missiles. For a discussion, see, Ernest J. Yanarella, *The Missile Defense Controversy: Strategy, Technology, and Politics, 1955-1972* (Lexington, KY: The University Press of Kentucky, 1977), p. 27.

7   Adams, p. 20.

Creating Insecurity I: Unilateral BMD Development and U.S. Security 71

for these offensive weapons. Fourth, advocates of BMD were unable to counter the growing 'logic' of deterrence. As Adams notes,

> ICBMs (made invulnerable) properly deployed by both sides, it was believed, could bring about a stable international environment. The most important task confronting the world was to slow down the arms race, allow both sides to acquire equalized invulnerable strategic deterrents based primarily on hardened or submarine-launched ballistic missiles and then eliminate the danger of nuclear war by de-emphasizing advanced technology which might upset the stable situation.[8]

Thus, while NIKE-ZEUS was demonstrated to be effective in the initial stages of testing,[9] and while the USSR was building a BMD system similar to ZEUS,[10] the first U.S. effort at BMD was never deployed.

The demise of NIKE-ZEUS and the increasing rhetoric of mutually assured destruction (MAD) doctrine are not coincidental and further discussion of their connection seems warranted. During the 1960s, the United States consistently attempted to articulate an offensive-oriented 'saturation parity' or 'mutual assured destruction'[11] as the most stable bilateral strategic policy available to the United States and USSR. Increasingly, this doctrine was viewed as an incontestable point in strategic thinking. It became imperative to 'teach' Soviet leaders the merits of this doctrine. Since Soviet research and development in missile defense had been a component of Soviet strategic thinking since the 1940s, an alternative to MAD was possible.[12] Given the perceived superiority of Soviet BMD research, *unilateral* adherence to MAD could have a deleterious effect on U.S. national security. Therefore, a concerted effort to: (1) teach the Soviets the 'logic' of MAD and (2) continue to research BMD technology in case the Soviets could not 'learn,' became the dual components of U.S. strategic thought throughout the 1960s. But it is important to note that according to adherents of MAD, deterrence and ballistic missile defense were contradictory policy options and could not be implemented simultaneously.[13] Jerome Wiesner articulates this point in late 1960. 'A missile deterrent system would be unbalanced by the development of a highly effective anti-missile defense system and if it appears possible to develop one, ... agreements should explicitly prohibit the development and deployment of such a system.'[14] Understanding this point, the U.S. government continued to fund

---

8 Ibid., p. 41.
9 Yanarella, pp. 64-65.
10 Adams, p. 38.
11 See, David Goldfischer, *The Best Defense: Policy Alternatives for U.S. Nuclear Security from the 1950s to the 1990s* (Ithaca, NY: Cornell University Press, 1993), p. 2.
12 Ibid., p. 107.
13 Ibid., p. 4.
14 Adams, p. 41.

research and development on BMD while simultaneously refusing to deploy the NIKE-ZEUS system.[15]

The problem with a U.S. strategic policy emphasizing MAD is that in order to succeed, its language must be understood and its doctrine employed by both sides. Without a good measure of trust that the opposing power wishes to adhere to MAD, there is always the possibility that defensive capabilities will be constructed that place the adhering state at a major disadvantage. As David Goldfischer makes clear,

> ongoing efforts in research and development reflect the provisional nature of adherence to MAD. It is simply assumed that if one side discerned a realistic chance to escape from assured vulnerability, it would defect from a MAD-based arms control regime. Episodic (and illusory) hopes for one's own escape from MAD have therefore been coupled to constant concern about the other side's efforts and plans. The result has been an ongoing search for better ways of penetrating defenses (e.g., nuclear cruise missiles, stealth technology, maneuverable reentry vehicles) that are already hopelessly overmatched and plans for new ways to protect retaliatory forces despite their existing capacity to survive an attack and inflict assured destruction many times over.[16]

The shortcomings of the MAD doctrine presented the United States with a perceived strategic imbalance by 1966. While 'the United States possessed at least a three-to-one superiority (1,446 to 470) over the Soviet Union in ICBMs and an ever greater superiority in terms of overall combat effectiveness,'[17] the USSR's emphasis on defensive technology was beginning to produce positive results and the Soviets had begun deployment of BMD technology.[18] U.S. reliance on 'assured destruction' now seemed to have placed the United States at a strategic disadvantage.

> In the area of BMD systems, the Soviets, after several abortive starts, had begun to deploy the Galosh ABM system around Moscow, as well as another type of defensive system (thought to be geared to the American bomber force) elsewhere in the Soviet Union. But, whatever the exact character of these systems and pace of their deployment by the Soviet Union, American defense planners, for the time being, were predicating

---

15 Ibid., p. 57.

16 Goldfischer, p. 58.

17 Yanarella, p. 127.

18 'The Soviet Union had begun placing a network of ABMs around Moscow early in 1964. Later in November the Soviets paraded a Galosh ABM during a holiday celebration.' Yanarella, p. 105. It was not until 10 November 1966 that official acknowledgment of the Soviet ABM system was made. 'McNamara announced that 'there [is] now considerable evidence that they [the Soviets] are deploying an anti-ballistic missile system.' The Soviet Galosh ABM system – as it was code-named by NATO – was believed to be composed of a network of radars and a two- or three-stage, solid-fueled interceptor missile designed for long-range, exoatmospheric interception of incoming ICBMs.' Yanarella, p. 118.

Creating Insecurity I: Unilateral BMD Development and U.S. Security 73

their strategic forces on the assumption that by the early 1970s the USSR would have deployed a heavy ABM protection around all its major cities.[19]

As a result of the perceived imbalance, the United States was faced with the need to research and deploy some form of BMD or accept an enemy with the *theoretical* potential to survive a nuclear attack. Responding to this new environment, the United States made clear to the Soviet Union that any BMD system they may have developed could easily be overwhelmed by U.S. offensive capabilities. A BMD system, however, might be appropriate for the newly-emerging Chinese nuclear arsenal – an arsenal without a second-strike capability. Toward that end, the United States once again considered a BMD system. While NIKE-ZEUS was now outdated, advances in missile and radar technology, and continuous R&D throughout the 1960s,[20] suggested that a 'thin' system could be deployed around major population centers (SENTINEL) to defend against a (smaller) Chinese attack. In addition, the possibility of protecting U.S. nuclear silos with a hard-point ABM system (SAFEGUARD), in an effort to demonstrate to the Soviet Union that the United States was committed to *assured* destruction, was being considered.

These second-generation policy options, and the political problems that lead to their demise, result in the eventual signing of the 1972 ABM treaty and the triumph of deterrence as a strategic doctrine. SENTINEL was doomed (politically) almost from the start. As an urban anti-missile missile system, SENTINEL was designed to launch nuclear-tipped interceptor missiles from fixed positions near large cities at incoming ICBMs. Soon after the deployment decision, the U.S. Army began locating possible deployment sites. The political movements from below,[21] in opposition to the establishment of these sites, resulted in a re-assessment of this deployment decision. Throughout 1969, as the Army continued to search for appropriate sites, national strike committees, community groups, and scientists fought SENTINEL deployment.[22] These groups, quite obviously, 'raised questions concerning the dangers inherent in erecting sites within residential areas – particularly the specter of accidental detonation at the missile site or at an altitude too low above the city, thereby obliterating the city it was supposed to protect.'[23]

---

19 Yanarella, p. 127.

20 The United States had been making modifications to NIKE-ZEUS, including the enhancement of radar systems and the addition of the faster SPRINT missile. This system was designated 'NIKE-X' and would become the urban defense system SENTINAL in the late 1960s.

21 I take the idea of 'political movements from below', from Alan Gilbert, *Must Global Politics Constrain Democracy: Great-Power Realism, Democratic Peace, and Democratic Internationalism* (Princeton, NJ: Princeton University Press, 1999), p. 4 and generally. Gilbert differentiates between a 'democratic internationalism from below' with a 'democratic internationalism from above'.

22 See, for instance, Yanarella, pp. 146-149.

23 Ibid., p. 147.

74   *Creating Insecurity*

Similarly, the SAFEGUARD program came under serious opposition from groups within the United States concerned by the seemingly exponential cost of the arms race and its negative effects on U.S. domestic society. While the U.S. was more successful in deploying SAFEGUARD, constructing sites near missile silos in North Dakota, plans for a nation-wide infrastructure were never fulfilled. In addition, protecting missile silos from harm appeared *not* to be an enhancement to national security but a condition for increased international instability. Realists, including Hans Morgenthau and George Kennan, argued against SAFEGUARD on the grounds that it was too expensive and would not lead to a better security position for the United States.[24] Kennan would argue before the Senate Foreign Relations Committee that 'a U.S. BMD deployment would lead the Soviets to doubt whether the United States really wanted strategic arms limitation.' Further, Kennan suggested that 'the expansion of SAFEGUARD could raise doubt and uncertainty in the Soviet Union about U.S. goals and intentions.'[25] The unilateral decision to deploy a BMD system like SAFEGUARD might very likely lead to increased international instability and move the world dangerously close to nuclear war.

With the United States and the Soviet Union moving towards a treaty on nuclear arms limitations,[26] a halt to deployment of BMD systems was required (an eventuality that came about with the 1972 ABM treaty).[27] The result of these arms control negotiations (and the freeze on BMD deployment) was the balance of terror outlined by the MAD doctrine. This doctrine would be the founding principle of Great Power strategic thought throughout the 1970s and into the 1980s. While the merits of a policy of deterrence that, if it failed, would result in the obliteration of both countries were open to serious critique by scholars, policy makers and citizens, the bi-polar world solidified by MAD remained stable throughout this period.

However, the strategy of deterrence would be seriously tested following the March 1983 public initiation of the Strategic Defense Initiative, or 'Star Wars' as its detractors would come to call it.[28] SDI was an ambitious attempt to break out of the environment of mutual destruction. Unlike previous BMD systems, it was

---

24 For Morgenthau's role in the policy debate, see, Yanarella, p. 156. For Kennan's role, see, Adams, p. 223. For a detailed discussion the realist concern with the development of BMD, see, Joel H. Rosenthal, *Righteous Realists: Political Realism, Responsible Power, and American Culture in the Nuclear Age* (Baton Rouge, LA: Louisiana State University Press, 1991), pp. 107-120.

25 Adams, p. 223.

26 These are often referred to as the Strategic Arms Reduction Talks.

27 *Treaty on the Limitation of Anti-Ballistic Missile Systems*, signed at Moscow, May 26, 1972, 23 UST 3435, TIAS No. 7503 (entered into force Oct. 3, 1972) [ABM Treaty], amended by Protocol of July 3, 1974, 27 UST 1645, TIAS No. 8276.

28 Steven Van Evera, 'Preface,' in *The Star Wars Controversy: An International Security Reader*, Steven E. Miller and Stephen Van Evera, eds. (Princeton, NJ: Princeton University Press, 1986), p. ix.

Creating Insecurity I: Unilateral BMD Development and U.S. Security 75

theorized (little of the technology had actually be developed) that SDI would intercept 'Soviet missiles in all four phases of flight, with a heavy emphasis on boost phase interception accomplished from space.'[29] (To be precise, two versions of SDI were contemplated. Star Wars I was a more ambitious 'Astrodome' version of SDI that included reliance on space-based weapons systems to protect U.S. territory from attack. Star Wars II was a more modest plan that upgraded the basic idea behind SAFEGUARD – an attempt to defend U.S. offensive capabilities.) Requiring that the United States withdraw from the 1972 ABM treaty, SDI was heralded as a national necessity by its proponents 'on both moral and strategic grounds.'[30] Those favoring the most ambitious plan argued,

> A comprehensive Star Wars I defense... will defend the United States against Soviet nuclear blackmail, protect American society from destruction should war break out, and provide a more moral basis for American defense, by removing American dependence upon threats to destroy others' civilian populations.[31]

Expressing the potential benefits accrued from the more limited SDI system, advocates suggested that such a BMD

> can enhance deterrence by better protecting American strategic forces from attack; can protect American conventional forces from nuclear or perhaps even conventional missile attack, thus deterring both conventional war and nuclear escalation during conventional war; can reduce American casualties in an all-out nuclear war; can demonstrate American resolve, thus inducing the Soviets to bargain more generously in arms control and other negotiations; can diminish the value of Soviet ICBMs and SLBMs by diminishing their effectiveness, thus inducing the Soviets to bargain away these weapons more readily in arms control negotiations; can create uncertainties about the results of a nuclear war that may help to deter a Soviet attack; can deter a limited Soviet nuclear attack by forcing the Soviets to use a larger number of nuclear weapons, which the Soviets may shrink from doing for fear of further escalation; and can protect the United States from accidental or unauthorized Soviet missile launches, or from ballistic missile attacks by third countries.[32]

In other words, the successful deployment of either version of SDI would allow the United States to break from the constraints imposed by mutual acceptance of 'assured destruction'. A technically-feasible BMD system 'would thereby restore American nuclear superiority, re-establish the credibility of the American nuclear threat, and extend American deterrence over Europe and other areas.'[33] If the Cold War was a stand-off between two superpowers with the ability to obliterate each other, then the construction of SDI would mean victory by default for the United

---

29 Ibid., p. xi.
30 Ibid., p. xvi.
31 Ibid., p. xvi.
32 Ibid., p. xvi.
33 Ibid., p. xvi.

76 *Creating Insecurity*

States. Conceivably, according to its advocates, the construction of a BMD system would mean the United States would have the freedom of action available to the great power in a unipolar system. However, for reasons similar to those that killed SENTINEL and SAFEGUARD, the BMD systems envisioned during the Reagan administration were not constructed. As the United States and the Soviet Union transitioned to a post-Cold War world during the Bush Sr. administration (1989-1993), the U.S. returned to a policy of limited research without deployment expectations.

The post-Cold War world provided proponents of BMD a new environment in which to advocate for the necessity of a defensive system. The reasons given for this renewed interest in BMD require special attention. Faced with pressure by Congressional Republicans, the Clinton administration created a '3+3 program' for BMD consideration.[34] Beginning in 1996, the United States would once again research and develop a system. 'If, after the first three years, no threat justified deployment, then development would continue so that the system would always be three years from deployment with up-to-date technology.'[35] While this initiative might have stopped serious debate on the issue, two events in 1998 would significantly alter the government's position and the pace of development on BMD. In July, the Rumsfeld Commission (the name given to the bipartisan Commission to Assess the Ballistic Missile Threat to the United States) released its findings on the proliferation of nuclear weapons technology and the threats posed to the United States by these emerging nuclear states. According to the findings of the Commission, 'North Korea or Iran could develop an ICBM within five years and with little warning.'[36] As if to underscore the accuracy of the study, North Korea launched a missile over Japan one month later. While the missile launch was a technical failure (it was intended to put a satellite into orbit – which did not succeed), the effect on policy makers in the United States was dramatic. In July of 1999, Clinton signed the National Missile Defense Act which stated that the United States was committed to deploying a BMD system 'as soon as technologically feasible.'[37]

Steven Miller locates seven repeatedly cited reasons for moving forward on a post-Cold War ballistic missile defense system. First, 'deployment is warranted by new missile threats.'[38] These threats no longer come from the USSR or China, but from smaller (potential) nuclear states. Second, these 'rogue states' may be undeterrable.[39] Third, the current inability to defend against ballistic missiles

---

34 George Lewis, Lisbeth Gronlund, and David Wright, 'National Missile Defense: An Indefensible System,' *Foreign Policy* 117 (Winter 1999/2000), p. 121.

35 Ibid.

36 Ibid., pp. 121-22.

37 Ibid., p. 122.

38 Steven E. Miller, 'The Flawed Case for Missile Defence,' *Survival* 43 (Autumn 2001), p. 96.

39 Ibid., p. 97.

Creating Insecurity I: Unilateral BMD Development and U.S. Security 77

creates incentives for proliferation – which creates instability.[40] Fourth, the new version of BMD will not be seen as a threat to Russia and China.[41] Fifth, because it is not a threat to Russia or China, BMD will not 'provoke nuclear build-ups' in these states.[42] Sixth, because the U.S. has the ability to consult with both allies and states like Russia and China, it is possible to construct a system that does not create an acute security dilemma.[43] Seventh, the political realities of the post-Cold War world are fundamentally different from those of the Cold War. Those insisting on adherence to the ABM treaty and defending deterrence as the *only* strategy for nuclear peace are dogmatically entrenched in the realities of a world that no longer exists. Advances in technology now permit development of a forward-deployed 'boost-phase' system[44] that solves many of the problems that plagued earlier versions without additional political costs.

These seven issues provide the political cover for the development and deployment of BMD. While the George W. Bush administration has yet to outline the systems that will be constructed, the United States withdrew from the ABM Treaty in June of 2002.[45] Furthermore, the United States has begun to construct radar systems in Alaska and to negotiate with other actors in order to expand its future radar and ABM capabilities.[46]

Realism and BMD Development

The potential for states to inflict harm on other states leads realists to seek out policies that provide necessary enhancements to national security. While security can never be assured by the policies they advocate, it is the purpose of the 'cautious

---

40 Ibid., p. 98.
41 Ibid., p. 100.
42 Ibid., p. 101.
43 Ibid., p. 102.
44 A boost-phase system could be constructed at various sites around the globe – near rogue states. It is designed to launch interceptor rockets at ICBMs in the early 'boost-phase' before an ICBM has reached the exoatmosphere. This is also the stage before an ICBM can deploy its warheads and possible decoys. A boost-phase system could employ the Navy Aegis Destroyer as a platform for launching the anti-missile missiles, thus reducing the political consequences of deploying a BMD system. However, as the discussion below suggests, it does not solve all of the problems associated with BMD deployment. For a discussion of 'boost-phase' systems, see, James M. Lindsay and Michael E. O'Hanlon, *Defending America: The Case for Limited National Missile Defense* (Washington, D.C.: Brookings Institution Press, 2001), pp. 147-151.
45 'Bush's Hang-Ups,' *The Economist* (December 15-21, 2001), pp. 10-11.
46 The complexities of these negotiations and problems they have caused to U.S. foreign relations are detailed in, 'Missiles Over the Moors,' *The Economist* (20 January 2001), p. 51; 'Missile Defense: A Shield in Space,' *The Economist* (3 June 2000), pp. 21-23; James Brooke, 'Greenlanders Wary of a New Role in U.S. Defenses,' *The New York Times* (18 September 2000), p. A6.

78 *Creating Insecurity*

paranoid' to outline the most harmful realistic consequences for any particular source of existential insecurity. To this, realists prescribe the most effective policies in order to combat the likelihood of these dangers. It might seem counter-intuitive, then, that a realist interpretation of the BMD debate consistently articulates the detrimental consequences of building such a system. But, close examination of realist tenets suggests that the requirement that states seek '*the most effective policy*' in any given situation has left realists to consistently rule out BMD as an enhancement to security. The policy-side of realism seeks to present a practical vision of policy alternatives – i.e., to argue for the most efficient and effective means to counter the most serious *realistic* (material) threat to national security. These limitations rule out advocacy of certain security policies even though they might appear to present short-term solutions to a problem of insecurity. Realists insist on policies that recognize both short-term and long-term consequences. We must live in the world as it is, not as we would like it to be[47] – and this point has policy implications. Policies must be chosen that recognize their effects on the international system. Emphasizing these issues, realists remain consistently skeptical of the benefits of ballistic missile defense. There appear to be two reasons why a consensus has emerged among realists against deployment of BMD. First, the implications for the balance of power in the system dissuade many from advocating BMD. Second, the depth and extent of the threat that emerges prior to and after deployment of BMD suggests reasons to forego the system as an enhancement to security. Together, the realist discussion of these points will challenge all seven claims (cogently articulated by Miller above) made by the policy making community in support of BMD.

First, realists are drawn to the concept of 'balance of power' in an effort to emphasize the effects of anarchy and the limitations on the power potential of each state. As the analysis of Waltz in chapter two makes clear, balance of power is both a repetitive historical condition and a necessary prescriptive component to an effective foreign policy. This issue appears as a central component in realist wariness to deploy a Cold War and post-Cold War BMD system.

Once the establishment of nuclear forces reached a level where both sides had second-strike capability, the international balance of power was preserved in the institution of MAD. Constructing the political world in this way, both the United States and the Soviet Union were considered to have created a (stable) bipolar arrangement. Deterrence is not a perfect policy – its failure results in devastating consequences – but even its detractors consider it stable, albeit it a stable system of terror.[48] If understood by all the necessary states (and this is an important requirement), MAD demonstrates how the costs of initiating a war outweigh the benefits. Indeed, while it is often difficult to differentiate between state policy

---

47 Kenneth N. Waltz, 'Reflections on *Theory of International Politics*: A Response to My Critics,' in *Neorealism and Its Critics*, Robert O. Keohane, ed. (New York: Columbia University Press, 1986), p. 338.

48 Goldfischer, p. 44.

Creating Insecurity I: Unilateral BMD Development and U.S. Security 79

makers and realist apologists of state power, on the issue of deterrence vs. missile defense, a distinction can be made. For instance, Paul Wolfowitz recently argued that 'the missile defences we deploy will be precisely that - defences. They will threaten no one. They will, however, deter those who would threaten us with ballistic missile attack.'[49] However, as Steven Miller correctly argues, '[this] does not conform to any known conception of deterrence. Indeed, by definition deterrence works via threats of retaliation whereas defences seek to defeat an attack or to neutralise the deterrent threats of others.'[50] An offensive attack cannot be considered a rational policy option because it would result in a net negative for the state. Therefore, once balance has been achieved in a bipolar system, instability occurs when one state seeks to defect from the 'deterrence game' being played. Unilateral deployment of BMD is one form of defection. Consider how Richard Betts weighs the Reagan-era decision to move ahead with SDI. '[The] U.S. advantage that plausibly could be achieved would be at best only one of degree (making the United States proportionally less vulnerable than the Soviet Union), not one of kind (making the United States and only the United States nearly invulnerable).'[51] Betts is suggesting that even an adequate defense does not promote the security of the United States. However, to this, it is necessary to recognize the likely impact that SDI will have on the stability of the system. Drell, Farley, and Holloway provide a succinct review of the instability invoked by unilateral deployment of BMD.

> The real risk of nuclear war is not a cold-blooded decision to initiate one, but what might happen under the pressures and suspicions of a crisis – an accidental triggering nuclear incident, miscalculation, loss of control by responsible leaders. An effective but imperfect ABM on one side would exacerbate the risk because the side that did have an ABM might calculate that it would be better off if it struck first and used the ABM defense to deal with the weakened response... Similarly, the side that did not have ABM might calculate that its situation would be better (however bad) if it struck first and avoided being caught trying to retaliate with a weakened force against the ABM defense.[52]

During Cold War crises, both the United States and the Soviet Union recognized the need for restraint. This need is demonstrated during the Cuban-Missile Crisis when the policy of deterrence was under considerable strain. One

---

49 Paul Wolfowitz, 'Prepared Testimony on Ballistic Missile Defense to the Senate Armed Services Committee,' p. 7. Cited in Miller, p. 103.

50 Miller, p. 103.

51 Richard Betts, 'Heavenly Gain or Earthly Losses? Toward a Balance Sheet for Strategic Defense,' in *The Strategic Defense Initiative: Shield or Snare?*, Harold Brown, ed. (Boulder, CO: Westview Press, 1987; reprint ed., The Bookings Institution, February 1988), p. 256.

52 Sidney D. Drell, Philip J. Farley, and David Holloway, 'Preserving the ABM Treaty: A Critique of the Reagan Strategic Defense Initiative,' in *The Star Wars Controversy*, p. 87.

80 *Creating Insecurity*

wonders if the outcome would have been different had the United States (alone) possessed a BMD system. While a counterfactual case study is beyond the scope of the present discussion, realists would likely have found the presence of such a system an aggravating condition and a further source of insecurity rather than an improvement in U.S. national security. Moreover, the development of a BMD system during the Cold War would have provided an *imperfect* defense of the United States alone. This system would have been of little use to NATO allies. Rather than enhancing the security of Western Europe, the unilateral decision to protect the U.S. mainland would have challenged the viability of the Alliance. If the United States possessed a preponderance of power in the international system, skeptical allies may have questioned their own security positions.[53] Great powers that attempt to break from the constraints of their constraining environments can be considered expansionist and induce other states to counter-balance.

A similar concern engages realists in the post-Cold War moment. Concerning the current U.S. design to construct ballistic missile defenses, John Newhouse suggests that 'Moscow, Beijing, and worried European capitals see in Bush's design a quest for unilateral advantage by a power already in full possession of the relevant strategic advantages.'[54] Seeking to enhance national security through the unilateral deployment of BMD, skeptics consistently argue that the United States will ultimately create situations defined by more insecurity rather than less. As Waltz reminds the international community, unipolar moments are not expected to last. At some point, states seek to balance against the power of others.[55] While this is not a law governing the behavior of states, our constructivist epistemology suggests that realists seek to emphasize this issue as a condition of their 'cautious paranoia'. It is a challenge to the policy maker to refrain from activities that promote counter-balancing tendencies. This point is particularly important in a post-Cold War world defined by a preponderance of U.S. power. Moreover, as the United States continues to demonstrate that it has the *will* to use its capabilities to fashion a world of its choosing, the dangerous consequences of unilateral BMD deployment would seem to grow.

Current U.S. desire to build a missile defense system may cause other international actors to undertake strategies designed to thwart what they perceive as expansionary U.S. policies. Charles Glaser articulates the negative possibilities that ensue from U.S. insistence on unilateral deployment of BMD.

---

53 Consider the problems associated with NATO/French relations when the United States was considered to a preponderance of power in that Alliance. See, Constantine A. Pagedas, *Anglo-American Strategic Relations and the French Problem 1960-1963* (London: Frank Cass Publishers, 2000), pp. 35-42; Anand Menon, *France, NATO and the Limits of Independence 1981-97: The Politics of Ambivalence* (New York: St. Martin's Press, 2000).

54 John Newhouse, 'The Missile Defense Debate,' *Foreign Affairs* 80 (July/August 2001), p. 100.

55 Kenneth N. Waltz, 'Structural Realism After the Cold War,' *International Security* 25 (Summer 2000), p. 28.

Creating Insecurity I: Unilateral BMD Development and U.S. Security 81

U.S. pursuit of nuclear superiority would fuel insecurity whether or not its NMD was effective. If NMD was effective, Russia and China would believe that they were vulnerable to U.S. coercion. If, as seems far more likely, NMD was ineffective, Russian and Chinese leaders would interpret dedicated U.S. efforts to achieve effective NMD as a signal of malign U.S. motives. Because they undoubtedly believe that nuclear deterrence is adequate to preserve U.S. security, they would interpret U.S. efforts to acquire nuclear superiority as indicative of expansionist motives. This is particularly likely given U.S. global conventional superiority and the absence of intense conflicts that threaten U.S. security. Competitive U.S. policies would lend support to hard-liners and nationalists who are competing for influence in Russia and China, and their increased influence would reinforce the signal sent by highly competitive U.S. nuclear policies.[56]

Echoing the realist concern that a great power is more secure when 'all of the major powers are secure,'[57] Glaser demonstrates the negative consequences of BMD deployment in the international environment. As he states, 'forgoing large-scale NMD seems preferable to risking what at best would be a new Cold War.'[58] Most importantly, from a realist perspective, alternative strategies for enhancing U.S. security are available.[59] Therefore, the possibility of increasing international instability outweighs the possible benefits. Even if, in the near term, Russia is incapable of countering the presence of BMD technology, it is necessary to consider the potential medium and long-term consequences. 'Russia will view NMD in terms of overall U.S. policy, which has included NATO expansion and military intervention in European conflicts in the face of Russian opposition.'[60] When, not if, Russia overcomes its current problems, it will expect an opportunity to participate more assertively in international politics. As Miller argues, 'it is very short-sighted to assume Russia's current financial problems will persist throughout the ten-to-twenty year time-frame of current US missile-defence plans.'[61] The perceived expansionism of the U.S. during its moment of unchallenged power will be among the policy considerations of a newly emergent Russia. In addition, even if BMD is not directed towards the overwhelming Russian ICBM forces, its deployment may be seen as the first stage in a more elaborate plan to defend against the Russian nuclear threat.[62] Expecting Russians to be 'cautious paranoids', many realists will argue they will 'employ worst-case analysis in assessing the adequacy of [their] core deterrent capabilities.'[63]

---

56 Charles L. Glaser and Steve Fetter, 'National Missile Defense and the Future of U.S. Nuclear Weapons Policy,' *International Security* 26 (Summer 2001), p. 64.
57 Ibid.
58 Ibid., p. 65.
59 I will discuss a number of these alternative strategies in the final section below.
60 Glaser and Fetter, p. 65.
61 Miller, p. 102.
62 Glaser and Fetter, p. 74.
63 Ibid., p. 75.

82 *Creating Insecurity*

Similarly, even if the United States expects China to modernize its small nuclear arsenal in the absence of U.S. BMD deployment, the nature and extent of its response might be altered dramatically.[64] 'China is likely to view NMD as part of a package in which Washington steps up its support for Taiwan, deploys TMD in the region, and calls for increases in Japanese military spending and operational capability.'[65] China has already warned that it views development of BMD technology as a threat to national security. Even though, in the short-term, China will not possess the capabilities to counter U.S. BMD systems, over the medium to long-term, China will play a more active role in international affairs. How they envision the United States will be an important factor in their foreign policy. As Glaser considers, 'Chinese leaders are inclined to see American policy – including support for international institutions and their universal norms, expansion of U.S. alliances, and improvements in U.S. and allied military capabilities – as designed to prevent China from achieving the great power status that they believe it deserves.'[66]

Both states have the potential to undermine U.S. security interests in the medium and long-term futures. As Miller argues, 'if relations with the United States sour, Moscow or Beijing could cause great mischief by promoting missile proliferation around the world and thereby multiplying the problems for defences.'[67] In addition, from a realist perspective emphasizing even the most rudimentary versions of rational-actor modeling, it is difficult to understand the decision to move forward on BMD deployment. 'In response to the first hint of Soviet missile defences in the 1960s, for example, the United States began to contemplate the deployment of 50,000 warheads. It was to avoid such expensive and fruitless interactions that both sides came to accept the ABM Treaty.'[68] It is difficult to understand why Russia and China would not contemplate such an offensive build-up in the face of U.S. BMD deployment *and* withdrawal from the ABM Treaty. 'Open minds could easily conclude that Russia and China are not likely to acquiesce passively to missile-defence deployments that further buttress American primacy while potentially undermining their own deterrent postures.'[69] As well, Russian and Chinese reactions to BMD deployment may increase the likelihood of an accidental launch by either state. With a BMD system in place, both powers might consider that the United States is more likely to engage in a first-strike. While this appears unlikely during the relative calm of normal international relations, during a crisis period, Russia and China may move to a heightened state of alert in an effort to be able to retaliate against a U.S. attack. Considering the present state of Russian command, control, and communication

---

64 As Miller argues, 'this interpretation is contrary to the explicit position of the Chinese government and simply ignores the possibility that US missile-defence efforts will affect the scale, pace and character of China's nuclear modernization.' Miller, p. 101.

65 Glaser and Fetter, p. 65. TMD stands for Theater Missile Defense.

66 Ibid., p. 84.

67 Miller, p. 102.

68 Ibid., p. 102.

69 Ibid.

systems,[70] this eventuality could have devastating consequences.[71] In other words, applying Cost-Benefit formulas, BMD is the least effective and most unreliable means to preventing an accidental launch by a major nuclear power, a point we will return to below.

The second realist principle that might be employed in an analysis of unilateral BMD deployment is an assessment of the depth and extent of the threat perceived by the United States. During the Cold War, the threat of nuclear annihilation presented both the United States and the Soviet Union with reason to desire defensive capabilities. However, recognition that offensive capabilities could always be enhanced to overwhelm any defensive system imagined (through the addition of decoys, pen-aids, multiple delivery mechanisms, or by simply increasing the number of warheads), made the ICBM threat too great. Even if it were possible to construct a perfect system that could grow with advances in offensive enhancements, realists would require the state to do a Cost-Benefit Analysis. Since any weapons system takes resources away from the development and deployment of other weapons systems, it remains to be seen whether the dollars spent on BMD would be better used by enhancing offensive nuclear capabilities in order to demonstrate to the opposing state that their BMD technology was insufficient to prevent second-strike annihilation. Glaser articulates this realist claim.

> The strongest Cold War argument against NMD was that even if the United States could build a missile defense that would work against deployed Soviet forces, the Soviets could defeat the U.S. NMD at a cost much smaller than the cost to the United States of building the defense in the first place. In other words, the cost-exchange ratio significantly favored the offensive forces and the preservation of retaliatory capabilities. The result of deploying NMD would be an arms race that left U.S. vulnerability undiminished, while greatly increasing the cost of U.S. and Soviet nuclear forces.[72]

On balance, then, the construction of BMD during the Cold War was seen by realists as a problematic and dangerous consideration when discussed in light of the overwhelming threat presented by the Soviet nuclear arsenal.

In the post-Cold War world, the extent of the nuclear threat envisioned by the United States is quite different. This, of course, is an understatement. As Thomas Friedman recently put it, the United States is insistent upon deploying 'weapons

---

70 Consider, for example, that in 1995, 'the detection by Russian radar of the launch of a Norwegian scientific rocket generated a warning of possible attack serious enough to trigger the first-ever activation of President Boris Yeltsin's 'nuclear briefcase.' Glaser and Fetter, p. 70.

71 According to Glaser and Fetter, most accidental launch scenarios with Russian ICBMs would overwhelm any BMD system. See the discussion at Ibid., p. 43.

72 Ibid., p. 59.

84 *Creating Insecurity*

that don't work against an enemy that doesn't exist.'[73] In a post-Cold War world defined by an overwhelming preponderance of U.S power (so much so that its allies are frequently chided for not being able to field resources capable of assisting the United States in crises),[74] the envisioned threats are negligible according to many realists. However, according to proponents of BMD deployment, these threats are real and growing. According to the 1998 Rumsfeld Commission report, North Korea, Iran, and Iraq (later to be termed the 'Axis of Evil') 'would be able to inflict major destruction on the U.S. within about five years of a decision to acquire such a capability.'[75] Similarly, the 1999 National Intelligence Estimate (a review amended in the aftermath of the Rumsfeld Commission report and the North Korean rocket launch) argued that 'during the next 15 years the United States will most likely face ICBM threats from Russia, China, and North Korea, probably from Iran, and possibly from Iraq.'[76]

Realists are skeptical of these states as threats to U.S. national security. Given the realist bias to examine material capabilities, the claim that these states are 'sources of insecurity' seems to ring hollow. Consider that North Korea, the country considered the most immediate threat in terms of its ability to construct an nuclear-tipped ICBM, 'is a small, impoverished nation of 23 million people whose entire gross domestic product is estimated to be less than 10% of the annual US defence budget.'[77] Since it seems equally likely that North Korea will disappear before constructing a viable ICBM system, '[the] American preoccupation with the North Korean threat inspires wide disbelief: many abroad simply cannot believe that the United States feels so threatened by such a weak and fragile state that it must undertake to deploy missile defences at vast expense.'[78] Further, as Miller states, it is a stretch to consider any of the current developments in the international system to be threatening to the United States.

> None of the threatening states whose behaviour is motivating American moves toward missile defence presently possesses either nuclear weapons or intercontinental ballistic missiles (ICBMs). Most do not possess any missiles with a range over 1,450 kilometres (900 miles). None has utilised solid-fuel rockets. None has extensive missile test facilities or the capacity to manufacture significant numbers of long-range missiles. Even in the worst case, none can have such capabilities for some years to come. In the

---

73 Thomas L. Friedman, 'The Rumsfeld Defense,' New York Times (13 July 2001), cited in Miller, p. 105.
74 Center for Defense Information, 'World Military Expenditures,' on the www at http://www.cdi.org/issues/wme
75 1998 Report of the Commission to Assess the Ballistic Missile Threat to the United States, reprinted in Lindsay and O'Hanlon, *Defending America*, p. 198. See the discussion of the Rumsfeld Commission at Glaser and Fetter, p. 44.
76 See, Glaser and Fetter, p. 45.
77 Miller, p. 97.
78 Ibid.

Creating Insecurity I: Unilateral BMD Development and U.S. Security 85

best case, most of the potential proliferators (who are few in any case) will never acquire ICBMs armed with weapons of mass destruction (WMD).[79]

Moreover, as one security analyst has recently argued, even if these states do obtain nuclear-tipped ICBMs, the United States is simply required to adjust its nuclear arsenal such that these states recognize they are now targets of a U.S. nuclear attack.[80] In other words, deterrence works as well against small states as it does against large superpowers. As Glaser argues, 'NMD would have virtually no ability to bolster deterrence of a rogue possessing only a vulnerable ICBM force, *because it should already be effectively deterred.*'[81]

Of course, the counter claim is that not only are these states intent on gaining nuclear weapons capable of harming the United States (either by launching an attack on the U.S. mainland or by preventing U.S. freedom of action abroad), but the leaders of these states are irrational and incapable of understanding the logic of deterrence. They will use nuclear weapons even if their use will result in assured annihilation. On this point, proponents of BMD seem to argue that these 'power-seeking' leaders do not understand the 'power' of others. This is not only a foolish claim, it is also quite dangerous. For, as Miller states quite clearly,

> Until the United States has deployed meaningful missile-defence capacities, it will necessarily rely on deterrence. Even when these defences are deployed, their perfect effectiveness cannot be assumed, which means that deterrence will continue to matter. Moreover, missile defences provide no protection against other means of delivery. Other WMD threats, against which the United States has little protection, must still be deterred. For these reasons, the [Bush] administration ought to be buttressing America's deterrent policy rather than questioning its effectiveness.[82]

Finally, it is necessary to consider by what means proponents of BMD rationalize their claims concerning its value. By employing a 'worst case analysis' to the proliferation of nuclear technology and the construction of ICBMs by 'rogue' states, policy makers and advocates of BMD are seeking to construct a *realist* vision of threats. Indeed, Bush administration officials now consistently claim to be advocating a 'new strategic framework' employing a 'new realism.'[83] What has occurred, however, is that these policy makers have employed a 'simple-minded, and erroneous, use of the game theoretic principle of "minimax."'[84] This principle

---

79 Ibid.

80 Interview with Dr. Gary L. Scott, Hatfield School of Government, Portland State University, 11 July 2001.

81 Glaser and Fetter, p. 67. *My italics.*

82 Miller, p. 98.

83 Jeffrey W. Legro and Andrew Moravcsik, 'Faux Realism,' *Foreign Policy* (July/August 2001), p. 80.

84 Bruce M. Russett, *No Clear and Present Danger: A Skeptical View of the U.S. Entry into World War II* (New York: Harper & Row Publishers, 1972), p. 67. While Russett

86 *Creating Insecurity*

'advises one to choose a strategy so as to minimize the chance of getting the outcome you regard as worst – but properly understood it does not mean bending all efforts to avoid very bad but very improbable events.'[85] Considering both the lack of any near-term threat from rogue states and the possibility that better solutions to medium and long-term threats already exist, realists see BMD deployment as both unhelpful and potentially harmful. Miller provides a succinct summary of a realist assessment of the BMD issue.

> Ultimately at issue in the present missile-defence debate is not whether or not to preserve the ABM Treaty but how best to protect the security of the United States and its friends and allies in a changing strategic environment. In the abstract, there is no reason to quarrel with the simple proposition that it is best to be defended. But the real question to ask about missile defences is: what benefit at what cost? At present, the answer seems to be that missile defences represent a high-cost remedy to a threat that is speculative, distant in time and uncertain in scale and character. Very expensive and very limited missile-defence capabilities will be acquired at the risk of provoking a variety of adverse diplomatic and strategic consequences. It is not at all clear that the net effect will be an improved security order for the United States.[86]

The United States possesses an assortment of material capabilities that might be harnessed in a response to nuclear rogues. For the realist, it is prudent to consider all options in both the assessment of threat and the construction of policy. Below we will consider realist policy options that offer a strategic alternative to unilateral BMD deployment. First, however, it is necessary to determine whether the picture that has been painted by the realists above tells the whole story of BMD. Since both state policy makers and realists offer a similar ontological focus on material threats, might the realist version of the BMD debate not look *too* similar to the version offered by the state? While such similarities do provide an opportunity for critical realists to engage the state in a security dialogue, it may be that their similar pictures of the world mask from view other sources of insecurity. Indeed, as the discussion above demonstrates, BMD policy advocates and realists argue over the extent to which material capabilities possessed by others are threats to the state. They do not inquire into (or problematize) the nature of that 'other' as defined by the state. Identity performances, at home and abroad, are left out of the policy analysis. This makes for a relatively 'clean' debate between state policy advocates and realists. However, it presents only certain security issues for review. Other issues remain outside their purview and require the addition of a political constructivist interpretation.

---

examines 'minimax' in terms of U.S. policy toward Vietnam, the logic of his argument seems appropriate for a discussion of U.S. policy toward BMD.

85 Ibid.

86 Miller, p. 107.

Political Constructivism and BMD Development

A political constructivist interpretation of the BMD debate is quite different from the interpretation offered by realists. While realists are interested in assessing changes in the balance of power and the extent to which other states possess material capabilities harmful to the United States (the extent of the threat), political constructivists are concerned with exploring how culture and identity inform the threat considerations that emerge in and advance the BMD debate. Three issues, in particular, engage political constructivists in their assessment of the issue. Rather than contradicting the realist critique, the following issues suggest how political constructivism might be included in a deeper security analysis. Combining the concerns of the realists above with the concerns of the political constructivists below will allow us, in the final section, to offer a more comprehensive security programme that reduces the potential threat posed by nuclear weapons. But first, it is necessary to outline three issues consistently raised by political constructivists: (1) how American political culture influences the BMD decision, (2) how actors construct the threats they then seek to counter, and (3) how U.S. identity (as the lone superpower) defines and expands its national interests.

First, the peculiarities of U.S. history, and the particular cultural references that arise from that history, engage political constructivists in their assessment of the policies surrounding BMD deployment. Blessed by geographical gifts and weak neighbors, the United States has been able to avoid the possibility that its territory could be invaded for more than a century. When combined with a moral claim that the United States is a hallowed community, the physical invulnerability of 'Fortress America' is both an empirical assertion and a deontological mandate. As such, during the Cold War, the presence of the Soviet nuclear arsenal created a measure of cognitive dissonance among those policy makers internalizing this particular view of American exceptionalism. Soviet weapons challenged the passivity of policy makers that did nothing to overcome the terror of MAD. Among proponents of BMD, it was considered un-American to challenge it.[87]

Moreover, the presence of Soviet ICBMs during the Cold War complicated the use of unilateral policies to overcome the constraints of bipolarity. The tradition of American unilateral foreign policy activity, in the face of the logic of deterrence, could be suicidal if not restrained. However, a culture that is in some way defined by a *manifest destiny* to rise to the role of superpower within 150 years of its birth

---

87 Consider, for example, the language used by Senator Steve Symms (R-Idaho), an advocate of SDI, when challenging legislation that would weaken development of BMD. 'If I were over in the Kremlin, I would say, if this amendment passes with this great momentum behind it, "Just stand firm, boys, because the Americans are weakening. They are voting on the Senate floor the same position we would like to see them take to demonstrate that they are weakening their position all the time."' Cited in Larry Pressler, *Star Wars: The Strategic Defense Initiative Debates in Congress* (Westport, CT: Praeger Publishers, 1986), p. 58.

88 *Creating Insecurity*

is not necessarily inclined towards restraint in its international activities.[88] Both strategically and morally, how could the 'Shining City on the Hill' cope with the threat of annihilation brought by the 'Evil Empire'? The moral dilemma presented to the United States was acute and often articulated in the public actions of key policy makers. Consider the language that Reagan was to employ when announcing development of SDI. 'What if a free people could live secure in the knowledge that their security did not rest upon the threat of instant U.S. retaliation to deter a Soviet attack, that we could intercept and destroy strategic ballistic missiles before they reached our own soil or that of our allies.'[89] It is expected that a politician would use cultural rhetoric to persuade an audience. However, the form and content of this rhetoric is important and reproduces that cultural vein that accepts the unique requirements of American exceptionalism. It is a re-affirmation of the fact that the United States represents the free world (the good) threatened by an aggressor (by definition, bad) willing to destroy it. If the United States is to protect this 'free world', a prerequisite is a return to 'Fortress America' – i.e., the ability to act without impunity in international affairs. These cultural cues are repeated over and over again in the promotion of Cold War BMD.[90] While this picture of American political culture does not represent all strands of the national political ethos, it does present the view offered by right-wing think tanks and policy centers with influence in Washington, DC.[91]

Even after the Cold War, the rhetoric of a besieged America is employed to advocate for deployment of ballistic missile defenses. In this way, a similar view of 'Fortress America' is re-articulated. As Newhouse argues, 'various members of the Bush administration judge relying on deterrence immoral: far better to defend society than to have to avenge it after a destructive attack.'[92] In this context, we can understand the politics of BMD proponents. '[The] mentality of the NMD partisans is a perfect fusion of isolationist and interventionist psyches [what might more

---

88 George Kennan speaks to the American tendency towards unrestrained foreign policies in George F. Kennan, *American Diplomacy*, expanded edition (Chicago: University of Chicago Press, 1984). See, especially, pp. 17-20.

89 Ronald Reagan, 'Speech on Defense Spending and Defensive Technology,' March 23, 1983. Reprinted in Miller and Van Evera, *The Star Wars Controversy*, p. 257. Bruce Jentleson, argues that 'during his 1984 re-election campaign, he accused his Democratic opponent, Walter Mondale, of being so misguided as to believe that the "Soviets were just people like ourselves." Reagan matched this demonic view of the enemy with classic American exceptionalism. America was "a shining city on a hill," the "nation of destiny," the "last best hope of mankind."' See, Bruce W. Jentleson, *American Foreign Policy: The Dynamics of Choice in the 21st Century* (New York: W.W. Norton and Company, 2000), p. 167.

90 The self/other distinction that emerges in this issue returns us to the approach taken by David Campbell, *Writing Security: United States Foreign Policy and the Politics of Identity*, revised edition (Minneapolis, MN: University of Minnesota Press, 1998).

91 See, for instance, the policy recommendations and the viewpoints represented at the Heritage Foundation, on the www at www.heritage.org

92 Newhouse, p. 99.

Creating Insecurity I: Unilateral BMD Development and U.S. Security   89

accurately be considered unilateralism]: We can build a shield over "our" country while preserving the right to intervene at will around the globe... the parochial and the imperial instincts are jointly served.'[93]

Investigating how American political culture influences debate on BMD is not undertaken simply as an historical exercise by political constructivists.. While an improved understanding of the BMD issue is obtained through this textual analysis, political constructivists are equally as interested in recognizing the potential that reflection plays in an improved policy debate. Again, to return to the writings of the constructivists explored in previous chapters, telling alternative histories is a political act. Emphasizing the boundedness of American cultural practices, political constructivists are challenging the parochial and ethnocentric conditions that persist. Given that we live in a world of our making, the opportunity to challenge cultural givens (those that confirm the moral necessity of BMD) is an important political addition.

An examination of the cultural construction of threats that require a subsequent state response in the form of BMD deployment represents another important political act undertaken by political constructivists. Here, the distinction between realism and political constructivism is intriguing. In a series of recent studies, political constructivists have demonstrated that the United States perpetuated its own identity by constructing enemies beyond its borders.[94] Similarly, if the above realist interpretation challenged the state claim that 'rogues' were threats on the grounds that few (if any) material capabilities could be measured that would support such a claim, the interpretation by political constructivists asks how 'rogues' come to be labeled in the first place. This addition to the BMD discussion is important. Realism provides an interesting and compelling analysis of the current lack of any material capabilities possessed by these rogues. But, realism is unprepared to investigate why these states are singled out as threats. Political constructivists, on the other hand, consider this point central to their investigation. In a recent critique of U.S. security policy, Legro and Moravcsik suggest that states labeled as rogues are more ideological threats than a material ones. 'These picayune foes are targeted not because they are the most powerful – or even minimally powerful – but because they are the least democratic and propagate the most hostile ideologies.'[95] In a similar approach to that of Campbell in *Writing Security*, Legro and Moravcsik articulate how the identity of the United States is challenged by these states. Moreover, a deeper analysis would consider how, in a post-Soviet world, the United States must locate an Other in order to maintain a

---

93 Christopher Hitchens, 'Farewell to the Helmsman,' *Foreign Policy* (September/October 2001), p. 70.

94 Again, see, Campbell, supra note 90 and Jim George, *Discourses of Global Politics: A Critical (Re)Introduction to International Relations* (Boulder, CO: Lynne Rienner Publishers, 1993).

95 Legro and Moravcsik, p. 81.

90 *Creating Insecurity*

sense of Self.[96] However insignificant the threat, rogues constitute a 'clear' boundary for American identity. This boundary maintains the unique qualities of American culture by representing that which is different as dangerous – and that which is dangerous as different. These representations reinforce each other. Danger is considered 'outside' while the outside is considered 'dangerous.'

More importantly, political constructivists recognize that if threats can be constructed they can be *de*-constructed and *re*-constituted. An interpretation of rogue states might be transformed through an examination of identity performances. Such a transformation could result in a view of these states as different but not necessarily hostile. While identities are necessary features of any culture, it is not the case that identities need be formed in (hostile) contrast to others. Recognition of difference is a healthy and necessary moment of definition for actors perpetuating a sense of self. It does not follow that these differences need be seen as threatening. Here, the emancipatory nature of political constructivism is most comfortable. Seeking to embrace a more reflexive approach to international politics, political constructivists challenge the standard (state) construction of threats and re-introduce and re-constitute hidden practices that have been marginalized by the official version. This activity is more than an academic exercise; it is hyper-political, requiring the state to re-conceptualize the boundary between Self and Other.

How political constructivists come to understand how U.S. identity influences its interests further expands this hyper-political exercise. On the issue of identity constituting interests, political constructivists and realists diverge. As noted above, realists insist that state interests are given.[97] Political constructivists, on the other hand, consider interests to be the result of particular identities.[98] Both the Cold War and post-Cold War attempt to build BMD systems seem to provide political constructivists with a measure of support for this view. During the early stages of the Cold War, for instance, the only system deployed by the United States (SAFEGUARD) was intended to defend ICBMs. If the United States identified itself as one of two superpowers caught in a bi-polar power struggle, it seems likely that a limited BMD system, designed to enhance deterrence, would be considered.

---

96 Consider both David Campbell, 'Violent Performances: Identity, Sovereignty, Responsibility,' in *The Return of Culture and Identity in IR Theory*, Yosef Lapid and Friedrich Kratochwil, eds. (Boulder, CO: Lynne Rienner Publishers, 1996), pp. 163-180; and Friedrich Kratochwil, 'Citizenship: On the Border of Order,' pp. 181-197.

97 Martha Finnemore's critique of this realist claim is straightforward. See, Martha Finnemore, *National Interests in International Society* (Ithaca, NY: Cornell University Press, 1996), pp. 1-3.

98 Again, see, Finnemore, generally; Ted Hopf, 'The Promise of Constructivism in International Relations Theory,' *International Security* 23 (Summer 1998), pp. 174-177; John Gerard Ruggie, 'What Makes the World Hang Together? Neo-Utilitarianism and the Social Constructivist Challenge,' *International Organization* 52 (Autumn 1998), pp. 862-864; and Paul A. Kowert, 'National Identity: Inside and Outside,' *Security Studies* 8 (Winter 1998/9 - Spring 1999), p. 2.

If deterrence was an appropriate (and stable) institution that would ensure the maintenance of the United States as a superpower, it is likely that a comprehensive BMD system would be more problematic. The ABM Treaty – and the legal codification of MAD – represents a clear articulation of both the United States and the Soviet Union as competing global superpowers. That the Reagan-era SDI program never came to pass is further support for this position. And, while both instances could be read as domestic policy options without sufficient support, the inclusion of a national identity variable seems to provide some insight into why both options had insufficient support.

Similarly, the current international environment has resulted in a re-assessment of American national identity. The United States no longer considers itself competing for world hegemony – *it has it*. As has been repeatedly suggested, the United States 'won the Cold War' and is now the 'indispensable nation'.[99] A new (burgeoning) identity, as the lone superpower, now pervades the policy making community. This identity is not constrained by the boundaries placed on Cold War America. As a result, the United States seeks to expand its interests in an effort to find some balance between its unrestrained national identity and its current capabilities. As Michael Klare argues, the resulting U.S. policy is 'designed to monopolize those critical elements of military power that will enable U.S. forces to prevail on any imaginable battlefield, now and in the future.'[100] Such a policy, of course, has a second component. 'By the same token, this strategy holds that all other states must forever be barred from attaining a similar position of advantage.'[101] A recent Joint Chiefs of Staff analysis makes clear the global parameters of this strategy. It advocates 'full spectrum dominance – a capacity of U.S. forces... to conduct prompt, sustained, and synchronized operations... with access and freedom to operate in all domains – space, sea, land, air, and information.'[102] Recognizing its indispensable nature, the United States has successfully re-identified its purpose in international politics.

This new identity – unbounded by external constraints – is reflected in the expansion of the national interest. The United States now has 'military advisors' in more than seventy countries.[103] Military interventions have increased dramatically since the end of the Cold War.[104] The United States now considers the territory of

---

99   'From Albright to All-murk,' *The Economist* (15 August 1998), p. 25.
100   Michael T. Klare, 'Permanent Preeminence: U.S. Strategic Policy for the 21st Century,' *NACLA Report on the Americas* 34 (November/December 2000), p. 12.
101   Ibid.
102   Newhouse, p. 105.
103   NPR, 'Morning Edition,' 13 May 2002, '"Advisors" Roles,' Eric Westervelt.
104   J. Patrice McSherry notes that 'U.S. Special Forces deployments in Latin America have actually increased from 147 in 1995 to some 200 today.' See, J. Patrice McSherry, 'Preserving Hegemony: National Security Doctrine in the Post-Cold War Era,' *NACLA Report on the Americas* 34 (November/December 2000), p. 27. On the more general problems with intervention, see, Stephen Van Evera, 'American

92   *Creating Insecurity*

the vanquished to be in its national interest. This includes protecting the oil fields around the Caspian Sea, eradicating terrorism in Afghanistan and the former Soviet republics, partitioning the former Yugoslavia, and expanding NATO into Eastern Europe.[105] It also means advocating 'regime change' in states unwilling to submit to U.S. demands.

The result of this unconstrained national identity – increasingly defined as victor of the Cold War and defender of the 'free world' – propels U.S. national interests closer into conflict with regional actors around the world. Moreover, as these regional actors are woefully inadequate as threats when considered alone, they must be grouped as a threatening force. Policy makers are required to group rogues in 'an Axis of Evil'. In addition, these policy makers have attempted to expand the antagonistic actors involved in terrorism.[106] The cultural cues represented in these actions should not be underestimated. Here, political constructivists seem able to say something profound about how language and politics work. The construction of the Axis of Evil is more complicated than a political psychology rendering would have it. By invoking the term 'axis', policy makers return the United States to its war against Germany, Italy, and Japan. By invoking the term 'evil', policy makers return the United States to its war against the Soviet Union. The result is a re-telling of the American fight against hostile and aggressive international forces. In terms of BMD advocacy, these policy makers claim American freedom of action will be deterred if the United States is incapable of defending against rogue missiles.[107] BMD becomes a necessary component of the American national interest. Without it, the United States is unable to protect and defend other interests abroad – interests that are influenced by an identity that sees the United States as a 'hegemonic stabilizer of the system.'[108] No doubt, from a material standpoint, the United States can play the role of hegemonic stabilizer. However, it does not follow that the United States must be defined solely as hegemonic stabilizer and defender of the free-world. Re-interpreting U.S. national identity to recognize its membership in a community of states with similar as well as competing interests would go a long way in challenging the official version of the United States. The challenge for political constructivists is to detail how the current national identity leads to an increased sense of insecurity by creating enemies where few exist.

     Intervention in the Third World: Less Would Be Better,' *Security Studies* 1 (Autumn 1991), pp. 1-24.

105   On NATO expansion, see, Waltz, 'Structural Realism After the Cold War,' pp. 36-38.

106   The most recent example is the Bush Administration's attempt to include Cuba in the terrorist camp. According to Undersecretary of State, John Bolton, 'Cuba should be added to the list of rogue states involved in making, or helping to make, weapons of mass destruction.' See, *The Economist*, 'Playing Softball in Havana,' (May 18-24, 2002), p. 35.

107   Miller, pp. 98-100.

108   McSherry, p. 26.

Enhancing Security

Balancing the disparate political visions (and the corresponding policy directives) offered by realists and political constructivists, a more robust security analysis is possible. In terms of U.S. BMD deployment, this balance occurs when we recognize the realist concern for maintaining adequate capabilities and the political constructivist concern for understanding the role identities play in the articulation of foreign policies. Neither approach, on its own, can provide a comprehensive critique of the U.S. decision to deploy ballistic missile defenses. In this final section, I will examine how the alternative strategies posed by realists to enhance nuclear security (without recourse to BMD) are complemented by the critique offered by political constructivists. Realists have offered several alternatives to the deployment of BMD in an effort to make the United States more secure in the face of the nuclear threat. These solutions are intended to supplement (rather than undermine) the strategy of deterrence. I will discuss three issues that both enhance national security and work within a realist strategy: (1) an agreement to de-alert nuclear weapons, (2) practical programs to reduce the proliferation of nuclear weapons and technology, and (3) diplomatic efforts to deal with potential nuclear rogues.

First, in the event of an accidental nuclear attack, proponents of BMD technology argue that defenses can be effective. An accidental launch is most likely to occur among the established nuclear powers that have developed sophisticated command and control systems. For example, the deteriorating Russian system is thought to be prone to an accidental of inadvertent launch because its intricate system is stretched beyond normal operating capacities. Realists have countered that such a launch would most likely overwhelm any BMD system.[109] But, it is their solution to the problem of accidental launches that is important in the current discussion. Realists advocate a series of policy options that are both more effective and efficient than BMD. An international agreement to 'de-alert' nuclear missiles would provide both the United States and Russia (and any other nuclear power) with a cost-effective means of preventing an accidental firing while maintaining a cogent deterrent. 'De-alerting would amount to de-mating, meaning the physical separation of missile warheads from launchers.'[110]

However, a successful agreement would require the United States to accept a regime to monitor the status of de-alerted nuclear missiles. Such transparency is not necessarily a problem. Cooperation that enhances self-help security promotion is valuable.[111] As long as realists could be relatively assured that opposing nuclear missiles had been successfully de-alerted, the security of the United States could be considered enhanced. The problem for realists is appreciating the challenge posed

---

109 Glaser and Fetter, p. 43.

110 Newhouse, p. 99.

111 Charles L. Glaser, 'Realists as Optimists: Cooperation as Self-Help,' *International Security* 19 (Winter 1994/95), pp. 50-90.

94   *Creating Insecurity*

by identity constructs. If policy makers in the United States continue to define the state as a global hegemon with unbounded freedom of action, it will be exceedingly difficult to bind the United States to any international agreement – even if that agreement appears in the interest of the state. Understanding the necessity of re-constructing identities, political constructivism is a further requirement. Here, the challenge is not the more practical concern of developing a verifiable international mechanism, it is manipulating the identity calculation so that such a mechanism would be recognized as in the interest of the state. As Legro and Moravcsik note, the Bush administration seems to believe that 'democracy promotion, economic integration, nonmilitary foreign aid, adherence to human rights, [and] multilateral cooperation'[112] are insignificant means of promoting the national interest. They conclude that the rhetoric of 'new realism', as it is employed by the Bush administration, is woefully naïve and simplistic. 'Any policymaker who relies only on the "realist" management of military power reveals a greater faith in simplistic theories than do academics.'[113]

We might be even more discerning. The realists presented in this chapter challenge the merits of BMD because they are committed to enhancing national security and recognize the sub-optimal level that BMD provides. Military power (in this case the development and deployment of a robust missile defense system) is one way to enhance security. But, it is neither the only realist alternative nor always the most warranted. Successful management of security might also include arms control agreements, increased transparency, and cooperative strategies. When a state refuses to recognize these options on the grounds that they run counter to the unilateral nature of a global hegemon, it does so by increasing its own insecurity. The predetermined consultations on BMD deployment with both allies and others (William Safire called it 'consultative unilateralism') have made the Bush administration appear both inflexible and uncooperative. Other states see in this behavior an unrestrained and unstoppable superpower. Consider a recent comment by Bush upon returning from meetings with European states concerned about BMD. 'With all due modesty, I think Ronald Reagan would have been proud of how I conducted myself. I went to Europe a humble leader of a great country, and stood my ground. I wasn't going to yield.'[114] Such comments have led Miller to argue that 'open minds could easily conclude that they were dealing with a closed-minded administration whose only real aim is gaining acceptance for predetermined policies.'[115]

---

112 Legro and Moravcsik, p. 81.
113 Ibid., p. 82.
114 Peggy Noonan, 'A Chat in the Oval Office,' *Wall Street Journal* (25 June 2001), cited in Miller, p. 103.
115 Ibid.

Creating Insecurity I: Unilateral BMD Development and U.S. Security   95

Second, realists have also encouraged the promotion of practical programs to reduce the proliferation of nuclear weapons and technology.[116] This has included successful programs to remove nuclear weapons from several Soviet republics and secure potentially problematic Russian weapons. However, the Bush administration has cut the necessary funds for the latter program and seems uninterested in the proliferation issue.[117] It is unclear why the relatively low-cost program (with potentially high benefits) was considered an unattractive means to enhancing national security. Legro and Moravcsik claim the Bush administration is 'skeptical of strategy and tactics not closely linked to military dominance.'[118] If this is the case, it is hard to understand how realists might respond. If realists are correct to argue for policies that enhance national security in the most effective and efficient way, the behavior of policy makers on this matter seems both foolish and dangerous. Again, we might consider what political constructivists offer as a possible solution to this conundrum.

Political constructivism emphasizes how actors construct and re-construct their identities through their foreign policies. In this case, Bush administration policy makers construct and re-construct American might and unilateral prowess by dissuading use of policy alternatives that require cooperative utterances. Insecurity, it would seem, is a result of activities that compromise unilateralism. For political constructivists, this insecurity is ultimately alterable. Because state actors construct their worlds, it is incumbent upon social actors to reflect on their insecurity in the hopes of altering it. Such reflection is not simply a means to deeper self-awareness.[119] The reflexive component of politics is a requirement for a broader, more democratic existence.[120] Recognizing that cooperative programs can also enhance security, U.S. policy makers might come to alter an unrestrained political identity that tends toward acts of hubris.[121] As has been demonstrated elsewhere,

---

116 Perhaps the most promising example is the Nunn-Lugar initiatives to reduce the threat of WMD. For a detailed discussion, see, 'Nunn-Lugar Threat Reduction Programs,' *Coalition to Reduce Nuclear Dangers* 2 (30 March 1998) at www.clw.org/pub/clw/coalition/brief10.htm

117 Indeed, recent diplomatic activities in South Asia suggest that India believes that in exchange for favorable comments regarding BMD, the United States is willing to allow states like India into the 'nuclear club'. See, for instance, Subhash Agrawal, 'NMD: India's Curious Response,' *Far Eastern Economic Review* (14 June 2001), p. 34.

118 Legro and Moravcsik, p. 81.

119 By this, I mean that the act of reflection is the engine which propels the dialectic forward.

120 Nicholas G. Onuf, 'The Politics of Constructivism,' in *Constructing International Relations: The Next Generation,* Karin M. Fierke and Knud Erik Jorgensen, eds. (Armonk, NY: M.E. Sharpe, 2001), p. 248.

121 Consider the argument by Alan Gilbert that a sophisticated realism cautions against acts of hubris in order to enhance security. See, Gilbert, pp. 12-13.

96   *Creating Insecurity*

the arrogant activities of great powers can undermine national security and leave a state less powerful than it might have been.[122]

Third, realists and others have attempted to improve U.S. nuclear security by employing diplomatic efforts to deal with potential nuclear rogues.[123] These diplomatic policies draw on realism's concern that states should discount ideological differences and concentrate on the material capabilities of others.[124] Rogues need not be destroyed militarily in order to enhance U.S. national security. In fact, a military solution to the rogue threat seems costly and unwarranted. While realists have offered alternative strategies that emphasize less destructive means, they are constrained by their negative vision of international politics from offering a more comprehensive approach.

Political constructivists recognize the potential for multilateral cooperation to enhance national securities. In so doing, they provide this analysis with an assortment of tools that promote more secure relationships. By way of example, we might consider the recent dismissal by the Bush administration of attempts to reach an agreement with North Korea on their nuclear program. Legro and Moravcsik provide a succinct summary of this dismissal.

> Consider the quick quashing of a deal, all but reached by South Korean President Kim Dae-Jung, for a far-reaching détente on the Korean peninsula, including significant restrictions on the North Korean nuclear program. Unfortunately, such a deal, designed to spur a positive evolution in North Korea's behavior, fit neither the [Bush] administration's reliance on military deterrence nor its justification for NMD.[125]

This example suggests that U.S. policy makers were unable to recognize that a change in the North Korean material interests could perpetuate a change in its antagonistic identity towards the United States (a point McSweeney emphasizes in his constructivist work above).[126] Further, policy makers were unwilling to reflect

---

122 See, Ibid., generally, but with specific attention to pp. 170-175; and Chalmers Johnson, *Blowback: The Cost and Consequences of American Empire* (New York: Henry Holt and Company, 2000).

123 Miller, p. 106.

124 As Hollis and Smith argue, '[this] is clear in Morgenthau's work, where he argues that the requirements of national interest drive out ideological considerations in the formulations of foreign policy.' See, Martin Hollis and Steve Smith, *Explaining and Understanding International Relations* (Oxford: Clarendon Paperbacks, 1991), p. 85; see, also, Hans J. Morgenthau, *Politics Among Nations: The Struggle for Power and Peace*, 5th edition (New York: Alfred A. Knopf, 1973), p. 7; and George F. Kennan, Memoirs 1950-1963, volume II (Boston: Little, Brown and Company, 1972), pp. 57-60.

125 Legro and Moravcsik, p. 82.

126 McSweeney argues that a change in material interests can change actor identities. His *Security, Identity and Interests: A Sociology of International Relations* relates this issue to the Northern Ireland peace talks. See, Bill McSweeney (Cambridge: Cambridge University Press, 1999), pp. 175-197.

on the potential that their identity (in opposition to North Korea) might be unduly hostile and indicative of increased insecurity between the two states.

Each of the examples above demonstrates how a more pluralistic approach, one that balances the negative vision of realism with the positive potential of political constructivism, offers a more comprehensive approach to security analysis. The goal of any security analysis is to find ways to improve and enhance national security. This discussion of unilateral BMD deployment demonstrates how a robust security policy cannot be constructed by relying solely on enhancements to material capabilities. Realism can offer a (necessary) critique of state policies that seek only to enhance capabilities without managing the overall security environment, but it is an incomplete tool because of its own bias towards a materialist ontology and a negative view of international relations. Recourse to political constructivism provides a positive approach to overcoming the insecurity that exists in the cultural milieu. In the following chapter, a second topic will be explored. The recent expansion of the U.S. war on drugs in the Andean region of South America represents another issue where U.S. policy makers may undermine national security by pursuing policies that actually create more insecurity.

Chapter 6

Creating Insecurity II: U.S. Policy Toward Colombia

As the above discussion concerning deterrence, ballistic missile defense, and U.S. policy suggests, a more comprehensive security framework allows for an understanding of how the United States may indeed create its own insecurity in an attempt to manage perceived international threats. This results from a process whereby the state acknowledges a material threat without simultaneously acknowledging ideational sources that play a role in the interpretation of that threat. In a similar way, the U.S. policy towards the illicit trade in drugs as it is manifested in U.S.-Colombian relations involves a compelling understanding of the existential issues at stake with very little mention of ideational issues that underpin certain aspects of the drug war. Keeping in mind that 'security' has a material *and* ideational dimension, insecurities are created when policy responses involve only one of the two dimensions. The following discussion begins with a review of the historical roots of the current political situation in Colombia and how U.S policy has developed to manage the security concerns that have emerged over the decades. A realist response to current U.S. policy can be situated within the state paradigm and thus provide an engaged criticism of U.S. drug policy in Colombia. The weight of this perspective demonstrates how realism provides a thorough account of the material concerns that emerge in the drug war. Indeed, a realist analysis is quite useful in demonstrating the limitations of U.S. policy to arrest the illicit trafficking of drugs. However, only the state-centric material account emerges through the realist lens. The subsequent inclusion of a political constructivist critique demonstrates the importance of offering an ideational account of the war on drugs. Of particular importance is an answer to the question concerning how the drug issue came to be framed as a criminal issue instead of one of public health. The drug war cannot be understood from an explicitly international perspective – one in which the U.S. and Colombia meet on the field of foreign policy. Rather, the arbitrary distinction between the international and domestic realms needs to be supplanted by what scholars have termed the domain of intermesticity. The political constructivist viewpoint that has been developed here attempts to link the issue of domestic political culture with state and (realist) concerns over the international drug trade. By balancing the two issues, it is hoped that a more comprehensive analysis can emerge.

Colombian History and U.S. Policy

The Colombian state has long been considered of strategic importance to the United States. At the turn of the last century, when Colombian intransigence stymied U.S. resolve to construct the Panama Canal, Washington policy makers found reason to foment rebellion in and support the independence of Panama. Throughout the Cold War, following the logic of NSC-68, 'U.S. security was seen as inextricably linked to promotion of the private enterprise system and unobstructed U.S. access to Third World economies and raw materials.'[1] As the Truman Administration would stress, 'U.S. security is the objective of our world-wide foreign policy today,' and 'U.S. security is synonymous with hemisphere security.'[2] Colombia, rich in petroleum and natural gas reserves, and strategically located between the Pacific and Caribbean, represented a key piece of this American grand design. By 1952, Colombia agreed to participate in a Mutual Defense Assistance Pact (MDAP) with the United States. In exchange for military assistance, the Colombian government would 'facilitate the production and transfer... of... strategic materials required by the United States' and would cooperate with the United States in limiting trade with the Soviet Bloc.[3] Throughout the Cold War, '[even] if it meant allying with authoritarian regimes or helping to overthrow democratically elected governments, the United States spent considerable effort pursuing its regional security objectives, above all preventing communism from gaining a foothold in the hemisphere.'[4]

Consistently over the past century, the United States has claimed a security interest in its relationship with Colombia. During this same period, the complexities of Colombian internal politics have substantially complicated U.S. policy.[5] With specific attention paid to issues that directly affect these foreign policy

---

1 J. Patrice McSherrey, 'Preserving Hegemony: National Security Doctrine in the Post-Cold War Era,' *NACLA Report on the Americas* 34 (November/December 2000), p. 29.

2 Draft Paper, 'Development of U.S. Latin American Policy in Terms of U.S. World Objectives, 1950-1955,' 9 November 1950, FRUS, 1950, 2: 634. Cited in Stephen G. Rabe, *Eisenhower and Latin America: The Foreign Policy of Anticommunism* (Chapel Hill, NC: University of North Carolina Press, 1988).

3 Edwin Lieuwen, *Arms and Politics in Latin America* (New York: Council on Foreign Relations, Frederick A. Praeger, 1960), p. 200.

4 Russell Crandall, *Driven By Drugs: U.S. Policy Toward Colombia* (Boulder, CO: Lynne Rienner Publishers, 2002), p. 7. For an extended discussion of U.S.-Colombian relations and how U.S. policy has formed to manage its interests in Colombia, see, Stephen J. Randall, *Colombia and the United States: Hegemony and Interdependence* (Athens, GA: University of Georgia Press, 1992).

5 Of particular interest is the period known as *La Violencia* that began as the East/West dynamic was emerging on the international stage. See, Gonzalo Sánchez and Donny Meertens, *Bandits, Peasants, and Politics: The Case of 'La Violencia' in Colombia,* trans. by Alan Hynds (Austin, TX: University of Texas Press, 2001). See pages 9-33 on what leads up to *La Violencia* – the period roughly from 1945-1960.

100 *Creating Insecurity*

developments, this section examines the origins of the guerrilla insurgencies, the connection between the cocaine trade and guerrilla/paramilitary organizations, and the creation of interdiction and eradication initiatives to reduce the amount of illicit drugs leaving Colombia for the United States.

As noted, the United States drew a parallel between access to strategic resources in Latin America and its ability to successfully wage a cold war against the Soviet Union. This overriding concern further required that the United States prevent leftist rebels from interfering with U.S. access to these materials and challenging the power of the state. By 1960, the Eisenhower administration 'identified Castro's Cuba as the major source of danger in the Caribbean.'[6] However, attention was also turned to 'political movements in such countries as Colombia, Venezuela, the Dominican Republic and Panama.'[7] The peculiarities of the Colombian guerrilla movements require special attention. These movements are an outgrowth of historical struggles over land reform and access to political power.

While the origins of guerrilla movements stretch back to the early 1920s, their rapid growth during the early years of the Cold War is of particular importance. The simultaneous emergence of 'La Violencia' in Colombia and the U.S.-Soviet split after WWII exacerbated the troubles in Colombia and solidified U.S. policy towards its weaker neighbor. By the 1950s, the United States saw it in its national interest to supply the Colombian state with arms and advisors to combat anti-government groups throughout the country.[8] With the introduction of U.S. military aid during the rule of General Rojas Pinilla an atmosphere of increased hostility and political unrest further destabilized the countryside. Although the introduction of this military hardware into the chaotic politics of Colombia cannot be said to have initiated the violence that had already begun, it can be argued with some degree of certainty that U.S. hemispheric security concerns legitimized Colombian state programs to eradicate the excluded elements of the domestic society. Rojas Pinilla's dictatorial rule emphasized the armed suppression of frequent political protests (using MDAP weapons)[9] and caused disparate excluded groups to band together. Between 1955 and 1957, communist and 'common liberal' guerrillas formed alliances and created 'Independent Republics' in rural portions of Colombia.[10] After the Rojas Pinilla regime and the subsequent formation of the *National Front* (a power-sharing arrangement between the Liberal and

---

6 Rabe, p. 138.

7 Ibid.

8 For a detailed and intimate history of the largest guerrilla movement in Colombia, the FARC, see, Luis Alberto Matta Aldana, *Colombia y las FARC-EP: Origen de la Lucha Guerrillera* (Nafarrao, Spain: Txalaparta Publishing, 1999). For a shorter account detailing the growth of the FARC see, Alfredo Molano, 'The Evolution of the FARC: A Guerrilla Group's Long History,' *NACLA: Report on the Americas* 34 (September/October 2000), pp. 23-31.

9 Rabe, p. 96.

10 Erma von der Walde and Carmen Burbano, 'Violence in Colombia: A Timeline,' *NACLA: Report on the Americas* 35 (July/August 2001), p. 24.

Conservative Parties that denied other political groups and parties access to the legislative process) the government of Colombia turned its attention to eradicating these 'Independent Republics' and the outlawed political groups they contained. This occurred as the United States decides to increase its assistance to the Colombian military. As a result of President Eisenhower's 1959 decision to assist Colombia with its domestic security concerns, 'in 1961 the United States sent its first military training team (MTT) to Colombia to help train the country's military in areas related to intelligence capabilities.'[11] In 1964, the Colombian military, with the assistance of the U.S. military,[12] bombed the town of Marquetalia and the surrounding populations (of south-central Colombia) in an effort to eliminate these separatist regions. Owing again to Cold War politics, the U.S. military seized this opportunity to hone its skills in the use of napalm.[13] Government offensives, however, were unable to defeat the guerrilla movements, which, later that year, mobilize as the Revolutionary Armed Forces of Colombia (FARC). Also in the 1960s, two other major guerrilla movements form, the National Liberation Army (ELN) and the People's Liberation Army (EPL).[14] By 1970, the situation in Colombia was tense but stable. Neither the Colombian armed forces nor the disparate guerrilla groups had the resources to achieve a military victory. As LeoGrande and Sharpe note, 'Throughout the 1960s and 1970s, Colombia's guerrilla wars were low-intensity affairs. None of the half-dozen guerrilla groups (which operated independently) could seriously challenge the armed forces for control of the state, but neither could the armed forces defeat the guerrillas, especially those with a well-established rural base.'[15]

With a political solution to rural poverty and inequality stymied by the exclusionary politics of Liberal/Conservative collusion, peasants and marginalized workers in Colombia increasingly recognized the economic benefits of supplying the growing international demand for illicit drugs to supplement meager incomes. In effect, an extralegal economic solution became a substitute for political reform. The growth of the drug trade and its origins in the political issues that initiated the rise of guerrilla movements further demonstrate how external political and market forces (largely from the United States) influenced the internal political and economic atmosphere of Colombia.

Colombia's participation in the international drug trade was inconsequential throughout much of the Twentieth Century. Only after drug use in the United States rose dramatically in the mid-1960s did Colombia begin to export large quantities of illicit drugs. While 'Colombian marijuana production mushroomed in the middle

---

11 Crandall, p. 24.
12 According to Alfredo Molano, the Colombian military was backed 'by Washington's National Security Doctrine and a $170 million U.S. loan.' See, Molano, p. 25.
13 von der Walde and Burbano, p. 24.
14 Molano, p. 26.
15 William LeoGrande and Kenneth E. Sharpe, 'Two Wars or One? Drugs, Guerrillas, and Colombia's New *Violencia*,' *World Policy Journal* 17 (Fall 2000), p. 4.

102　　　　　　　　　　　　*Creating Insecurity*

and late 1960s as a result of growing U.S. demand,'[16] it was not until the early to mid-1970s that the 'epicenter of marijuana production in the hemisphere shifted to Colombia.'[17] In an early example of the 'balloon effect',[18] U.S. efforts to eradicate the marijuana industry in Mexico resulted in beneficial market entry for Colombian growers and traffickers.

> By the end of the 1970s Colombia accounted for some 70 percent of the marijuana reaching the United States from abroad. Between 30,000 and 50,000 small farmers along Colombia's Atlantic coast came to depend directly on marijuana cultivation for their livelihood, while at least another 50,000 (seasonal pickers, transporters, guards, bankers, and such) made some part of their living from it.[19]

Similarly, and again as a result of international market forces, Colombian entry into the cocaine market was a consequence of increased U.S. consumer demand during the mid-1970s as well as U.S.-led marijuana eradication programs during the same period. During the Carter and Reagan administrations, increased awareness of a domestic drug problem resulted in more aggressive U.S.-led interdiction and eradication campaigns in the 'source' Andean countries. In the late 1970s, the United States and the Colombian military cooperated in the eradication of the Colombian marijuana trade (mainly in the northern 'Guajira' region along the Atlantic Coast). However, these eradication efforts would presage myriad problems with the militarization of drug policy. Important for our consideration, these eradication efforts came at a high cost to the local population. In addition, 'to the extent that enforcement efforts in the Guajira were successful, they tended merely to displace drug cultivation and transport activities to other parts of the country, such as the Eastern Plains and the Amazonian jungle, rather than eliminating them.'[20] This seemingly mundane example of a domestic 'balloon effect' would have lasting consequences for Colombia. Pushing the drug trade south and east meant pushing drug cultivation into areas protected by the largest guerrilla movements. In addition, by directly involving large components of the Colombian military, police, and judicial agencies on the front lines of the 'drug war', the United States involved these government agencies in activities susceptible to corruption.[21]

16　Bruce M. Bagley, 'Colombia and the War on Drugs,' *Foreign Affairs* 67 (Fall 1988), p.73.

17　Bagley, p. 73.

18　The idea of the 'balloon effect' is often used to describe the problem of attacking drugs in one area only to find them emerge in another. See, LeoGrande and Sharpe, p. 2.

19　Bagley, p. 74.

20　Ibid., p. 80.

21　Ibid. This problem reaches its apogee, perhaps, in the presidency of Ernesto Samper, who was funded by and largely beholden to drug money. See, Francisco E. Thoumi, 'The Impact of the Illegal Drug Industry on Colombia,' in *Transnational Crime in the*

Creating Insecurity II: U.S. Policy Toward Colombia

Shortly after the marijuana eradication efforts in Colombia, U.S. coca eradication programs in Peru and Bolivia hastened the development of sophisticated coca-processing plants inside Colombia and turned significant tracts of rural acreage within Colombia into coca cultivation regions. These eradication efforts demonstrate the further militarization of U.S. drug policy. Following the 1986 signing of National Security Decision Directive No. 221, 'which identified drugs as a threat to the United States and, by implication, hemispheric security,'[22] U.S. eradication and interdiction programs increased in frequency and became more invasive. As a paradigmatic case, Operation Blast Furnace demonstrated how U.S. and Andean militaries were to work together in the eradication effort. Constructed by U.S. embassy officials in La Paz, Bolivia, as early as 1985, the joint U.S.-Bolivian counternarcotics effort known as 'Operation Blast Furnace' was launched in July of 1986. Supplied with U.S. Black Hawk helicopters and 160 U.S. troops,[23] special Bolivian police units entered the 'Chapare' region of Bolivia in an effort to destroy coca production facilities and eradicate large tracts of coca plants.

> Blast Furnace pursued three objectives. First, cocaine-processing laboratories... would be closed down. Second, this action would disrupt cocaine processing and consequently reduce the demand for coca leaves. Third, the price of coca leaves would fall below production prices thus forcing peasants to turn to crop substitution programs.[24]

Unfortunately, except for undermining the Bolivian constitution,[25] invigorating anti-American protests throughout the region, and reducing the short-term price of the coca leaf, Operation Blast Furnace was largely ineffective. 'As soon as the U.S. troops left... the price of coca leaves jumped back to pre-Blast Furnace levels.' Additionally, 'the total hectarage under cultivation increased concomitantly over the next three years.'[26] Another unintended consequence of Blast Furnace (and similar operations in Peru including 'Operation Verde Mar' and 'Operation Condor' as well as the broader Andean initiative 'Operation Snowcap')[27] was the

---

Americas: An Inter-American Dialogue Book, Tom Farer, ed. (London: Routledge, 1999), p. 134.

22 William O. Walker III, 'A Reprise for "Nation Building,":' Low Intensity Conflict Spreads in the Andes,' *NACLA Report on the Americas* 35, (July/August 2001), p. 26.

23 Eduardo Gamarra, 'Bolivia,' in *International Handbook on Drug Control*, Scott B. MacDonald and Bruce Zagaris, eds. (Westport, CT: Greenwood Press, 1992), p. 107.

24 Ibid., p. 108.

25 Ibid.

26 Ibid.

27 Operation Verde Mar was created to eradicate coca in the Upper Huallaga Valley of Peru in 1979, Operation Condor was created to interdict the trafficking of coca from the Upper Huallaga Valley of Peru in 1985, and Operation Snowcap was created in 1987 and involved U.S. DEA agents in nine Latin American countries in an attempt to assist in eradication and interdiction programs. For a discussion, see, Laura Vasquez, 'Peru,' in *International Handbook on Drug Control*, pp. 212-217.

104 *Creating Insecurity*

regional 'balloon effect.' While Colombia had been a transport center for the cocaine trade, U.S. eradication and interdiction policies in Peru and Bolivia pushed coca cultivation further into remote regions of Colombia.

Throughout the 1980s and early 1990s, U.S. efforts focused on eliminating the 'narcotrafficking' cartels in Medellin and Cali. While the U.S. and Colombian effort to dismantle these cartels was largely successful, the resulting effects on the cocaine industry demonstrated how U.S. policy designs were inadequate and incomplete. LeoGrande and Sharpe summarize the point nicely when arguing that 'smashing the cartels did not reduce the flow of drugs. It simply changed the structure of the industry, creating space in the market for many new small and intermediate producers.'[28] In addition, having pushed coca cultivation and cocaine production into rural Colombia, U.S. policy demonstrably increased the strength of the leftist guerrilla groups. The FARC, for instance, grew from a force of barely 3,000 in 1985 to a force of between 16,000 and 20,000 by 2000.[29] Most devastating, however, the disparate right-wing death squads – remnants of the Conservative Party's campaign to prevent land reform efforts in the 1940s – used their newly gained access to drug trafficking to finance increasingly brutal attacks on peasants in rural areas. In 1995, Carlos Castaño officially brought many of these groups together as the Self-Defense Units of Colombia (AUC). The resulting right-wing paramilitary offensives against FARC-controlled coca cultivation areas in the south as well as the solidification of AUC regions in the north dramatically increased political violence and further destabilized efforts to bring about a peaceful solution to the political crises.[30]

As Cold War hostilities gave way to the complexities of the post-Cold War world, U.S. eradication and interdiction policy changed little. The Bush Administration (1989-1993) created the Andean Drug Strategy in 1990 as a response to concerns that military strategies could not be effective unless they could be coordinated at a regional level (a weak policy response to the seemingly law-like balloon effect). Quixotically, recognizing the limitations of a

---

28 LeoGrande, and Sharpe, p. 2.

29 Martin Hodgson, 'The Coca Leaf War,' *The Bulletin of the Atomic Scientists* 56, (May/June 2000): 40. Russell Crandall follows Ricardo Vargas Meza and suggests that the FARC's growth can be measured using the following numbers: 1986- 32 fronts and 3,600 members; 1995- 60 fronts and 7,000 members; 2000- 85 fronts and 18,000 members. Crandall, p. 91 citing Ricardo Vargas Meza, 'The Revolutionary Armed Forces of Colombia (FARC) and the Illicit Drug Trade,' (Cochabamba, Bolivia: Acción Andina, June 1999).

30 See, Nazih Richani, *Systems of Violence: The Political Economy of War and Peace in Colombia* (Albany, NY: SUNY Press, 2002), pp. 104-113 for a detailed discussion of the political economy of paramilitary groups in Colombia. Richani notes that recent drug finds in AUC-areas 'confirm the thesis that the AUC is becoming a narco-trafficking organization with its involvement in the processing, packaging, and marketing of cocaine.' (p. 108). See, also, Von der Walde and Burbano, pp. 26-27 for a brief account of AUC activities.

Creating Insecurity II: U.S. Policy Toward Colombia   105

predominantly military response to the illicit drug trade, the Bush administration actually *increased* militarization. Military aid to Colombia, already on the increase during the Reagan administration, increased to $500 million between 1989 and 1993.[31] Increased militarization occurred, as well, during the Clinton Administration, which supplied Colombia with over $1 billion prior to 2000. So, too, did the ineffective nature of the military response to coca cultivation and cocaine production in the Andean region. As a result, U.S. and Colombian officials found it necessary to unveil 'Plan Colombia', a $7.5 billion anti-drug initiative that emphasizes further military means to eradicating and interdicting illegal drugs. While funding for the multi-year plan was to involve many states and international agencies, the Plan's teeth involved a $1.3 billion U.S. aid package to the Andean region. Of the $860 million allocated to Colombia, $519 million would be for military assistance and just $3 million would be for the peace process.[32] Rather than the final offensive in the war on drugs, Plan Colombia represents the dire situation present in Colombia at the turn of this century. As Walker notes, 'Plan Colombia cannot be understood, let alone implemented, in isolation from the totality of the situation in Colombia. In spring 2001, even before a significant infusion of Plan Colombia aid had begun, the country was facing an unemployment rate of approximately 20%; as much as 40% of the countryside was not fully in government hands.'[33] Since Colombia covers a land mass about the size of Texas and California combined, it is not unrealistic to contend that by the end of the century, Colombia was a failed state.[34] Further evidence for such consideration is supplied by the fact that as a direct result of the drug war,

> [the] internal migration of perhaps two million people, better characterized as dislocation if not exile, was exceeded only in Sudan and Angola. Human flight of the privileged classes, with its attendant and burgeoning capital flight, to North America and Europe was continuing apace; and foreign investors were growing more reluctant by the day to continue business as usual.[35]

---

31 Walker, p. 27.

32 Crandall, pp. 154-155.

33 Ibid., p. 28.

34 See, for instance, Robert H. Jackson, *Quasi-states: Sovereignty, International Relations and the Third World* (Cambridge: Cambridge University Press, 1990). While this takes liberties with a definition that has traditionally been used to describe state in Sub-Saharan Africa, the dire situation in Colombia cannot be underestimated in the eyes of U.S. officials. Even if it is remembered that the Colombian state has rarely been in control of the whole country at any one time, the perception in Washington, D.C. during the construction of Plan Colombia was that Colombia was imploding. See, Crandall, p. 149 for a longer discussion of U.S. concerns. As our theoretical discussion of security suggests, empirical evidence is only one part of a broader security calculus. A psychological (or, more broadly, ideational) understanding of the situation is something quite different but equally as important.

35 Walker, p. 28.

106 *Creating Insecurity*

Moreover, of the $519 million in military assistance from the United States, over 80% ($416 million) will fund the Colombian state's attempt to regain areas lost to guerrillas and drug producers in the south of the country.[36] Considering that it was the United States that created Plan Colombia for all intents and purposes,[37] it seems clear that the approach to the illegal trade in narcotics mirrored that taken during the Cold War.

The history of U.S. security policy towards Colombia over the past sixty years demonstrates an attempt to fit Colombia into a 'national security' paradigm constructed during the Cold War and re-tooled as a reaction to social problems in the United States and the emergence of Colombia as a dominant player in the production of cocaine. Three issues, in particular, largely define the nature of U.S. policy proposals and programs. First, the United States has consistently sought to externalize domestic considerations. During the Cold War the United States placed Colombian insurgencies in the context of East/West issues. Doing so, the specific political dynamics of U.S/Soviet relations were externalized to the South. While it might be argued that the Cold War was already an external issue for the U.S., it is important to remember works such as David Campbell's *Writing Security* that demonstrates how U.S. domestic identity was largely formed through a perception of anti-communism at home as well as abroad. In the case of Colombia, the domestic conflict between an elite-controlled government and predominantly rural guerrilla movements was envisioned as a micro-example of the macro-Cold War. As well, the United States externalized its domestic social and political problems involving illicit drug use. Unable or unwilling to deal with the domestic demand side, the United States found 'the problem' to be located in an external environment- the source countries of the Andean region.

Second, the United States has consistently endeavored to define its policy problems by recourse to increased militarization. Repeatedly during the Cold War, the United States aided the Colombian military in its war against leftist insurgents. These policies often antagonized actors involved in the conflicts and reduced the effectiveness of already fragile Colombian institutions. Although the source of Colombia's violence involves a much more detailed review of the actors involved, the inability on the part of the U.S. to envision non-military strategies as central to the Colombian crisis is striking. Likewise, as the demand for drugs increased beginning in the 1970s, the U.S. responded with military assistance and intervention in these 'source' countries. Indeed, as the Cold War ended, 'intermestic' issues like the illegal drug trade gained credence for a hegemon seeking a new reason to remain involved in Colombia.[38]

Third, U.S. policy makers have often given confusing and contradictory statements when attempting to distinguish between policies intended to combat guerrilla insurgencies and those intended to reduce the supply of illegal drugs.

---

36 Crandall, p. 155.

37 Ibid., pp. 149-150.

38 Ibid., p. 10.

Creating Insecurity II: U.S. Policy Toward Colombia 107

While social scientists rarely take policy makers at their word, just how confused the policy directives become during the latter part of the Cold War suggests how the policies of containing communism merged with the policies to fight the drug war. During the Reagan-era Cold War, Elliott Abrams and other high-ranking officials were explicit in making a link between the war on drugs and the war against leftist insurgents. In early 1987, Abrams would argue before Congress that 'MAP funds for Colombia strengthen the government's antinarcotics programs and at the same time assist it in dealing with the increasingly violent insurgents who have rejected the government's peace initiatives.'[39] Similarly, Barry McCaffrey, drug czar during the Clinton Administration and former U.S. commander of SOUTHCOM, has argued that 'Colombia is losing the drug war because it cannot eradicate coca in the areas under guerrilla control, and it is losing the guerrilla war because the Colombian armed forces are out-gunned by insurgents flush with the 'taxes' they collect from coca growers.'[40] In this way, McCaffrey insists that Plan Colombia is the answer to the 'twin ills' that afflict the country. However, Plan Colombia has been advertised as a comprehensive plan to eradicate and interdict drugs – not a counterinsurgency initiative.[41] Indeed, its approval by Congress required that the executive branch significantly separate the two issues.[42] Yet, to add to the confusion, the United States and the Colombian military have pushed for and begun the eradication of coca cultivation areas in the south of Colombia-regions controlled by the FARC – instead of the eradication of the larger and more integrated fields of northern Colombia- regions controlled by the right-wing AUC. Moreover, in the present context, and after the events of 11 September, the drug/leftist insurgency connection has become mired in the language of the war against terrorism.[43] While officials as early as the first Bush administration used the

---

39 Elliott Abrams, 'U.S. Interests and Resource Needs in Latin America and the Caribbean,' United States Department of State, Bureau of Public Affairs, Washington, D.C. April 1987.

40 LeoGrande and Sharpe, p. 1.

41 Marc Cooper, 'Plan Colombia: Wrong Issue, Wrong Enemy, Wrong Country,' *The Nation* 272 (19 March 2001): 11-18. Of course, the Colombian military is far more direct in their assessment of the initiative, 'We don't differentiate between counterinsurgency and counter-narcotics operations – they're the same thing.' (Lt. Col. Jose Leonidas Munoz, commander of the 90th Battalion), cited in Hodgson, p. 41. See the more engaged discussion of Plan Colombia in Crandall, p. 149.

42 This is most clearly represented in the need for State Department Certification. See, 'Drugs, Latin America, and the United States,' *The Economist* (7 February 1998), pp. 35-36.

43 See the recent hearing before both the House and Senate. U.S. Congress, House, Committee on International Relations, *International Global Terrorism: its links with illicit drugs as illustrated by the IRA and other groups in Colombia.* Hearing before the Committee on International Relations, 107th Congress, 2nd session, 24 April 2002; and U.S. Congress, Senate, Committee on the Judiciary, *Narco-Terror: the worldwide connection between drugs and terrorism.* Hearing before the Subcommittee on

108 *Creating Insecurity*

rhetoric of 'terrorism' to define the activities of the FARC,[44] such language now takes on added significance. In a recent article, Russell Crandall notes that, 'following the terrorist attacks on United States soil, the taboo against counterinsurgency assistance has vanished.'[45] Linking FARC rebels to coca cultivation in regions controlled by this group and further labeling them 'terrorists' lends *official* legitimacy to counterinsurgency campaigns that have been unpopular since the Vietnam era. Perhaps most importantly, it also renders the stated 'separateness' of the guerrilla and drug issues irrelevant.

If this brief history of Colombia and the corresponding U.S. security policies created to manage it suggest anything, it is that further analysis is required in order to understand and critique the current 'drug war'. In the following section, I will explore how realism might be employed to analyze this war on drugs. As with the previous chapter, this section demonstrates how the traditional approach to security studies offers a necessary but incomplete understanding of a complex issue.

Realism and the War on Drugs

Realists are committed to viewing the world as full of potential threats. Their place as the 'cautious paranoids' at the security table is welcomed by state actors employing a similar materialist interpretation of the dangers that exist beyond its borders. Further, realists and state actors place central importance on defending the national interest – albeit for different reasons and with different interpretations of that interest.[46] These similarities in world views and policy orientations make a realist critique of U.S. drug policy a necessary component of a larger and more comprehensive engaged security analysis.

As a public health issue, drugs can be interpreted as a national security problem. The effects of cocaine use in the United States can be measured in higher crime rates, lost productivity, premature mortality, etc. The issue represents what

---

Technology, Terrorism, and Government Information of the Committee of the Judiciary, 107th Congress, 2nd session, 13 March 2002.

44 Michael J. Kryzanek puts the point nicely when arguing that 'descriptions of ties between leftist FARC (Revolutionary Armed Forces of Colombia) rebels and drug lords have been used by the Bush administration to lend support to the Colombian government's war against the Medellin Cartel. The objective is clearly to paint the rebels as criminals and terrorists with little interest in government reform.' Michael J. Kryzanek, *Leaders, Leadership, and U.S. Policy in Latin America* (Boulder, CO: Westview Press, 1992), p. 143.

45 Russell Crandall, 'Clinton, Bush and Plan Colombia,' *Survival* 44 (Spring 2002), p. 168.

46 The collection of essays brought together by Hans J. Morgenthau in *Truth and Power* provides some direction as to the differences that exist between realists and state power brokers over the term 'national interest'. See Hans J. Morgenthau, *Truth and Power: Essays of a Decade 1960-1970* (New York: Praeger Publishers, 1970).

Creating Insecurity II: U.S. Policy Toward Colombia   109

Harold and Margaret Sprout regard as a 'functional limitation' on state power.[47] As drug use continues to grow, it undermines the social fabric of the state and draws precious resources that might have been used for more productive ends.

Therefore, when U.S. policy makers consistently sought to view the drug issue as a supply-side problem, thereby externalizing the issue and making the problem largely one of production and trafficking, realists could offer a critique of the policies enacted and be understood by those state policy makers. In a telling description of the drug problem, Bagley and Tokatlian offer a realist summation that mirrors many of the state concerns.

> By 1989 substance abuse in the U.S. work force (including both illegal drugs and alcohol) cost the U.S. economy an estimated $200 billion annually in lost production and productivity, job – and transportation – related accidents, and health care. Meanwhile, the enormous profits derived from the illicit trade fueled the growth of violent criminal organizations whose economic resources, political influence, and firepower gave them the wherewithal to destabilize, to intimidate, or, in some cases, to manipulate various national governments in the region.
>
> Rising concern in the 1980s over the economic and social consequences of the drug 'plague' at home and the growing power of the international drug rings abroad drove both the U.S. executive branch and Congress to regard narcotics trafficking as a national security problem.[48]

So close was the realist interpretation of the drug problem to that of the state that Bagley and Tokatlian would argue that '[realist] analyses unquestionably inspired the successive antinarcotics bills passed by Congress in the 1980s.'[49] Cautious paranoids, limited by a world-view defined by anarchical relations between states, are predisposed to view the drug issue as 'international' in origin. Drawing on a materialist ontology and empiricist epistemology, and following this bias to view threats as external to the state, realist policy direction focuses on source country production of illicit drugs – measuring production capacities, interdiction rates, and acreage fumigated. A quasi-war can likely be constructed. Producers, traffickers, and (most importantly) those that protect these groups might be defined as enemies intent on harming the U.S. population and, by default, undermining U.S. national interests.

Considering the potential harm to U.S. interests and the construction of an 'enemy', realists might contemplate how to bring to bear the power of the United States against that enemy. Given realism's proclivity to define power in military

---

47 Harold and Margaret Sprout, *Toward a Politics of the Planet Earth* (New York: Van Norstrand Reinhold Company, 1971), pp. 198-200.

48 Bruce M. Bagley and Juan G. Tokatlian, 'Explaining the Failure of U.S.-Latin American Drug Policies,' in Jonathan Hartlyn, Lars Schoultz, and Augusto Varas, eds., *The United States and Latin America in the 1990s: Beyond the Cold War* (Chapel Hill, NC: The University of North Carolina Press, 1992), pp. 215-216.

49 Ibid., p. 217.

110   *Creating Insecurity*

terms, it seems likely that once a national security danger had been clearly envisioned, realists would develop policy proposals similar to those of the United States. Certainly, this would be the focus of what Alan Gilbert has termed 'official realism' – a version of realism that remains an apologist for state power and disengages from moral thinking.[50] Official realism is often more concerned with being policy relevant than with critiquing state policy.

However, this view of realism seems overly simplistic and warrants a deeper interpretation on our part in order to offer a materialist account that can balance the ideational one to follow. While there is no doubt that realist tenets have been employed by the state in its war on drugs, a more sophisticated version of realism, one that recognizes the requirements of a just policy and considers economic variables,[51] would continue to challenge the policy makers' version of the issue. Realists insist on pursuing the national interest as it is reasonably and rationally defined.[52] This often means that something more than a military/strategic viewpoint needs to be considered. Those realists committed to being critical yet engaged have emphasized the importance of including an economic account of the drug war to more fully understand why state policies have been so limited in their effectiveness. Tokatlian emphasizes how the perception of drugs as an external evil quickly translated into policy proposals and initiatives following a 'politico/strategic logic.' 'This logic discards the underlying economic-commercial basis of the traffic and emphasizes a language high in moral content in order to wage a 'war on drugs.''[53] By perceiving the drug issue as emanating from abroad and representing a destructive force on the domestic social fabric, U.S. policy makers were intellectually constrained in viewing the 'war on drugs' as the only appropriate policy response.

> The concept of war demands that the predominant instruments should be of a coercive-repressive nature. In this logic, there is no room for the suggestion that demand may be generating that supply. Consequently, not only is the commercial-financial aspect of the drug traffic concealed (or ignored, depending on your point of view), but a clear political objective is revealed" e.g., to transfer the costs of the war to the countries where the illegal drugs are cultivated, produced and processed.[54]

---

50 Alan Gilbert, *Must Global Politics Constrain Democracy?: Great-Power Realism, Democratic Peace and Democratic Internationalism* (Princeton, NJ: Princeton University Press, 1999), p. 12.

51 Alan Gilbert addresses this more 'sophisticated realism' and its interest in the 'common good' at Ibid., p. 12.

52 Hans J. Morgenthau, 'Another Great Debate': The National Interest of the United States,' *The American Political Science Review* 46, 4 (December 1952), p. 978.

53 Juan G. Tokatlian, 'National Security and Drugs: Their Impact on Colombian-U.S. Relations,' *Journal of Inter-American Studies and World Affairs* 30 (Spring 1988), p. 134.

54 Ibid., p. 134-135.

Creating Insecurity II: U.S. Policy Toward Colombia

Finally, bringing economic considerations into a realist analysis of the war on drugs leads scholars to demand that the state recognize the ineffective nature of overwhelmingly militaristic policies. Consider that, 'while spending on eradication and interdiction programs has grown from a few million dollars in the early 1970s to billions annually today, the street price of a pure gram of cocaine has dropped from $1,400 to under $200 during that time.'[55] While the political process seems to require more money to be spent on foreign eradication and interdiction, the structure of the market 'invariably thwarts Washington's best efforts to suppress supply.'[56] 'Drugs are so cheap to produce, the barriers to entry are so low, and the potential profits are so enormous that market forces invariably attract willing growers, producers, and traffickers.'[57] A brief synopsis of the economics of the Colombian cocaine trade illustrates the near futility of U.S. policy to date.

> Even if the United States could significantly cut coca acreage, the market structure for cocaine would undermine the drug war in another way. Most of the markup on drugs occurs after they enter the United States; the actual costs of growing and processing illegal drugs abroad are a tiny fraction of their street price. In 1997, the price of the coca leaf needed to make a pure kilo of cocaine was $300. Refined and ready for export from Colombia, it was worth $1,050. The cost of smuggling that kilo into the United States raised its price in Miami to $20,000, and black market distribution costs raised its retail price in Chicago to $188,000. This means that even an incredibly successful crop eradication program that tripled the price of coca leaf to $900 would raise retail prices in the United States imperceptibly.[58]

A more sophisticated realist approach that develops a twin understanding of the military and economic considerations affecting U.S. policy seems to offer a number of reasons for the United States to re-think its policy toward Colombia. By implementing strategies after developing only a cursory understanding of the issues at stake,[59] state policy makers have been unable to develop comprehensive policy approaches to manage the illicit drug trade. Sophisticated realists have been able to fill in this understanding of the issue and demonstrate in stark terms the limitations of state policy, i.e., *they do not work*!

Yet, even after a more comprehensive picture is painted that provides nuance to the state version of the drug war, many questions remain to be answered. Indeed, if realists have been able to articulate *why* the drug war has met with little success,

---

55 LeoGrande and Sharpe, p. 2.

56 Ibid.

57 Ibid.

58 Ibid.

59 The [official] 'realist' picture of the drug problem outlined by Bagley and Tokatlian demonstrates how shallow the state version was. Their analysis suggests how a more detailed picture could point out many of the concerns raised in this section. While the authors do not differentiate between an official and sophisticated realism, their subsequent analysis of the drug issue clearly demonstrate how useful a more sophisticated realist interpretation might be. See Bagley and Tokatlian, pp. 216-222.

112   *Creating Insecurity*

the question as to *how* drugs became labeled as a security threat rather than a domestic health issue remains outside the realist purview. Further, the domestic (security) issues that are reflected in the national (security) strategies pursued by the state seem not to have a place in the realist account. These domestic security issues often draw on cultural norms and identity performances that are best analyzed from the point of view of a political constructivist.

Political Constructivism and the War on Drugs

A different set of questions engages those scholars working in the political constructivist tradition. Rather than focusing on the material environment that makes up the U.S.-Andean drug trade, political constructivists might begin an investigation of the drug war by investigating how U.S. collective identity is reflected in its Andean policies. For example, the language employed to define the policy problem is inherently political and demonstrates how U.S. cultural practices are reinforced and reproduced in the policies proposed. To begin an investigation of this sort, it is possible to find examples of the importance of language in addressing the drug issue. While political constructivists will take their arguments further, it is interesting to note that even realists see in U.S. domestic practices an underlying sense of insecurity. Juan Tokatlian, for example, explores the extent to which language becomes political when investigating the drug issue. He argues that much like the vehement *anti-communist* rhetoric that prevailed during the Cold War, drug use 'produced a broad consensus as to its origins.'[60] And, like communism, the drug problem 'comes from abroad, whether or not as the result of a conspiracy to undermine the foundations of U.S. society.'[61] Even in the early years of Cold War, realists recognized that the government emphasized its external origins. However, taking a broader look at domestic society, political constructivists articulate the strength of the identity performances that ensued. Consider the reproduction of the 'external enemy' in instances of popular culture. The villains in the popular 1980s television drama, *Miami Vice*, are Latin American drug runners in fast-moving cigar boats penetrating the sovereign waters of south Florida. Colombian drug lords directly challenge Tom Clancy's protagonist, Jack Ryan, in the both novel and film *Clear and Present Danger*. Similarly, drug traffickers threaten the U.S. Drug Czar's family in the film *Traffic*. These three representations provide only a small glimpse into how broader culture consumed and interpreted the illicit trade in drugs.

The emergence of a specific sociological language further reinforces the perception that the 'evil' exists outside U.S. cultural and political boundaries. 'Such is the case with the term *drug trafficking*, which suggests the external dimension of the issue: i.e., that the core of the problem is the *traffic in* and

---

60 Tokatlian, p. 134.
61 Ibid.

Creating Insecurity II: U.S. Policy Toward Colombia   113

transport of drugs, rather than their consumption.'[62] The attempt to externalize the drug problem reached a frenetic state in the late 1980s. In 1988, a House bill required President Reagan to order the U.S. military to 'seal the borders to drug smugglers' and to 'substantially halt' the flow of illegal narcotics into the United States within 45 days.'[63]

At its most sophisticated, the externalization of the drug threat is coupled with the threat of communism. Before a Senate hearing in 1984, U.S. Customs Commissioner William Von Rabb gives voice to the 'narcoguerrilla' theory. 'Drugs have become the natural ally of those that would choose to destroy democratic societies in our hemisphere through violent means.'[64] Alleging that (*communist*) Cuba and Nicaragua were financing insurgent revolutions throughout Latin America with drug money, Von Rabb reproduced Cold War anti-communist ideology in the new fight against illicit drugs. Similarly, the above comments by Elliott Abrams suggesting the FARC connection to drugs paints these rebels as drug traffickers intent on creating, in Rep. Benjamin Gilman's words, a '"narco-state" just three hours by plane from Miami.'[65]

Moreover, as Cold War hostilities began to ebb, military planners (especially those in SOUTHCOM who initially resisted becoming active players in the drug war) came to see the challenge of illicit drugs as a replacement for the challenge posed by communist guerrillas. Their need for a stable and productive identity seems to play out in their transition to anti-narcotics players.

> For the U.S. military, the drug war served as a rationale, not only to maintain but to expand military-to-military relations across the hemisphere, and ensure a U.S. troop presence through a variety of counter-narcotics training programs and joint operations. Defining the problem as a narcoguerrilla threat... allowed the U.S. military to employ the same low-intensity conflict strategies they had used in fighting Communism.[66]

Russell Crandall has cogently argued that the move from Cold War concerns about communism to the post-Cold War concerns about drugs must be seen in light of a U.S. identity as 'hegemonic protector' in the hemisphere. 'The hegemonic presumption is the belief on the part of the United States that it has a right – and often an obligation – to intervene in the affairs of its own backyard, whether it be in the name of security, economic interests, or anticommunism.'[67] Stable identity

---

62 Ibid.

63 Cited in Bruce Michael Bagley, 'The New Hundred Years War?: US National Security and the War on Drugs in Latin America,' *Journal of InterAmerican Studies and World Affairs* 30 (Spring 1988), pp. 168-9.

64 Coletta Youngers, 'Cocaine Madness: Counternarcotics and Militarization in the Andes,' *NACLA Report on the Americas* 34 (November/December 2000), p. 18.

65 Comment of Rep. Benjamin Gilman, cited at Ibid.

66 Ibid., p. 17.

67 Crandall, *Driven By Drugs*, p. 11.

114 *Creating Insecurity*

constructs require that actors manage 'cognitive dissonance' when the environment changes rapidly as it did at the end of the Cold War.

In all of these cases, the discourse that emerges places the problem beyond the United States. Drugs come to be seen as a 'threat' in the same way that Soviet ICBMs were during the Cold War. Similarly, the drug trafficker becomes analogous to the soldier in the Red Army. Both the capability (drugs/ICBMs) and the willing agent (trafficker/communist soldier) are present in the resulting national security issue. But why should the drug issue be framed in this way, why was it not reasonable to argue that drugs were really a domestic health concern analogous to polio or any other public health issue that mobilized the nation to act?

Much like the draconian policy responses in the early days of the AIDS crisis, illicit drug use was framed as an immoral act by key figures with the resulting *securitization* that can often occurs. Criminal drug sellers and traffickers as well as morally weak users were considered to exist at the margins of society. This led many actors to view the drug issue as a moral one. As a 'civilizing crusade' the war on drugs reproduces and reinforces a particular strain of American political culture.[68] It is not unwarranted to argue that the drug war became another crusade like previous crusades exporting Christian values, outlawing gambling, and prohibiting alcohol consumption.[69]

Perhaps most powerful, the moral content of the policies developed to stop the drug trade suggest that drug traffickers are not simply targeting Americans, but are targeting *innocent* Americans. Claims that 'our children' are at risk and 'America's future' is being compromised strengthen the purpose of U.S. policy and perpetuate an image of the United States as under attack by actors intending on doing intentional harm to the nation. When George W. Bush claims that drugs rob Americans of their 'innocence, and ambition, and hope,'[70] he not only signals the need to respond to this external problem, he also reproduces the capitalist ideology of a hard-working, industrious, and energetic America. This is not to suggest that the President's remarks are inaccurate. Drug abuse is a serious problem for the individuals who engage in it and for the broader society that must manage it. However, it is one thing to claim that illicit drug use is detrimental to individual and collective well-being and something quite different to couch it in criminal language like 'robbery'.

---

68 See, for instance, the discussion of nativism in Dale T. Knobel, *'America for the Americans' The Nativist Movement in the United States* (New York: Twayne Publishers, 1996); and Walter Benn Michaels, *Our America: Nativism, Modernism and Pluralism* (Durham, N.C.: Duke University Press, 1995).

69 In addition, this tendency to couch foreign policy initiatives in moral language is explored in depth by George F. Kennan, *American Diplomacy*, expanded edition (Chicago: University of Chicago Press, 1984).

70 Daniel Lazare, 'A Battle Against Reason, Democracy and Drugs: The Drug War Deciphered,' *NACLA Report on the Americas* 35 (July/August 2001), p. 14.

Creating Insecurity II: U.S. Policy Toward Colombia 115

Externalizing the criminal aspects of the drug issue also seems to play to the political philosophies most cherished by Americans. Consider the problems associated with initiating a domestic war on drugs akin to the one being fought in Colombia. Or, to frame the argument another way, consider the likely consequences of maintaining drugs as a security threat and fighting the demand side rather than the supply side. If you will, a *drug scare* instead of a *red scare*. For a state founded on political liberty and limited government interference, a domestic war on drugs would be both unpopular and potentially destabilizing. It is not surprising that domestic legislation to fight this war seeks to limit its negative consequences by targeting already marginalized groups thus reducing domestic strife while simultaneously demonizing groups already suspect in the minds of the dominant political constituency.[71] Stronger prison sentences for 'crack cocaine' possession (common among African-Americans because of its cheaper market price) are meted out than those for similar amounts of cocaine powder possession. As Alan Gilbert notes, 'crack offenders receive *ten* times the sentence for sale or possession as "ordinary" cocaine users. This policy alone has resulted in the disproportionate jailing of young blacks (the government has sentenced approximately a third of young men between nineteen and thirty-four to some jail time or is currently prosecuting them).'[72]

The long-term effects of drug legislation on American politics are striking but proportionally limited to marginalized groups, leaving political institutions in the control of groups perpetuating mainstream cultural values. 'For African-American men between the ages of 20 and 29, almost one in three are currently under the thumb of the criminal justice system.'[73] The racial bias of domestic drug incarcerations reaffirms the nativist impulse in the United States to define others as threatening to the self. As with Japanese internment during WWII and post-11 September incarcerations of Arab-Americans, the African-American male has become the domestic source of drug insecurity.

> African-Americans do not use drugs more than white people; whites and blacks use drugs at almost exactly the same rates. And since there are five times as many whites as blacks in the United States, it follows that the overwhelming majority of drug users are white. Nevertheless, African-Americans are admitted to state prisons at a rate that is 13.4 times greater than whites, a disparity driven largely by the grossly racial targeting of drug laws. In some states, even outside the old Confederacy, blacks make up 90% of drug prisoners and are up to 57 times more likely than whites to be incarcerated for drug crimes.[74]

---

71 George E. Pozzetta, ed. *Nativism, Discrimination, and Images of Immigrants* (New York: Garland Publishers, 1991).

72 See, Gilbert, p. 200.

73 Graham Boyd, 'The New Drug War is the New Jim Crow,' *NACLA Report on the Americas* 35 (July/August 2001), p. 19.

74 Ibid., p. 21.

116   *Creating Insecurity*

It is striking that dominant political groups have been spared so much of the deleterious consequences of drug use. While the purpose of these laws has been to deter criminal activities associated with illicit drugs, the result of these laws seems to be as much about retaining the perception of an innocent America under attack as it is about incarceration. By limiting the domestic problems of illicit drugs to a predominantly African-American male core group, the United States seems able to focus on drugs as a security threat rather than a public health problem. By understanding the drug threat as emanating from external drug traffickers and domestic African-American males, it is possible to avoid direct discussion of the economic features of the drug trade. Here again, Tokatlian provides a summary of the problems associated with waging a war on drugs at home.

> To define the problem as an economic one of demand and consumption would mean that the consuming countries would have to become the site of stronger, more repressive measures. In the United States, implementing such measures would carry undesirable social costs, infringing upon established civil liberties and rights and, possibly, leading to social conflict. Imposition of draconian measures, in order to transfer the battle from the foreign to the domestic front, is a dismaying prospect. Such measures would also imply an increase in control over the domestic financial establishment, which would interfere with and upset powerful political and economic interests at home.[75]

For the political constructivist, it is necessary to include an understanding of domestic political culture and how this culture assists in focusing an issue for the state. The nativist influence in the United States and the identity performances that flow from this strain of thought have severely limited domestic debate on illicit drugs. Moreover, while all actors recognize that the drug issue has both a demand and a supply side, the prevailing cultural practices in the United States have accentuated supply side responses at great cost to the demand side. To expand on the concerns raised by Tokatlian, a very different American political culture would be required in order to wage a domestic war on drugs. In addition, a political culture that seeks to limit government influence over individuals is hard-pressed to engage in the types of welfare-oriented domestic programs necessary to resolve demand side public health concerns over the use of drugs. The following discussion notes the necessity of balancing this interpretation of the drug problem with the interpretation offered by realists.

Enhancing Security

Balancing the disparate political visions offered by realists and political constructivists (and their corresponding policy directives), a more robust security analysis is possible. In terms of U.S. drug policy, this balance recognizes the realist

---

75 Tokatlian, p. 135.

concern over the potential for drug use to diminish state power.[76] While reduced U.S. capabilities from Colombian drugs might seem to be an excessively paranoid vision given the practical limitations on the trafficking of illicit drugs and the size and scope of both the U.S. population and economy, prudent state agents are required to recognize their theoretical potential for harm.

In addition, realism's tendency to focus on defining a (material) problem and offering a (material) solution supplies a policy analysis with a necessary practical grounding. International crises occur in real-time. States require policy responses that can be constructed rapidly and lend themselves to a construction appropriate for the technological and bureaucratic tools available. In the case of the war on drugs, measurement of the absolute and relative capabilities of the Colombian drug community is an integral part of a broader analysis. Moreover, a (sophisticated) realist analysis regarding the ineffective nature of state policy is a necessary component of a larger critique. As noted, the inability of the United States to demonstrate any real success in the war on drugs suggests that valuable resources are being misapplied. Realists are wary of any ill-conceived policy that expends limited resources on an initiative of questionable merit. The inclusion of an economic discussion points out the quixotic nature of the policies administered by the state.

More than anything, a realist inquiry highlights the insufficiency of U.S. policy. By focusing on the state-initiated problem in the source country, realism articulates the shortcomings of that policy. However, realism does not provide a solution to state insecurity; nor is its assessment of the problem complete. The addition of a political constructivist approach balances the story of the drug war. Its emphasis on how actors construct and re-construct their identities through foreign policies locates an essential strand of insecurity in the cultural milieu. More to the point, it locates enhancements to security in this same cultural milieu. If insecurity is a result of identity performances that are inculcated in racism and nativism, then (owing to the social construction of our world) it is incumbent upon social actors to reflect on this source of insecurity in the hopes of altering it. Of course, this does not mean that 'thinking' about a more secure world creates one. The environment in which actors exist makes certain constructions more likely than others.[77] Racism, classism and the political ideologies that perpetuate them will continue to undermine efforts to achieve a more egalitarian society, and this has a consequence

---

76 See the discussion of 'functional limitations on power' by Harold and Margaret Sprout at supra note 40.

77 Robert Cox makes this clear when drawing out the environmental constraints on 'emancipatory' or 'critical' international relations theory. He writes, 'its utopianism is constrained by its comprehension of historical processes. It must reject improbable alternatives just as it rejects the permanency of the existing order.' Robert W. Cox, 'Social Forces, States and World Orders: Beyond International Relations Theory,' in *Neorealism and its Critics*, Robert O. Keohane, ed. (New York: Columbia University Press, 1986), p. 210.

118   *Creating Insecurity*

for the security calculus. I hope to have demonstrated that these issues directly relate to security. While the issues involved in understanding American political culture might not play a role in the material understanding of threat (a place where realism plays a central role), they do inform the ideational sources of insecurity. And, without recognizing how states come to interpret the security threats that realists and state policy makers locate, a comprehensive security calculus remains incomplete. A return to the economic considerations involved in the drug issue brings this point home.

The introduction of market explanations demonstrates two important elements overlooked by state actors. First, large groups of Colombians are reliant on selling coca leaves in order to survive. Their 'ontological security', to use McSweeney's term, is tied to their ability to sell coca leaf to the myriad small-time producers throughout Colombia. Having been marginalized by the 'legitimate' political process, large segments of the rural population find it necessary to engage in this illicit cultivation. It is not uncommon for the small farmers to argue 'What's the point of planting yucca if nobody will buy it? At least with coca I make just enough to feed the family.'[78] The identities of these marginalized groups (as *outlaw* coca farmers) are connected to their material interests (survival) in coca cultivation. Changing those interests would consequently change their identities. This, in turn, would enhance U.S. national security by removing the market incentives now present to grow coca.

However, altering current interests would mean finding a solution to poverty in Colombia. A stronger U.S. foreign/security policy would pressure the government to take the peace process seriously and forego trying to win the political fight through a military victory. The current 'democratic' and economic system that marginalizes large segments of civil society in Colombia and distributes land and other forms of wealth unequally, does not constitute an environment conducive to U.S. security interests. Here, the realist inclusion of economic variables seems most important. Such a system constrains the choices for marginalized groups. Their ability to achieve basic ontological security is severely compromised.[79] And, without marginalized groups able to achieve ontological security, U.S. security is compromised by the economic logic of coca production.

Moreover, as U.S./Colombian initiatives result in further disruption to these marginalized groups, they are pushed deeper into unpopulated regions of Colombia. Their survival-choices become even more constrained. At this point, peasant economic interests converge with the political interests of both guerrilla and paramilitary groups. These groups come to represent the only possible protection for coca-producing farmers – and their collective interest is *protection from* the state (and United States). In a very real way, U.S. and Colombian

---

78 Statement of 33 year old coca farmer Abelando. Cited in Hodgson, p. 45.

79 The idea of 'ontological security' (as it is being discussed here) is explored by Bill McSweeney, *Security, Identity and Interests: A Sociology of International Relations* (Cambridge: Cambridge University Press, 1999), pp. 154-155.

Creating Insecurity II: U.S. Policy Toward Colombia 119

strategies make it inevitable that coca farmers define their interests in opposition to their government. This analysis suggests that not only is U.S. policy ineffective, it is also counter-productive. U.S. policy creates insecurity. The eradication of coca plants actually increases the incentives for market entry and strengthens the position of extra-legal armed political movements. Thus, employing a balanced approach, realists and political constructivists, together, counter state policy initiatives arguing that alleviating rural poverty through democratic reforms and micro-development assistance is actually a *stronger* security tool than current eradication and interdiction efforts.

Second, on the domestic front, a political constructivist analysis of the drug war questions U.S. identity performances and the interests they engender. By demanding a critique of U.S. cultural practices, which challenges the drug war as a foreign war and suggests its domestic importance in defining an 'other', political constructivists reflect on how the drug war reinforces racism and the negative effects of capitalism at home. By transferring the domestic effects of the drug war onto a predominantly poor African-American sector of the population, U.S. society is able to define drugs as something existing on the 'outside', harming a cultural constituency that is largely 'innocent'.

This reflective activity is more than a passive study in cultural attitudes. Political constructivists are insistent that they play an active role in the political process – the object of their study. They challenge the policy maker to answer for domestic poverty and the concomitant racism that reaffirms it. The same measures that go into alleviating poverty abroad become possible solutions to the domestic demand side of the drug war. More to the point, the activities of the political constructivists demand a constant form of critique in order to construct a more democratic existence where marginalized groups are given opportunities to participate in political and economic reforms.[80]

On both points, the balance between realists and political constructivists offers radical solutions to the problems of illicit drug production and use. When sophisticated realism and political constructivism are both recognized as necessary rhetorical tools for the construction of an engaged critique of state policy, the resulting policy recommendations challenge dominant state practices. Uncovering the relationship between contingent identities and material interests becomes a central feature of a more comprehensive understanding of the drug issue. By doing so, engaged scholars can demand more of the state than has been traditionally thought.

---

80 See, for instance, David Campbell, *Writing Security: United States Foreign Policy and the Politics of Identity*, revised edition (Minneapolis, MN: University of Minnesota Press, 1998).

Chapter 7

Creating Insecurity III: Democracy, Globalization, and Protests from Below

Ballistic missile defense and the war on drugs represent two policy debates that benefit from a broader analytic discussion concerning the origins of insecurity. In both cases a balanced approach that maintained the need to account for both material and ideational security provided a more comprehensive critique of state policy than either realism or political constructivism could provide on its own. Additionally, it was possible to critique the state from an *engaged* position – to speak to the state employing a language fitting its world view while introducing marginalized issues previously neglected by security analyses. A similar approach might be taken in an investigation of democratic security in the United States. More specifically, how the state has responded to protests from below concerning economic globalization points to an instance of created insecurity. Historically, the United States has engaged in the twin policies of promoting global capitalist institutions and the spread of procedural democracy around the globe. It is argued, quite forcefully by its adherents, that the promotion of democracy and the spread of capitalist values lead to a more secure world. Indeed, a broad consensus among politicians, academics, and business leaders has emerged that the promotion of liberal capitalist democracy is in keeping with core American interests at home and abroad and allows states to live in peace with one another. This consensus is often referred to as the 'democratic peace.' The following discussion examines its merits as a state security strategy. Realists and political constructivists have serious reservations about the promotion of the democratic peace, but for widely divergent reasons. Yet, as the discussion below makes clear, a critique of the democratic peace employing a balance between sophisticated realism and political constructivism points to instances of insecurity that remain unacknowledged by the state. These instances are, perhaps, most acute when attention is turned to the state response to protests from below against globalization from above. A diverse group of protestors including labor union members, environmentalists, community organizers, transnational non-governmental organization advocates, political progressives, and nationalists have voiced concern about the manner by which the United States and other governments have pursued global economic integration. Their collective voices, in the form of street demonstrations, have been met with repressive tactics by states unwilling to participate in deeper democratic practices. It is this inability or unwillingness to engage protests from below in democratic discourse that implicates the state in creating insecurity by undermining

Creating Insecurity III: Democracy, Globalization, and Protests from Below 121

democratic security. In order to understand this moment of insecurity, the following section investigates theoretical arguments surrounding the democratic peace and the form of economic globalization it engenders. It also briefly examines how the U.S. government has suppressed dissent at home. Following this history, a sophisticated realist response and a political constructivist response will be considered. The final section brings both approaches together in order to offer a more comprehensive critique of state practices.

A History of the Democratic Peace and U.S. Policy

After World War II, the United States put together a world economic order centered on what John Gerard Ruggie terms 'embedded liberalism.'[1] Liberal trade and monetary policies would transform a world of rival states into a pacific union of cooperative actors. In addition to a new economic order, procedural democracies were thought to be the political equivalent of liberal capitalism and were promoted with increasing zeal. The twin strategies of promoting liberal capitalism and procedural democracy came to embody the mainstream features of U.S. foreign policy.[2] Buoyed by its three pillars (the World Bank, the IMF, and the GATT Rounds), this international economic order would not only keep the peace, it would also allow states to prosper. Serious attention in academic circles was paid to the merits of promoting democracy and liberal capitalism as a long-term strategy for enhancing international security. Throughout the 1990s, the literature on the democratic peace – as it is commonly called – countered standard realist claims that domestic structures are irrelevant in our attempts to understand international violence. Following Kant's notion of a perpetual peace among law-abiding republics[3] it was generally argued that political science had located the nearest thing to an empirical law of the relations among states. Due to their respect for civil liberties, private property, and equality before the law, citizens of democratic states are predisposed to follow pacific problem-solving techniques in resolving potential conflicts and eschew the use of warfare among them. In an oft-cited

---

1 John Gerard Ruggie, 'International Regimes, Transactions, and Change: Embedded Liberalism in the Post-war Economic Order,' in Stephen D. Krasner, ed., *International Regimes* (Ithaca, NY: Cornell University Press, 1983), pp. 204-214.

2 This is a sweeping generalization of post-World War II U.S. policy. While it may have been the norm, there were serious deviations from that norm. The United States undermined many democratic governments in its Cold War with the Soviet Union. For a detailed discussion of U.S. foreign policy see, Alan Gilbert, *Must Global Politics Constrain Democracy?: Great-Power Realism, Democratic Peace, and Democratic Internationalism* (Princeton, NJ: Princeton University Press, 1999). For a more detailed discussion of the international order put together by the United States, see, G. John Ikenberry, *After Victory: Institutions, Strategic Restraint, and the Rebuilding of Order After Major Wars* (Princeton, NJ: Princeton University Press, 2001), pp. 163-214.

3 Immanuel Kant, 'Perpetual Peace,' in Immanuel Kant, *Political Writings*, Hans Reiss, ed. (Cambridge: Cambridge University Press, 1970), pp. 93-130.

122 *Creating Insecurity*

article expounding the possibilities of a democratic peace, Michael Doyle points to a speech by Ronald Reagan in 1982 before the British Parliament. 'President Reagan proclaimed that governments founded on a respect for individual liberty exercise "restraint" and "peaceful intentions" in their foreign policy.'[4] Juxtaposed to this democratic restraint, 'the aggressive instincts of authoritarian leaders and totalitarian ruling parties make for war.'[5] Citizens of democratic regimes, 'appreciate that the benefits of trade can be enjoyed only under conditions of peace.'[6] Hence, the processes of global democratization and economic globalism were to go hand-in-hand with the creation of a more stable international future.

The solution to international violence had been found not in a standard realist concern for state balancing or hegemonic leadership but rather in this 'global process of democratization'[7] whereby democratic regimes 'treat each other differently.'[8] Bruce Russett cogently summarized the potential utility of the democratic peace. 'The spread of democratic norms and practices in the world, if consolidated, should reduce the frequency of violent conflict and war.'[9] Individual states could enhance their national security environment through the perpetuation of like national democratic structures around the world. This, in turn, would lead to a better environment for global economic growth, allowing democratic states to reap the rewards of national political structures through the potential for increased vertical legitimacy between government and citizen.[10]

The study of a democratic peace among states demonstrates an improved understanding of 'security' beyond the Cold War definition so often linked to military and strategic issues. This can be seen not only in the academy but also in policy statements of officials acknowledging a link between greater security and democracies. By recognizing the connection between democracy and security, these scholars and policy makers have brought something quite valuable to the security table. However, a deeper investigation of democratic peace studies and the practices of the United States in response to democratic dissent suggest a need to qualify much of the work that has been done. Consider the observation of Mark Rupert who argues that 'some kinds of democratic peace might be potentially

---

4 Michael W. Doyle, 'Liberalism and World Politics,' 80 *American Political Science Review* (December 1996), pp. 1151-69; reprinted in Charles W. Kegley, *Controversies in International Relations Theory: Realism and the Neoliberal Challenge* (New York: St. Martin's Press, 1995), p. 83.

5 Ibid.

6 Ibid.

7 Karen L. Remmer, 'Does Democracy Promote Interstate Cooperation? Lessons from the Mercosur Region,' 42 *International Studies Quarterly* (March 1998), p. 25.

8 Anne Marie Slaughter-Burley, 'Law Among Liberal States: Liberal Internationalism and the Act of State Doctrine,' 92 *Columbia Law Review* (1982), pp. 1907-1996.

9 Bruce Russett and William Antholis, 'Do Democracies Fight Each Other? Evidence from the Peloponnesian War,' 29 *Journal of Peace Research* 4 (1992), p. 416.

10 For a discussion of vertical legitimacy and its importance in this regard, see, Kalevi J. Holsti, *The State, War, and the State of War* (Cambridge, UK: Cambridge University Press, 1996).

Creating Insecurity III: Democracy, Globalization, and Protests from Below 123

worthy political projects, but for that potential to be realizable a radical recasting of the terms in which the discussion is conducted will be required.'[11] While a democratic peace may provide some security for the state, a robust national security programme that enhances democratic security appears lacking.

A review of the fight over the practices of the World Trade Organization (WTO) suggests a reason to be concerned about the form of democracy that is emerging in the world today. The global effort from below to re-examine and re-construct the global economic regime that the United States put into place after WWII offers a particularly striking example of the creation of insecurity due to sectarian over national interests and particular economic security over democratic security.

In November of 1999, over fifty thousand people arrived in Seattle, Washington in the northwest corner of the United States to protest the convening of the 'Millennium Round' negotiations of the WTO.[12] These protestors from below represented a diverse cross-section of society including 'environmentalists, labor unionists, advocates of Third World debt relief, consumer activists, indigenous peoples' groups, farmers, Lesbian Avengers, religious groups, student anti-sweatshop activists, animal rights defenders – a rich stew representing, by some estimates, over 700 various grassroots organizations from many countries.'[13] According to these groups seeking to change the way global economic decisions are made from above, the WTO decision-making procedures represent the dangerous side of procedural democratic practices and neoclassical economic thinking. WTO decision-making procedures remain explicitly beyond the deliberative environment of citizens – international civil society is prevented from participating in WTO decision-making.[14] One avenue for democratic debate is thus thwarted by member states of the WTO. Another avenue, domestic debate, however, is severely limited to citizens wishing to prevent efforts to foment globalization from above. By creating fast-track authority, empowering trade representatives, and limiting dissent, states have managed to circumvent deliberative steps in the democratic process.[15] These democracies-in-name-only are

---

11 Mark Rupert, 'Democracy, Peace, What's Not to Love?' in Tarak Barkawi and Mark Laffey, *Democracy, Liberalism, and War: Rethinking the Democratic Peace Debate* (Boulder, CO: Lynne Rienner Publishers, 2001), p. 155.

12 This discussion provides a cursory review of the events in Seattle. For a detailed discussion of state tactics to repress democratic protest, see, Kevin Danaher, ed., *Democratizing the Global Economy: the Battle against the World Bank and International Monetary Fund* (Monroe, ME: Common Courage Press, 2001).

13 Mark Rupert, *Ideologies of Globalization: Contending Visions of a New World Order* (London: Routledge Press, 2000), pp. 149-150.

14 Martin Köhler, 'From National to the Cosmopolitan Public Sphere,' in Daniele Archibugi, David Held, and Martin Köhler, eds. *Re-imagining Political Community: Studies in Cosmopolitan Democracy* (Stanford: Stanford University Press, 1998), p. 232.

15 For a discussion of state policies that limit deliberation at home, see, Ralph Nader and Lori Wallach, 'GATT, NAFTA, and the Subversion of the Democratic Process,' in Jerry

124 *Creating Insecurity*

thus able to deflect any serious discussion of who benefits from globalization from above. Manfred Bienefeld articulates this point.

> Some take comfort in the thought that countries generally only enter such agreements voluntarily, but this is to ignore the fact that what appears to be voluntary is often tinged with more than a hint of blackmail and coercion. Moreover, these governments in question frequently do not represent the national interest in any real sense. In fact, governments dominated by small global elites or by international capital, often seek to enter such agreements to protect their interests from domestic political challenges.[16]

Member states of the WTO have created a system whereby democratic deliberation is disallowed at both the national and international level. This has had the effect of disrupting much of the democratic legislation that states have implemented over the years. Consider Nader and Wallach's assessment of WTO rules.

> Under WTO rules, for example, certain *objectives* are forbidden to all domestic legislatures, including the U.S. Congress, the state legislatures, and county and city councils. These *objectives* include providing any significant subsidies to promote energy conservation, sustainable farming practices, or environmentally sensitive technologies. Laws with *mixed goals*, such as provisions of the U.S. Clean Air Act that implement the international ozone agreement (which bans the import and sale of products made with ozone-depleting production methods), conflict with the WTO's requirements. In addition, the WTO trumps provisions in pre-existing international agreements, including environmental treaties that conflict with trade rules.[17]

A brief example of such an instance is provided by the GATT ruling in the U.S. Mexico Dolphin/Tuna Case. In 1991, a GATT dispute-resolution panel ruled against the U.S. ban on tuna imports from Mexico and Venezuela. For many, 'the GATT panel's ruling... reflects the tendency of most trade specialists to view any restrictions on trade for environmental purposes as setting a dangerous precedent that could destroy the entire world trade system.'[18] This suggests that in an era defined by liberal capitalism and democratic peace – where 'the individual nation-state always finds itself overstretched'[19] – the procedural democratic institutions that hold elite-governed polities together are becoming fractured in the face of globalization from above.

Mander and Edward Goldsmith, eds. *The Case Against the Global Economy* (San Francisco, CA: Sierra Club Books, 1996), pp. 92-107.

16 Manfred Bienefeld, 'Capitalism and the Nation State in the Dog Days of the Twentieth Century,' *Socialist Register* (1994), p. 103.

17 Nader and Wallach, p. 96.

18 Gareth Porter and Janet Welsh Brown, *Global Environmental Politics*, second edition, (Boulder, CO: Westview Press, 1996), p. 134.

19 Hans-Peter Martin and Harald Schumann, *The Global Trap: Globalization and the Assault on Democracy and Prosperity* (London: Zed Books, 1996), p. 9.

Creating Insecurity III: Democracy, Globalization, and Protests from Below   125

The immediate political result is two-fold. First, democratic pressure from below demands access to political debates that circumvent even the procedural institutions that offered cover to elite decision-making. Second, state authorities then employ more direct means of coercion to counter these demands. Such action-reaction scenarios are defined nicely by Alan Gilbert as 'anti-democratic feedback'.[20] Anti-democratic activities by the United States and member states occurred regularly at WTO meetings throughout the latter half of the 1990s and into the new century. Such anti-democratic feedback was demonstrated against the cross-section of activists in Seattle, too. In response to the large citizen response and isolated acts of violence by self-proclaimed anarchists, 'the city's mayor declared a state of emergency, put downtown under a curfew, and called in state police and National Guard troops. Meanwhile Seattle police unleashed clouds of tear gas, pepper spray, and rubber bullets – along with the more traditional boots and batons – at demonstrators and bystanders. Although protests continued on subsequent days, mass arrests by riot police in gas masks and body armor enabled the delegates to go about their business.'[21] Subsequent meetings of globalization delegates for the WTO, IMF, and World Bank in North America and Europe have led to similar protests and violent reactions from the state. This has led more recent meetings to take place in isolated locations like Doha, Qatar, where political space to protest is nonexistent.

The actions taken by the United States against citizen protestors in Seattle and elsewhere demonstrate the limits of democratic governance in the state. How sophisticated realists and political constructivists might respond to these actions points the way forward to a more comprehensive critique of state policies to limit dissent.

Sophisticated Realism and the Democratic Peace

In 1969, during the height of the Vietnam War, Reinhold Niebuhr defended both his opposition to the war and his adherence to realism by stating, 'realism means particularly one thing, that you establish the common good not purely by unselfishness but by the restraint of selfishness. That's realism.'[22] What makes the Niebuhr approach to realism so intriguing is that he recognizes that 'sophisticated realism starts from underlying ethical judgments about a common good.'[23] For Alan Gilbert, such an introduction 'provides a comparatively elaborate, empirical – and social theoretical – critique of the oligarchic structure of contemporary "democracies" that can lead to unjust, even genocidal wars.'[24]

---

20 Gilbert, p. 28.
21 Rupert, *Ideologies of Globalization*, p. 150.
22 Reinhold Niebuhr, *Christianity and Crisis*, 17 March 1969, p. 50. Cited in Gilbert, p. 105.
23 Gilbert, p. 110.
24 Ibid.

126 *Creating Insecurity*

A realist argument concerning the purpose and importance of *national* security programmes need not be linked to arguments for the common good. Indeed, the standard realist argument against the democratic peace is that it simply does not understand the importance of anarchy.[25] However, a comprehensive critique of the democratic peace and globalization from above requires that the *national* in national security be linked to some notion of the common good. Sophisticated realists are in a good position to make this necessary link. Because realists take a state-centric approach to the study of security, their ability to appreciate the requirements of national security strategies is given *a priori*. The field of Security Studies has traditionally sought to understand *national* security rather than *elite* security, *ruling-class* security, *regime* security, etc. Traditional security theorists (often espousing realist tenets), as well as those working in critical security studies, recognize the state as fundamentally important to understanding the security problematique (albeit for different reasons).[26] As has been argued in the first part of this book, the state is the primary locus of security. States, in the words of Scott and Carr, 'have a moral obligation to their own citizenry.'[27] In essence, this requires theorists to consider how national security strategies are linked to an understanding of the common good rather than sectarian interests.

In a powerful critique of realist thought, Jack Donnelly recognizes that even a 'realist' like Machiavelli 'reveals the coincidence of justice, the common good, and the interests of the prince.'[28] Working through the Machiavaellian argument, Donnelly writes

> A prince may acquire a state through force, fraud, or fortune. To maintain it securely 'it is necessary to have the people friendly.' But this is relatively easy, for in contrast to the elite, who 'desire to command and oppress,' the people want only not to be oppressed.

---

25 For a detailed critique of the democratic peace from a standard realist position, see, for instance, Mark W. Zacher and Richard A. Matthew, 'Liberal International Theory: Common Threads, Divergent Strands;' and Joseph M. Grieco, 'Anarchy and the Limits of Cooperation: A Realist Critique of the Newest Liberal Institutionalism,' in Kegley, *Controversies in International Relations Theory*. See, also, Tarak Barkawi and Mark Laffey, eds., *Democracy, Liberalism, and War: Rethinking the Democratic Peace Debate*; and Christopher Layne, 'Kant or Cant: The Myth of the Democratic Peace,' 19 *International Security* 2 (Fall 1994), pp. 5-49. These works represent but a small sampling of the critiques available on the democratic peace literature; they are quite comprehensive in their critique of the approach to international security and I will not discuss them here. My concern is with outlining the sophisticated realist argument that Alan Gilbert links to some notion of the common good.

26 For a good discussion of Critical Security Studies and the need to recognize the state as central to security discussions, see, Keith Krause and Michael C. Williams, *Critical Security Studies* (Minneapolis, MN: University of Minnesota Press, 1997), pp. vii-xvi.

27 Gary L. Scott and Craig L. Carr, 'Are States Moral Agents?,' *Social Theory and Practice* 12 (Spring 1986), p. 75.

28 Jack Donnelly, *Realism and International Relations* (Cambridge, UK: Cambridge University Press, 2000), p. 172.

Creating Insecurity III: Democracy, Globalization, and Protests from Below   127

To maintain his state, a prince need only look after the interests of the people. 'For when men are well governed, they do not go about looking for further liberty.'[29]

While the introduction of a Machiavellian argument complicates our task due to the need to further link an understanding of the common good to deliberative democracy, the argument still holds. Taking this interpretation of Machiavellian realism forward, it can be recognized that ensuring adequate national security (including *economic security* for all citizens)[30] is a component of the common good. Indeed, without ensuring (securing) the economic interests of all citizens, the state engages in some form of economic oppression against some segment of its citizenry. By so doing, national security is sure to be undermined. Consider the following passage by Paul Hirst who draws a parallel between those marginalized citizens of Western Democracies and state instability.

> The main threats to western societies are no longer external and organized but internal and diffuse. They are nonetheless real for that, but centralized bureaucratic structures [buffering procedural institutions] cope badly with these more amorphous threats of crime and drug addiction, for example, that this can hardly provide them with a convincing *raison d'être*. The real problems stem from the failure to sustain full employment and from the side-effects of collectivist welfare. In the USA, in the UK, even in Germany we face the growing reality of a two-thirds versus one-third society. The notion of an 'underclass' is both graphic and yet absurd, since its members will not accept their 'place' at the bottom. A differentiated society cannot work if elementary freedoms of movement and association for all are to be preserved. Unless effective work and welfare are offered, in a way that both targets and empowers the members of this 'class', then the way is open to an escalating conflict between crime and deviance and disablingly authoritarian measures which aim at the protection of the majority. The members of the 'underclass' are not stupid. They know that wealth and success are in part capriciously distributed; that is, that they depend on the chances of social position and geographical location. Property will never be legitimate unless it offers real welfare – that is, a stake in society – to all in return.[31]

For sophisticated realists, the connection seems quite clear. Economic globalization from above creates insecurity for the state when it undermines the economic well-being of citizens within that state. If the state in question professes to be a democracy, and if that democracy represses citizen dissent and undermines initiatives to improve the livelihood of segments of the population, then an instance of insecurity appears likely. The question that needs to be asked, however, is how has it come to be that a political system founded on the idea of the rule of the masses now means an electoral decision between elite-governing groups? How has

---

29 Ibid.
30 For a discussion of economic security see, Barry Buzan, Ole Wæver, Jaap de Wilde, *Security: A New Framework for Analysis* (Boulder, CO: Lynne Rienner Publishers, 1998), pp. 95-118.
31 Paul Hirst, *From Statism to Pluralism: Democracy, Civil Society, and Global Politics* (London: UCL Press, 1997), p. 40.

128   *Creating Insecurity*

democratic governance been framed in procedural terms outside an argument for the common good? A political constructivist interpretation offers the best way into answering these questions.

Political Constructivism and the Concept of Democracy

Democratic governments in concert with other democratic governments promote their security by forming an *international* pacific union. Contra structural realists,[32] domestic politics matter! This claim by theorists working in the democratic peace tradition seems to hold a good percentage of the time. Indeed, according to Michael Doyle who studied the period from 1790 to the present, there have been no wars among *liberal* states[33] A later study, by Bruce Russett and William Antholis, argues that the emergence of a norm against fighting other democracies was apparent as far back as Ancient Greece.[34] And, while these authors note the 'normative difference' between 'twentieth-century liberal representative democracies' and 'Greek city-state democracies,'[35] they are willing to overlook these differences in order to make their more general point concerning pacific relations between democracies. R. J. Rummel argues that we can make even bolder statements concerning the notion of a democratic peace. According to Rummel, 'the more freedom that individuals have in a state, the less the state engages in foreign violence.'[36] Here, liberal democrats not only maintain a peace between each other, they are more pacific creatures.

These studies represent a small sampling of the use of terms in the democratic peace literature. If correct, their works suggest that liberal, democratic regimes do indeed enhance their security through a 'zone of peace'. Yet, how terms in these studies are employed suggests a reason to further investigate the claims made. In order to examine more closely what is going on within the democratic peace and globalization from above, it seems necessary to differentiate between the positivist epistemology employed by democratic peace theorists and a constructivist epistemology that seeks to problematize the constants at issue in their work.

The writings of Michael Doyle are a good place to start. To repeat Doyle's claim: liberal states have not gone to war with one another since 1790. In defining *liberal*, Doyle is following Kant in outlining four essential institutions present in liberal regimes:

1.   market and private property economies

---

32 See, for instance, the claims made most recently by Kenneth N. Waltz, 'Structural Realism After the Cold War,' *International Security* 25 (Summer 2000), pp. 5-42.

33 Doyle, 'Liberalism and World Politics Revisted,' p. 88.

34 Russett and Antholis, p. 415.

35 Ibid, p. 418.

36 R. J. Rummel, 'Libertarianism and International Violence,' *Journal of Conflict Resolution* 27 (March 1983), p. 27.

Creating Insecurity III: Democracy, Globalization, and Protests from Below 129

2. polities that are externally sovereign
3. citizens who possess juridical rights
4. 'republican' (whether republican or parliamentary monarchy) representative government.[37]

The presence of these four essential institutions allows a 'pacific union' to develop among similar states. The fourth institution is central to this discussion. Quite subtly, Doyle has collapsed the term democracy into that of liberalism and thereby allowed a conception of 'Western liberal democracy' to emerge from Kant's institutional framework. The presence of a representative government becomes synonymous with democracy. While there is much support for this in the literature, it distorts our understanding of that important term *democracy*. Schumpeter argued that democracies exist when there is a circulation of party elites. Robert Dahl demands that political equality and party competition provide support for democracy. Doyle is following these interpretations. 'The Schumpeter-Dahl axis... treats democracy as a mechanism, the essential function of which is to maintain an equilibrium [between] two or more elite groups for the power to govern society.'[38] But doing so deflects a more sophisticated understanding of the political issues involved in understanding the relationship between democracies and pacific relations. Barkawi and Laffey offer a cogent analysis of the historical differences between these terms.

> Historically, democracy and liberalism have taken different forms and meant different things to different people, with different implications for institutional forms and the relative power of publics and elites. A fixed definition of democracy or liberalism will reflect a particular historical moment; a particular set of social, political, economic, and social circumstances; and a particular understanding of what being democratic or liberal entails. *Struggles over the meanings of democracy, liberalism, and their institutional forms comprise much of the political history of the Western liberal democracies, a history obscured by the stipulated institutional or procedural definition used in the DP debates.*[39]

The authors articulate the degree to which the positivist epistemology employed by democratic peace theorists undermines the historical contingencies of terms like 'democracy' and 'liberalism'. Following John Dryzek, Barkawi and Laffey argue that 'democracy should be understood as a project, as the product of political struggle over the degree to which publics can participate in and shape the conditions of their lives. Democracy is about *popular rule*. Liberalism, in contrast, is about the construction of a particular kind of *social order*, organized around the

---

37 Doyle, 'Liberalism and World Politics Revisted,' p. 92 at table note a.
38 C.B. Macpherson, *Democratic Theory: Essays in Retrieval* (Oxford: Oxford University Press, 1973), p. 78. Cited in Bruce Cumings, 'War, Security, and Democracy in East Asia,' in *Democracy, Liberalism, and War*, p. 136.
39 Tarak Barkawi and Mark Laffey, 'Introduction: The International Relations of Democracy, Liberalism, and War,' in *Democracy, Liberalism, and War*, p. 13. *My italics.* Please note that the authors shorten the term 'democratic peace' to 'DP'.

130 *Creating Insecurity*

individual and his or her rights.'[40] This distinction is important and reflects an understudied component of the democratic peace. It also suggests how a constructivist epistemology that takes seriously the meaning of terms and their coherence within broader social practices is required if we seek to offer a better understanding of democratic security.

Dryzek's contention that democracy is about *popular rule* is particularly important to this discussion. While it is not necessary to return to a rendering of the Ancient Greek *demos* in order to understand 'popular rule', it is important to note that something more than electoral majorities or procedural institutions is required when examining 'democratic' regimes. The essential institutions noted above seem insufficient for judging democracies. Indeed, in an odd way, the institutions listed above are neither necessary nor sufficient conditions for democratic governance-although they do provide a good description of some (but not all) forms of liberalism.

A return to the work of Isaiah Berlin will illustrate this point. In his famous essay on the various components of liberty,[41] Berlin distinguishes between negative and positive liberty. *Freedoms from interference* might best be described as negative liberties. Positive liberties relate to one's ability to make important decisions for one's life. To some degree, the use of the term 'liberal democracy' by authors working in the democratic peace tradition (and detailed in Kant's four institutions) spell out Berlin's notion of 'negative liberty'. Individual rights (emphasized in institutions 1, 3, and 4 above) provide the basis upon which social order might emerge. But, remember Dryzek's desire to differentiate between *political rule* and *social order*. While the institutions above relate quite well to liberalism – 'a particular kind of social order, organized around the individual and his or her rights'[42] – they must be distinguished from democracy which has to do with governance issues (political rule, authority) rather than social order. Democracy does not necessarily follow from a social order based on individual rights emphasizing negative freedoms, although one can certainly see how an electoral or procedural democracy based on the institution of one-person-one-vote correlates well with a social order based on individual rights and negative freedoms.

A liberal polity might emerge that fulfills Kant's essential institutions and offers *representative* access to politics for its citizens. In this case, we can speak of a liberal, representative democracy but we have done something significant to the term 'democracy'. These polities have become defined 'in terms of essentialized and ahistorical understandings of market democracy.'[43] As Barkawi and Laffey caution, 'whether or not a particular polity is democratic cannot be determined

---

40 Ibid, p. 14; see also John Dryzek, *Democracy in Capitalist Times* (Oxford, UK: Oxford University Press, 1996).
41 Isaiah Berlin, 'Two Concepts of Liberty,' in Michael Sandel, ed. *Liberalism and its Critics* (New York: New York University Press, 1984), pp. 15-36.
42 See, Barkawi and Laffey, p. 14.
43 Ibid, p. 16.

Creating Insecurity III: Democracy, Globalization, and Protests from Below   131

simply by pointing to the presence of a particular set of institutions.'[44] This holds not only for the presence of those essential institutions recognized by Kant, but also for electoral institutions that create the illusion of *popular rule*. A liberal, representative democracy might offer the franchise to its citizens without fulfilling the promise of positive liberty – a say in one's life plan – as discussed by both Berlin and Dryzek.[45] Elite-dominated decision-making procedures may control the classic question of who gets what behind a façade of electoral privilege for the masses. Moreover, focusing on the presence of institutions to describe a polity as a 'liberal democracy' is insufficient. For political constructivists, 'it is necessary to conceptualize how the received meanings of liberal democracy [are] understood by the actors themselves.'[46]

Alan Gilbert offers an alternative view of today's democratic regimes by arguing that in reality a number of these regimes are 'oligarchies with parliamentary forms.'[47] This alternative view of democracies including the United States represents the procedural democracies of the democratic peace. These polities 'do not represent the fundamental interests of their citizens.'[48] (In other words, they do not promote a common good but rather their own sectarian- elite-interests.) Elite actors in such states have engaged in an 'oligarchic distortion of – and defeat for – democracy.'[49] Rather than popular rule, 'democratic' opinion is... oligarchically stimulated (the *threat of external enemies, construction of political options*).'[50] With particular attention paid to the actions of the United States, and in contrast with what Gilbert terms the *Doyle-Keohane Critique of Realism* (the democratic peace), 'Powerful oligarchies with parliamentary forms have... widely "intervened" against democracies, for instance, the U.S. overthrow of the Arbenz regime in Guatemala, Mossadegh in Iran, Goulart in Brazil, Allende in Chile, and the like.'[51] Similar readings of U.S. policies during the Twentieth Century can be found in the works of William Robinson and Mark Rupert.[52] All three authors wish

---

44 Ibid, p. 15.
45 Here, again, the similarity between Berlin and Dryzek is striking. Berlin writes, in defining positive freedom, 'I wish to be the instrument of my own, not of other men's acts of will.' (p. 23) Dryzek argues that democracy (linked to popular rule) is 'the degree to which publics can participate in and shape the conditions of their lives.' (p. 14).
46 Himadeep Muppidi, 'State Identity and Interstate Practices: The Limits to Democratic Peace in South Asia,' in *Democracy, Liberalism, and War*, p. 52.
47 Gilbert, p. 12.
48 Ibid.
49 Ibid.
50 Ibid, p. 61.
51 Ibid, pp. 64-65.
52 William I. Robinson, *Promoting Polyarchy: Globalization, US Intervention, and Hegemony* (Cambridge: Cambridge University Press, 1996); Mark Rupert, *Producing Hegemony: The Politics of Mass Production and American Global Power* (Cambridge: Cambridge University Press, 1995), Mark Rupert, *Ideologies of Globalization*.

132   *Creating Insecurity*

to re-claim an understanding of 'democracy' that relates to something beyond capitalist polyarchies.

Paying close attention to the way that the term 'democracy' is employed at various historical periods becomes a necessary feature for investigating the claims made by democratic peace theorists. Gilbert's frustration with the use of the term democracy to connote a form of political rule not linked to some notion of the common good is emblematic of the problem currently facing studies of democracy. Hirst speaks for many when he arguing,

> Conventional representative democracy has become little more than a plebiscite that chooses and legitimates the rulers of a big governmental machine that is out of control, it that it is largely unaccountable and cannot tackle major social problems. The crisis of citizen participation and of effective accountability of government to society is all too obvious. Democracy needs to be renewed.[53]

Similarly, Robinson's concern that rather than promoting democracy abroad throughout the Cold War, the United States has attempted to maintain hegemonic leadership by installing and supporting elite rulers insulated by procedural institutions reflects a desire to re-tell current history beyond the operational boundaries of the democratic peace. In all of these cases, the claim is being made that '[f]etishizing democracy is problematic for analysis, because in addition to ignoring the significant changes democracy has undergone historically, it directs attention away from broader processes of social change and their consequences for both what democracy is and how it works.'[54] It seems necessary then, to pay particular attention to what democracy means. Distinguishing between procedural democracy and deliberative democracy helps in this endeavor.

Critical theorists are quick to put out the substantive reduction in intellectual weight that is afforded to a term like 'democracy' when it is reduced to an electoral or procedural form. Consider Mark Rupert's claim.

> Reducing democracy to 'polyarchy' – defined primarily in terms of more or less extensive franchise and competitive elections within particular territorial states – this literature articulates a hegemonic project wherein the scope of democratic self-determination is circumscribed within the electoral systems of liberal capitalist states. This results in forms of democracy 'in which a small group actually rules and mass participation in decision-making is confined to leadership choice in elections carefully managed by competing elites.'[55]

The ideological nature of those advocating a procedural definition of democracy becomes central to a re-telling of the democratic peace. For Rupert, democratic peace literature 'is ideological in the dual sense that it obscures social relations and processes from the view of their participants, and by disabling critical

---

53 Hirst, p. 42.
54 Barkawi and Laffey, p. 15.
55 Mark Rupert, 'Democracy, Peace, What's Not to Love?,' p. 154.

Creating Insecurity III: Democracy, Globalization, and Protests from Below   133

analysis it implicitly promotes the interests of groups privileged by those relations.'[56] Moreover, and this is the point I wish to argue further in a discussion of deliberative democracy, 'it becomes difficult to imagine radical democratizing projects that might seek to construct more participatory relations within and between capitalist social formations, transformative processes that might generate postliberal and conceivably postcapitalist forms of social life.'[57]

Definitions that seek to operationalize the term 'democracy', therefore, not only limit our collective understanding of the term and remove from its meaning a historical link to popular rule, but they also perform a political act by re-enforcing a particular view of the purpose and limits of politics. The distinctly Western, liberal, representative form of procedural democracy employed by advocates of globalization from above and the democratic peace is, in many ways, 'democracy lite'. It is a form of democracy that requires a weak or shallow understanding of the polity. An institutional analysis (highlighted by the essential institutions above) is all that is necessary in order to make causal claims about the relationship between states. 'Procedural democracies' can be easily utilized in statistical analysis. However, such an approach is also quite limiting.

> A liberal conception of democracy is assumed to be applicable to the entire period of the DP. If this were not the case, statistical comparison of cases from, for example, the nineteenth, twentieth, and twenty-first centuries would be invalid. Such an assumption explicitly denies the significance of changing institutional forms, and hence of historical context, for the nature and meaning of democracy. To the extent that changes in the meaning and institutional forms of democracy are acknowledged, they are seen primarily as a matter of coding; implicitly, the more democracy changes, the more it stays the same.[58]

It seems under such limiting conditions that an alternative form of democracy (often competing throughout these historical periods) with the procedural form might provide a vision of democratic rule that counters this ahistorical view. Such an alternative view is not a truer form of democracy but it does uncover hidden sources of insecurity inaccessible to theorists working in the democratic peace tradition. A rendering of democracy that looks beneath institutional forms and demands that democratic governance relate in some meaningful way to popular rule for the common good challenges ahistoricism and depoliticization. It becomes more than an issue of coding – there is a qualitative difference in the purpose and motivation of democratic values and norms when a society moves from popular franchise to popular rule.

Deliberative democracy is a '*self-governing* community' of citizens who rule and are ruled in turn. For Aristotle, such a community becomes 'an agency of the common good at least in the modest sense that political activity has to bear a discernable relationship to the good of citizens as each understands it, and perhaps

---

56 Ibid.
57 Ibid.
58 Barkawi and Laffey, pp. 14-15.

134 *Creating Insecurity*

in the stronger sense that citizens should participate democratically in the forging of the *political* good.'[59] This idea of the common good radically changes what constitutes political life. Politics becomes the exercise of a cooperative, free life based on pursuit of a common good. Practical, democratic deliberation serves to uncover this common good based on diverse claims to justice.[60] Gilbert's reading of Marx as an advocate for democratic internationalism founded on a notion of the common good is telling.

> He [Marx] extended the Aristotelian idea of a common good to include democratic internationalism; communists would make the 'common interests of the proletariat independently of all nationality' a linchpin of their political strategy and conception of justice. This internationalism is democratic because it envisions widespread pressure from below to check the predatory policies of one's own (even a parliamentary) government. It is also internationalist in the stronger sense that citizens of one nationality empathize with resistance to oppression by those of another. They put common moral interests above the policies and 'interests' of the nation's elite.[61]

Democracy, in the above passage, relates to deliberative pressure from below on state elites that may be functioning within broadly defined procedural democratic institutions. But, as Gilbert discusses, in order to investigate the presence of 'democratic norms and values' it is incumbent upon the scholar to do more than acknowledge institutional variables. Here, we begin to see the reflexive activities of political constructivists at work. Political constructivists attempt to locate a discursive space where substantive deliberation occurs concerning political alternatives within the boundaries of the common good. The maintenance of this discursive space – whereby diverse groups within a polity transcend the 'tyrannies of particular interests' and seek the common good represents *democratic security*. This, in turn, might be discussed in terms of a broader national security programme.

Enhancing Democratic Security

While democracy might be thought to benefit all citizens, economic globalization from above has winners and losers. The concern of many critics is that theories underpinning global economic policies conflate procedural democracies with deliberative democracies seeking a common good. When viewed in conjunction with the processes of economic globalization, a certain inevitability thesis emerges from the political rhetoric of the state. By reducing economic debates, on the one hand, to advocates for free-trade and international growth (neoclassical economics), and on the other hand, to all other (marginalized) economic policies,

---

59 Alan Gilbert, *Democratic Individuality* (Cambridge: Cambridge University Press, 1990), p. 27.
60 Ibid, pp. 27 and 263-264.
61 Ibid, p. 285.

advocates for globalization from above deflect a number of issues that deliberative democrats wish to raise. For mainstream economists, those advocating globalization from above, 'globalization must be accepted as a *fait accompli*... It cannot be based on any positive benefits, since these accrue only to a minority, while the majority is threatened with an open ended, permanent decline in its standard of living.'[62] Simultaneously, the inevitability thesis concerning globalization is analogous to the unitary view of the state supplied by democratic peace theorists and state policy advocates who suggest that the spread of procedural democracies leads inevitably to a world without war. Thus, neoclassic economic policies become the 'inevitable' outgrowth of the democratic peace just as procedural democracies become the 'inevitable' outgrowth of neoclassical economics. The case of the United States is illustrative. In pursuit of policies that enhance economic globalization from above, the United States has framed democracy in procedural terms and limited deliberative democratic movements by repressive means.

In a cogent critique of neoclassical economics, George DeMartino evaluates how policy formation has been co-opted by particular interests and removed from the deliberative arena. '[Policies] that emerge in a society are taken to reflect the preferences of its citizens. This maneuver requires a simplistic view of politics and policy formation, one that effaces enduring divisions of class, race, gender, etc.'[63] The approach taken by neoclassical economists mirrors that taken by democratic peace scholars. 'At worst, this model of governance is predicated upon a conception of the nation as a unified actor with consistent preferences, so that all citizens are seen to value and benefit equally from a particular policy choice.'[64] 'By analogizing the state as a unified economic actor, [neoclassical] theorists are spared consideration of the deep conflicts over values and interests that permeate all societies. Hence, a nation's policies can be taken as simply reflecting the national will.'[65] The thought that sectarian interests might manipulate democratic institutions is eschewed for a more parsimonious rendering of a rational actor model of decision-making that claims to uncover and promote the 'national will'. The synergy between neoclassical economics and procedural democratic thinking enables both approaches to move forward outside the bounds of democratic deliberation. As Rupert notes, 'the power of transnationally mobile capital to override democratic processes and public deliberations has increased manifoldly along with the growth of international liquidity and the sophistication and speed of exchange in world financial markets.'[66]

Under such conditions, a more comprehensive critique of U.S. policy that can balance sophisticated realist concerns for *national* security and political

---

62 Bienefeld, p. 99.
63 George DeMartino, *Global Economy, Global Justice: Theoretical Objections and Policy Alternatives to Neoliberalism* (London: Routledge Press, 2000), p. 204.
64 Ibid.
65 Ibid, p. 205.
66 Rupert, 'Democracy, Peace, What's Not to Love?' p. 164.

136 *Creating Insecurity*

constructivist attempts to problematize 'democracy' is necessary. Critically investigating the considerations of power that remain hidden in a review of democracy in its procedural form uncovers instances of insecurity. Democratic security (defined as an understanding of democratic governance that takes seriously the idea of a *common good*) is not necessarily enhanced by globalization from above. Consider that 'inequalities have been deepening as the neoliberal project has unfolded; the wealthiest 20 percent of the world's people received 74 times as much income as the poorest 20 percent in 1997, up from a ratio of 60 to 1 in 1990 and 30 to 1 in 1960.'[67] For Rupert, this suggests that 'liberal capitalist democracy is not all that democratic, and the contemporary liberalizing world appears actually to be moving away from the cosmopolitan vision of self-determination and mutual respect presented in the more normative versions of the democratic peace. Instead, transnational liberalization is bringing with it an unprecedented global hierarchy of wealth and power.'[68] If this assessment is correct, then national security strategies will suffer from the twin problems of internal and external actors disenfranchised by a political and economic system that dictates policy from above and remains antagonistic to their interests.

For sophisticated realists, this presents a problem for the long-term maintenance of national security. Without recognizing the importance of adhering to the common good, states undermine their viability as actors responsible for the well-being of their citizens. For political constructivists, problematizing democracy demonstrates that in a real sense democratic security is undermined by the hegemonic practice of oligarchies with parliamentary forms. Both critiques require something more of the state. Globalization from above (the elite-dominated approach to free-trade and democratic peace) and globalization from below (the deliberative democratic approach to fair trade and the common good) represent two broad security programmes. However, only the latter can provide a long-term enhancement to national security. Globalization from below requires that states take seriously their obligation to act in the best interest of their citizens (not the best interests of a segment of their citizens – no matter how large a percentage of the population this might be). This requires an 'international egalitarian perspective'[69] that challenges globalization from above and radically re-constitutes democratic practices.

---

67 Ibid, p. 166.
68 Ibid.
69 DeMartino, p. 207.

Chapter 8

Creating Insecurity IV: Regime Change, WMD, and the Invasion of Iraq

The combination of 11 September 2001, a new pre-emptive national security strategy, and the worldwide war on terrorism culminated in the desire of the United States to galvanize the international community to support the removal of Saddam Hussein from power in Iraq. Euphemistically referred to as *regime change*, the George W. Bush Administration pushed the world community to take military action against Iraq in order to eliminate his suspected stockpiles of weapons of mass destruction. While it remains unclear exactly when the U.S. administration conceived of the need to remove the Iraqi dictator from power, the swift military build-up in the Persian Gulf and the frantic diplomatic efforts from September of 2002 through February of 2003 demonstrated a near 'inevitability' to U.S. policy. When the invasion of Iraq finally happened, it seemed to be a surprise to few, including the Iraqi regime, its soldiers, and its citizens.

Critics of the U.S. decision to invade Iraq, however, recognized quite quickly that the potential for creating insecurity was at least as great as any post-war enhancement to national security. Both realists, espousing their traditional 'cautious paranoid' vision of world politics, and political constructivists, drawn to how the debate was being framed and the political issues being explored, questioned the strategic efficacy of U.S. policy. The negative potential for disrupting U.S. security goals caused realists to critically evaluate the Bush Administration's war policies. Simultaneously, seeking to challenge the motives of the Administration to perpetuate a sustained superpower mentality, political constructivists located hidden sources of ideational insecurity. Perhaps even more than the discussions concerning BMD, the Drug War, and democratic security, U.S. policy to 'liberate' Iraq provides an instance of state practice that unintentionally creates insecurity while attempting to manage national security concerns. In the analysis that follows, a brief historical discussion of the U.S. rationale(s) for war will be explored. While it has been argued that a strategic rationale for war remained absent during the run up to the war, state policy makers offered various reasons why a war was necessary and required immediate attention. Following the state version of the events leading to war, a realist interpretation demonstrates why cautious paranoids found fault with the arguments put forth by the state. This discussion details the traditional realist reliance on containment and deterrence when faced with an enemy endowed with WMD. In addition, realists recognized the potential that unintended political and military

138   *Creating Insecurity*

complications could undermine the U.S. security position in Iraq and lead to a long and costly campaign to achieve a suitable strategic outcome. Then, a political constructivist interpretation of the political milieu in the period prior to the war considers how specific identity performances provide an understanding of cultural sources of insecurity beyond the realist interpretation. Finally, the two approaches are brought together in order to offer a balanced analysis of U.S. policy toward Iraq. As with the applications above, realists and political constructivists find common ground in the antipathy toward state actions. However, their theoretical points of departure require that we balance both positions rather than attempting to subsume one into the other.

The United States and a *Casus belli* for War with Iraq

The origins of the decision to go to war to remove Saddam Hussein from power are less clear than might otherwise be thought. Unlike previous wars where a single event came to be thought of as the precipitating cause,[1] the claim that Saddam Hussein represented a clear and immediate danger to the United States seems to have multiple and, at times, competing origins. Some argue that a neo-conservative clique of intellectuals and policy makers arrived at this conclusion long before George W. Bush became President of the United States. Once in the halls of power, their ideas could be put into practice. As if to lend credence to this view, many in the Administration found the events of 11 September 2001 to represent a reasonable excuse to unveil the already planned removal of Saddam Hussein.[2] Vice President Richard Cheney, Deputy Defense Secretary Paul Wolfowitz, Chairman of the Defense Policy Board Richard Perle, Chief of Staff to the Vice President I. Lewis Libby, Under Secretary of Defense for Policy Douglas Feith and others in the Administration may have been considering how to remove the dictator from power years before the eventual war. Emerging from documents like the *Defense Planning Guidance* put together by Cheney and his staff when the Vice President was Defense Secretary during the first Bush Administration (1989-1992), the rationale for war can be viewed as a need to keep Iraq from developing nuclear weapons while simultaneously ensuring the hegemonic position of the United States after the Cold War.[3]

Alternatively, the war against terrorism might be seen as substantially changing the strategic playing field of the United States. In this reading, a fundamental

---

1   For a discussion of 'precipitating cause' and war see, Joseph S. Nye, Jr., *Understanding International Conflicts: An Introduction to Theory and History* (New York: Addison Wesley Longman, Inc., 2000).

2   See, for instance, the discussion in Bob Woodward, *Bush at War* (New York: Simon and Schuster, 2002), pp. 48-50.

3   See, for example, Todd S. Purdum, 'The Brains Behind Bush's War Policy,' *New York Times*, 1 February 2003, sec. B, p. 9; and Michael R. Gordon, 'Serving Notice of a New U.S., Poised to Hit First and Alone,' *New York Times*, 27 January 2003, sec. A, p. 1.

Creating Insecurity IV: Regime Change, WMD, and the Invasion of Iraq 139

change in U.S. military strategy seems to provide the rationale for war. The need to launch pre-emptive strikes against possible foes replaced *deterrence* and *containment* as the new cornerstone of U.S. strategic thinking. Such a change is necessary because of 'new threats' that undermine the old paradigm pertaining to state behavior in international anarchy. The basis for such a change in strategic direction can be found in *The National Security Strategy of the United States of America*[4] requiring that threats be removed before they become serious enough to undermine U.S. freedom abroad or diminish national security at home.[5] Threat transcendence becomes the goal of such a policy rather than threat mitigation. During the run up to war an attempt was made to connect the Saddam Hussein regime to international terrorist groups including al Qaeda. With the connection made, it was thought the United States would have a clear *casus belli* for war. Iraq represented a striking example of a state that could be neither contained nor deterred. Because the regime survived at the margins of legitimacy, actors (specifically, Saddam) could not be categorized as *rational*. They were neither interested in the survival of Iraq as a state nor their own survival, but, rather, bent on the destruction of their enemies without regard for their own well-being. The inability to view Saddam and his cadre as rational actors meant they could never *learn* the rules of international relations. Moreover, they would be willing to interact with non-state security threats including terrorists. 'Containment is not possible when unbalanced dictators with weapons of mass destruction can deliver those weapons on missiles or secretly provide them to terrorist allies,' Bush would declare in a speech at West Point in June of 2002.[6] Secretary of State Colin Powell would continue this theme in late January of 2003 before the *World Economic Forum* in Davos, Switzerland. Given Saddam's 'clear ties to terrorist groups, including al Qaeda,' not going to war would allow him to 'pass a weapon, share technology, or use these weapons [WMD] again.'[7] For thinkers like Wolfowitz, the possibility that states and terrorists may act together changes the security calculus of the state. 'Containment and deterrence goes back to an era when the only use of force we worried about was one in which the use of force could be directly

---

4   George W. Bush, *The National Security Strategy of the United States of America* (Washington, D.C.: Government Printing Office, 2002).
5   The official term is 'anticipatory self-defense.' See, Jeffrey Record, 'The Bush Doctrine and the War with Iraq,' *Parameters* 4 (Spring 2003), p. 6.
6   Cited at ibid, p. 6.
7   'Powell on Iraq: We Reserve Our Sovereign Right to Take Military Action,' *New York Times*, 27 January 2003, sec. A, p. 8; For a continuing discussion of the Bush Administration's views, see, Mark Landler and Alan Cowell, 'Powell, in Europe, Nearly Dismisses U.N.'s Iraq Report,' *New York Times*, 27 January 2003, sec. A, p. 1. Later in January, the Bush Administration attempted to make the link between the Iraqi regime and terrorism even stronger by positing a further link between Iraq and Ansar al-Islam, Islamic extremists operating in northern Iraq. See, David Johnston and Don Van Natta, Jr., 'U.S. Focuses on Iraqi Links to Group Allied to Al Qaeda,' *New York Times*, 30 January 2003, sec. A, p. 9. It was thought that this link would bolster Colin Powell's pending presentation to the U.N. Security Council.

140 *Creating Insecurity*

associated with a country, and that country had an address... The whole thing that terrorists introduce is that you not only do not see the threat coming but you do not know where it came from.'[8] Echoing the American concern, Prime Minister Tony Blair of Britain argued that 'despite sanctions, the policy of containment has not worked sufficiently well to prevent Saddam from developing these weapons. I am in no doubt that the threat is serious and current, that he has made progress on weapons of mass destruction and that he has to be stopped.'[9] Jeffrey Record sums up the new *National Security Strategy* and the Bush Administration's view that containment and deterrence were insufficient policy options.

> The Bush Doctrine postulates an imminent, multifaceted, undeterrable, and potentially calamitous threat to the United States – a threat that, by virtue of the combination of its destructiveness and invulnerability to deterrence, has no precedent in American history. By implication, such a threat demands an unprecedented response.[10]

A war to remove Saddam from power represents such an *unprecedented response*. By explicitly stating pre-emption as the new strategic doctrine and proceeding to foment regime change in Iraq, the United States would not only remove a 'substantial' threat in the Middle East, but it would also signal to other possible 'rogue states' the potential harm that follows from not participating in a U.S.-led world order.

A third, and perhaps related, condition for going to war was thought to be the sustained desire and escalating attempts by the Iraqi regime to acquire a sophisticated WMD program. Throughout the period leading up to the invasion of Iraq, the United States and its strongest ally Great Britain sought to convince skeptical allies and the greater world community that Iraq possessed various WMD assets in violation of United Nations Security Council Resolutions. In early September of 2002, the U.S. Administration claimed that Iraq had attempted to purchase 'specially designed aluminum tubes' to be used in the processing of uranium for nuclear weapons.[11] Later in September, the Administration followed Britain in reporting that Saddam Hussein was attempting to smuggle uranium into Iraq from Niger in West Africa.[12] In October, the President asserted that Iraq was 'less than a year away from building a nuclear weapon.'[13] It was further suggested that the Iraqi military was 'continuing to produce chemical and biological agents capable of causing mass casualties, including mustard gas, sarin, anthrax and botulinum toxin.'[14] Later, Vice President Cheney would argue that Iraq 'has, in

---

8   Cited in Gordon, p. 1.

9   Warren Hoge, 'Blair Says Iraqis Could Launch Chemical Warheads in Minutes,' *New York Times*, 25 September 2002, sec. A, p. 1.

10   Record, p. 6.

11   Michael R. Gordon and Judith Miller, 'U.S. Says Hussein Intensifies Quest for A-Bomb Parts,' *New York Times*, 8 September 2002, sec. 1, p. 1.

12   Hoge, p. 1.

13   Record, p. 8.

14   Hoge, p. 1.

Creating Insecurity IV: Regime Change, WMD, and the Invasion of Iraq 141

fact, reconstituted nuclear weapons.'[15] Intelligence reports claimed that a new and more dangerous command and control structure for WMD deployment was being put into place in Iraq.[16] For advocates of war as a policy to remove Saddam Hussein, this claim added weight to the notion that the dictator was too ruthless to be allowed to remain in power. Taken as a whole, the weight of these assertions was thought to provide a sufficient pretext for war. Since each of these actions was in violation of numerous U.N. resolutions, officials in the United States felt reasonably assured that the international community would back a further resolution to go to war.

The origins of the decision to go to war will be debated for decades and the rationales given above are meant only as an introduction to the two critiques that follow. A thorough history of U.S. policy cannot be written so soon after the war. Such an undertaking will be left to historians and policy analysts armed with 'Freedom of Information' writs and years of hindsight. In the hyper-political environment of the period immediately after the war, attempts to explain why the United States decided to push the war option so aggressively have become tangled in political charges that policy makers engaged in outright lies, inaccurate intelligence reviews, and misleading statements in order to justify war. When the Iraqi regime did not use WMD during the war and when these illegal weapons remained unaccounted for long after the official end to hostilities, many of the claims concerning the immediacy of the threat posed by Iraq seemed unfounded at best. As intelligence reports were analyzed more closely, evidence concerning uranium procurement from Africa, aluminum tubes for nuclear purposes, the connection between Iraq and al Qaeda, as well as the presence of mobile chemical and biological weapons factories was deemed inaccurate.[17] The governments of both the United States and Great Britain would spend months after the war attempting (internationally) to keep the peace in an Iraq that was suffering from an acute power vacuum and (domestically) defending themselves against charges that intelligence used to justify military action had been manipulated.

In the arena of international diplomacy, the decision to go to war in Iraq without the consent of the United Nations caused a rift between the United States and many countries including Germany, France, and Russia. The shaky political and security environment in Iraq after the removal of Saddam was complicated by tensions concerning how and in what capacity the United Nations would participate in the rebuilding of the country. Special peacekeeping forces that might

---

15 Eric Schmitt, 'Cheney Asserts No Responsible Leader Could Have Ignored Danger from Iraq,' *New York Times*, 25 July 2003, sec. A, p. 10.

16 Hoge, p. 1.

17 James Risen and David E. Sanger, 'After the War: C.I.A. Uproar; New Details Emerge on Uranium Claim and Bush's Speech,' *New York Times*, 18 July 2003, sec. A, p. 1; 'The Government, the BBC and WMD: What Did You Do In the War, Alastair?' *The Economist*, 5 July 2003, p. 47; 'Intelligence and Iraq: The War Isn't Over for Tony,' *The Economist*, 12 July 2003, p. 49; and 'Iraq, Niger, and Uranium: Spies Fall Out,' *The Economist*, 12 July 2003, p. 50.

142   *Creating Insecurity*

have had more success in preventing the random violence that followed the war remained in France, Germany, and elsewhere due both to the diplomatic tension created on the road to war and the intransigence of the United States in relinquishing political power at war's end.[18]

A Realist Interpretation of U.S. Policy

The realist emphasis on material security threats allows the cautious paranoid to engage the state in an analysis of security policy. The Bush Administration's attempt to securitize the threat posed by Saddam Hussein and his WMD presents realists with an opportunity to assess the extent to which the decision to go to war can be seen as an enhancement to the national security of the United States. As with the previous applications, the realist response to U.S. policy has been quite critical. Five arguments against the decision to go to war have consistently been raised by realist scholars who find military action to be a moment of created insecurity. First, the strategic logic of containment and deterrence worked against the Iraqi regime contra the stated views of the Bush Administration. Pre-emption against Iraq might be effective but it cannot be considered as sure a strategy as some might think. Second, if it is the case that Saddam Hussein has WMD, a military invasion and the stated goal of 'regime change' provide the dictator with a rational-choice to use these illegal weapons or smuggle them out of the country to be used by other actors demonstrating antagonism toward the United States. Third, any war that begins in Iraq could quickly spread out of control and ignite other conflicts in the region. Turkey's stated policy to intervene should the Kurds attempt to establish themselves in the northern region of Iraq, Syria's concern at being cornered by Israel and a U.S. occupied Iraq, or Iran's similar concern at being flanked by U.S. forces on its east and west could corrupt the war strategy of the United States and lead to multiple security problems throughout the Middle East. Fourth, the United States would appear to be a rogue superpower bent on global hegemony. This perception could have deleterious consequences for the medium and long-term interests of the United States and prompt terrorists to engage in violent acts within the U.S. in a form of *blowback*.[19] Fifth, while a military victory over the Iraqi army appeared certain from a calculus of capabilities, maintaining the integrity of Iraq after the war would prove too much for the United States. Kurds in the north, Shi'ite in the south, Saddam loyalists, fundamentalist guerrillas, as well as common criminals and the requirements of rebuilding twenty years of neglected and damaged infrastructure would overwhelm U.S. efforts to win the peace. Each of these objections to U.S. war plans might be examined further.

---

18 Elaine Sciolino, 'France and Germany Consider Possible Roles in Postwar Iraq,' *New York Times*, 29 July 2003, sec. A, p. 10.

19 See, Chalmers Johnson, *Blowback: The Costs and Consequences of American Empire* (New York: Owl Books, 2000) for a discussion of the *blowback* syndrome.

The first realist critique of U.S. policy counters the claim that containment and deterrence have not been effective strategies towards Iraq. In a *Foreign Policy* article published just prior to the war, John Mearsheimer and Steven Walt argued that the 'belief that Saddam's past behavior shows he cannot be contained rests on distorted history and faulty logic.'[20] Their argument draws upon the historical record in an attempt to demonstrate that even Saddam Hussein could be considered a rational actor and likely to follow the logic of deterrence. Reviewing the history behind the initiation of war against Iran in 1980 and Kuwait in 1990, Mearsheimer and Walt show that on both occasions 'he attacked because Iraq was vulnerable and because he believed his targets were weak and isolated. In each case, his goal was to rectify Iraq's strategic dilemma with a limited military victory.'[21] Against Iran, Hussein considered, with good reason, that the revolution of 1979 would lead to Iranian support of the majority Shi'ite population in Iraq. Further, the ascendance of fundamentalists in Tehran would lead them to take-over key Gulf islands controlled by Iraq.[22] 'Tensions mounted throughout 1979 and the first half of 1980, especially as the Iranians made no secret of their desire to export the Islamic revolution to Iraq as well as Sa'udi Arabia and the Gulf states.'[23] For realists, the origins of this war can be located in the weakness of the Iraqi position vis-à-vis Iran and the opportunity afforded Iraq in the tumultuous moments after Khomeini came to power. 'Although the war cost Iraq far more than Saddam expected, it also thwarted Khomeini's attempt to topple him and dominate the region. War with Iran was not a reckless adventure; it was an opportunistic response to a significant threat.'[24] Moreover, prior to the Bush Administration's campaign toward war, the link between a realist interpretation of Saddam's motives and the U.S. position had been quite close. Throughout the eight year struggle, the United States recognized the need to support Iraq against the hegemonic behavior of Iran.

In December 1983 Donald Rumsfeld, the American administration's special envoy to the Middle East, visited Saddam and gave him a handwritten letter from President Reagan. In November 1984, after other friendly gestures on both sides, diplomatic relations between the two countries were restored and Foreign Minister Tareq Aziz visited Washington, delivered a message from Saddam to President Reagan and met with Vice President George Bush....
Both sides were acting in accordance with the unwritten rules of an alliance of convenience.[25]

---

20 John J. Mearsheimer and Stephen M. Walt, 'An Unnecessary War,' *Foreign Policy* 134 (January/February 2003), p. 52.

21 Ibid, pp. 52-53.

22 Ibid, p. 53.

23 Marion Farouk-Sluglett and Peter Sluglett, *Iraq Since 1958: From Revolution to Dictatorship*, revised edition (London: I.B. Tauris Publishers, 2001), p. 256.

24 Mearsheimer and Walt, p. 53.

25 Saïd K. Aburish, *Saddam Hussein: The Politics of Revenge* (New York: Bloomsbury Publishing, 2000), pp. 228-29.

144   *Creating Insecurity*

Even during the Iraqi invasion and occupation of Kuwait in 1990, Mearsheimer and Walt argue that 'a careful look shows Saddam was neither mindlessly aggressive nor particularly reckless.'[26] 'He chose to use force because he was facing a serious challenge and because he had good reasons to think his invasion would not provoke serious opposition.'[27] Assuming that he had the implicit support of the United States, Saddam chose to invade Kuwait in order to overcome Iraq's weak position after the war with Iran.[28] Even when the United States and its allies began their liberation campaign, Saddam, rather than acting irrationally, attempted to sue for peace – making it clear he 'was willing to pull out completely.'[29]

Beyond Saddam's behavior in the wars, Mearsheimer and Walt argue that still more evidence suggests that the dictator has been and remained deterrable. 'First, although he launched conventionally armed Scud missiles at Saudi Arabia and Israel during the Gulf War, he did not launch chemical or biological weapons at coalition forces that were decimating the Iraqi military.'[30] Evidence suggests that he refrained from using these weapons because of U.S. threats to retaliate if such weapons were deployed.[31] 'Second, in 1994 Iraq mobilized the remnants of its army on the Kuwaiti border in an apparent attempt to force a modification of the U.N. Special Commission's (UNSCOM) weapons inspection regime. But when the United Nations issued a new warning and the United States reinforced its troops in Kuwait, Iraq backed down quickly.'[32]

The historical record also suggests that the issue of '[deterrence] has worked well against Saddam in the past, and there [was] no reason to think it [would not] work equally well in the future.'[33] As Richard Betts put it, '[reckless] as he has been, he has never yet done something Washington told him would be suicidal.'[34] As for containment, a similar historical treatment suggests that realists are correct on this point as well. The long Cold War with the Soviet Union suggests that containment is an ugly yet effective strategy against nuclear armed states. 'Containment may not be enough to prevent Iraq from acquiring nuclear weapons someday. Only the conquest and permanent occupation of Iraq could guarantee that. Yet the United States can contain a nuclear Iraq, just as it contained the Soviet

---

26   Mearsheimer and Walt, p. 54.

27   Ibid.

28   Ibid. The Iraqi losses were staggering. Over 105,000 dead and 300,000 wounded. "The financial losses too were staggering. Iraqi reserved had disappeared: $35 billion was owed to the West, $11 billion to the USSR and, in addition to outright cash grants and gifts of oil produced in the Neutral Zone, more than $40 billion to Kuwait and Saudi Arabia.' See, Aburish, p. 259.

29   Mearsheimer and Walt, p. 54.

30   Ibid, p. 55.

31   Richard K. Betts, 'Suicide From Fear of Death? (Possible War between the US and Iraq),' *Foreign Affairs* 82 (January/February 2003), p. 39.

32   Mearsheimer and Walt, p. 54.

33   Ibid, p. 56.

34   Betts, p. 38.

Creating Insecurity IV: Regime Change, WMD, and the Invasion of Iraq   145

Union.'[35] In an eerie example of the realist choice to rely on containment and deterrence when faced with a hostile enemy, Jeffrey Record tells of the following exchange between President Truman and Major General Orville Anderson.

> In the earliest years of the Cold War, before the Soviet Union exploded its first atomic bomb, there were calls in the United States for preventive war against another evil dictator. The calls continued even after the Soviets detonated their first bomb in 1949. Indeed, in the following year, the Commandant of the Air Force's new Air War College publicly asked to be given the order to conduct a nuclear strike against fledgling Soviet atomic capabilities. 'And when I went to Christ,' said the Commandant, 'I think I could explain to Him that I had saved civilization. With it [the A-bomb] used in time, we can immobilize a foe [and] reduce his crime before it happened.'
> President Truman fired the Commandant, preferring instead a long, hard, and, in the end, stunningly successful policy of containment and deterrence.[36]

If containment could work against a state as powerful as the USSR for over four decades, it appeared that the immediacy of the threat posed by Saddam had been exaggerated. Further, deterrence and containment seemed to mitigate the threat without placing American troops on the battlefield.

The second claim raised by realists skeptical of the U.S. pursuit of war draws further on rational actor logic. Accordingly, the actions of the United States, in pushing for regime change, provide Saddam with one of the only instances when the use of WMD appears reasonable. Richard Betts puts the point succinctly. '[If] a U.S. invasion succeeds, Saddam will have no reason to withhold his best parting shot – which could be the use of weapons of mass destruction (WMD) inside the United States.'[37] Without reference to an attack inside the United States, Mearsheimer and Walt concur. 'Saddam thus has no incentive to use chemical or nuclear weapons against the United States and its allies – *unless his survival is threatened.*'[38] 'Regime change in Baghdad... probably means an end to Saddam Hussein. And he will not go gently if he has nothing left to lose. If a military assault to overthrow the Iraqi regime looks likely to succeed, there is not reason to doubt Saddam will try to use biological weapons where they would hurt Americans the most.'[39] Here, realist critics of U.S. policy are playing their traditional role as 'cautious paranoids.' While it turned out that the Iraqi regime did not deploy WMD against coalition forces, the logic of the realist argument holds. Indeed, what distinguishes the cautious paranoia of realism from the policy makers' position is the coherence of thought in the realist view. Realism attempts to place threats into a larger theoretical picture of world politics. Policy makers attempt to sell ideas, no matter how ungrounded those ideas might be. In the case of regime change, '[the Administration is] in the business of selling a preventive war, so they must try to

---

35 Mearsheimer and Walt, p. 56.

36 Record, p. 19.

37 Betts, p. 34.

38 Mearsheimer and Walt, p. 55. *My italics.*

39 Betts, p. 36. Such a claim follows analysis by Tenet and the CIA in October of 2002.

146 *Creating Insecurity*

make remaining at peace seem unacceptably dangerous. And the best way to do that is to inflate the threat, either by exaggerating Iraq's capabilities or by suggesting horrible things will happen if the United States does not act soon.'[40] For Betts, the argument can be summed up in the following way. 'By mistakenly conflating the immediate and long-term risks of Iraqi attack and by exaggerating the dangers in alternatives to war, the advocates of a preventive war against Saddam have miscast a modest probability of catastrophe as an acceptable risk.'[41]

If Saddam decided not to use his cache of WMD as a parting shot to the United States, it seems equally likely that he could proliferate them beyond Iraq in order to cause mischief long after he was gone. An imminent attack on Iraq might have the immediate effect of introducing chemical and biological agents to other rogue states like Syria. Such an occurrence would create a heightened level of insecurity within Israel and undermine peace plans. In the immediate aftermath of the war, the bewilderment of U.S. officials searching for WMD was met with an equally paranoid vision of the potential danger these weapons might pose if they had been scattered beyond Iraq. While realists found any connection between Saddam and terrorists groups like al Qaeda highly implausible prior to the war, the likelihood that an alliance of convenience might be formed during or after the war made for increased insecurity. Jeffrey Record details the difference between the Iraqi dictator and bin Laden while also noting the potential for events to substantially alter the political calculations.

> Both Saddam Hussein and Osama bin Laden may hate the United States, but the former is a secular dictator on the Stalinist model who has never hesitated to butcher Muslim clerics, whereas the latter is a religious fanatic who regards secular Arab regimes as blasphemous. Other than hatred of the United States, they do not have a common agenda, though the history of international politics is replete with very strange bedfellows.[42]

Echoing this logic, Betts provides a realist assessment of the potential to be harmed by WMD after a war for regime change has begun.

> Saddam may not be crafty enough to figure out how to strike the American homeland. Iraqi intelligence may be too incompetent to smuggle biological weapons into the United States and set them off. Or Saddam's underlings might disobey orders to do so. The terrorists to whom Iraq subcontracts the job might bungle it. Or perhaps American forces could find and neutralize all of Iraq's WMD before they could be detonated. But it would be reckless to bank on maybes. Washington has given Saddam more than enough time to concoct retaliation, since he has had months of notice that the American were coming.[43]

---

40 Mearsheimer and Walt, pp. 58-59.
41 Betts, p. 35.
42 Record, p. 10.
43 Betts, p. 37.

Creating Insecurity IV: Regime Change, WMD, and the Invasion of Iraq   147

We see in the realist concern over the proliferation of WMD a similar concern to that of state policy makers. Strikingly, the solution to the threat posed by these weapons [for the state policy maker: *going to war*] becomes the instance of increased insecurity when interpreted through the lens of the realist world view. The realists employ a rational actor model of decision making to the possible use of WMD. The time to use these weapons, according to this view, is when state actors feel they have nothing left to lose – when they have been backed against the wall. A war prefaced on regime change presents just such a moment. More importantly, given the realist desire to look to medium and long-term consequences of security policies, the decision to remove Saddam from power in Iraq will demonstrate to future rogue leaders the logic of utilizing WMD when confronted with similar demands. So, even if Saddam does not use his own cache, the lesson for future Saddams is given. This represents a further instance of created insecurity for the United States.

Wars do not normally go as strategists envision. The third possible negative consequence of a war to remove Saddam Hussein addresses the potential for other actors to become involved in ways that complicate and undermine the U.S. war effort. Prior to the beginning of hostilities, demonstrations in Egypt, Jordan, Turkey, Syria and Pakistan and the Palestinian Territories demonstrated how unpopular the potential war was viewed by the majority of citizens/subjects in these states. Realists could envision a number of scenarios whereby a prolonged and deadly war with high civilian casualties and urban street fighting would lead to unintended regime change of a different kind in countries throughout the region. In addition to street protests potentially overwhelming the political institutions of various states in the region, it was unclear exactly what a number of actors in Iraq would do as the war unfolded.

In the north, would the Kurds defy American warnings and pronounce the creation of an independent Kurdistan? If so, the Turkish government had long warned Washington that such an occurrence would lead to Turkish forces in Iraq. While not as vociferous, Iran might also have an incentive to become involved in northern Iraq. In the south, would the Shi'ite population, long repressed by the regime in Baghdad, seek revenge on the Sunni population? Would such an occurrence lead to Iranian involvement? Would either of these events lead to a massive population exodus into neighboring states like Jordan? Could a humanitarian crisis develop whereby neighboring states would be required to become involved militarily?

Moreover, if Saddam launched Al Samoud missiles into Israel would the Israeli government be as restrained in their actions as they were in 1991 when Saddam launched Scuds in an attempt to draw Israel into the war and disrupt the international coalition allied against him? If not, how would Palestinians, Egyptians, Jordanians, and Syrians react?

None of the possible scenarios above came to pass during the war. However, the realist focus on the regional aspects of a war to remove Saddam Hussein from power suggests a need to contextualize individual instances in world politics. The concern for many realists was the potential destabilizing effect that such a war

148 *Creating Insecurity*

would have on relations with other states in the region and on the domestic politics of these states. Here, realist warnings did come to pass, although the long term effects will not be known for some time. In Pakistan, fundamentalists gained political space in parliament due to anti-American sentiment and the impending war on Iraq. Similar strains could be seen in the domestic politics of states like Turkey and Indonesia.[44] If realists are correct and power balances power, then might the United States not find itself confronted by states unwilling to submit to American hegemony in the Gulf? If so, the medium and long term security environment might be much more problematic than an Iraq led by Saddam Hussein.

A similar concern over deleterious external consequences animates the fourth realist critique of U.S. policy. Waging a war outside the U.N. system would make the United States appear to be a rogue superpower bent on global hegemony. If states come to see the United States in this light, the global war on terrorism will suffer. Once cooperative nations will neglect to participate in the gathering and dissemination of intelligence. Further, the probability that terrorists will attack the United States will increase in an example of Chalmers Johnson's notion of blowback.[45] As Record argues, '[pursuit] of the neo-conservative agenda of permanent American primacy via perpetual military supremacy, and, as a matter of doctrine, an aggressive willingness to use force preemptively, even preventively, to dispatch threatening regimes and promote the spread of American political and economic institutions, invites perpetual isolation and enmity.'[46] It was this isolation and enmity that most concerned former National Security Advisor Brent Scowcroft. Seeing the real threat to national security in the persistence of terrorists to attack American interests, Scowcroft echoed the view of many Republicans outside the neo-conservative clique in Washington in arguing that an unpopular war on Iraq would undermine the war on terrorism.[47]

After the terrorist attacks of 11 September 2001, a global war on terrorism would require more assets than the United States could provide on its own. While the vast intelligence gathering capabilities and overwhelming military prowess of the United States is acknowledged, a successful war on terrorism requires human intelligence from disparate regions of the globe. Human intelligence rests on perceptions of legitimacy – providing sources with information because doing so appears just. Undermining this legitimacy by occupying Iraq and appearing as a 'unilateralist, overbearing hyperpower'[48] leads irreparably to a loss of the 'hearts and minds' of those with knowledge of terrorist activities.

In addition, by appearing to be an unrestrained hyperpower, the United States invites more marginalized and angry voices to participate in hostile acts. At this

---

44 Husain Haqqani, 'The Ripple Effect: Turkey, Pakistan, and Indonesia,' *Foreign Policy* 137 (July/August 2003), p. 62.
45 See, Johnson, pp. 3-33.
46 Record, p. 16.
47 Brent Scowcroft, 'Don't Attack Iraq,' *The Wall Street Journal*, 15 August 2002, sec. A.
48 Record, p. 16.

Creating Insecurity IV: Regime Change, WMD, and the Invasion of Iraq   149

point, realists focus on the willingness to harm rather than the capabilities to harm. It is not that the United States does not have enough resources to fight a war in Iraq while simultaneously fighting a war on terrorism. Rather, it is the reaction to fighting the former that undermines success in the latter. By appearing unrestrained, the United States offers the best recruiting tool available to terrorist groups.[49] Husain Haqqani examines how this realist concern developed after the war.

> The war in Iraq has definitely increased the number of radical Muslims believing in the inevitability of a clash of civilizations and the need to stand up and be counted for their religious fellowship. Radical Islamists have started building the argument that the United States offers nothing by way of ethical ideas and has become arrogant as a result of its military dominance. This argument finds even greater resonance in the context of the Iraq war. What is new following the collapse of Iraq's secular Arab nationalist regime is a process of cooperation and convergence between radical Islamists and secular nationalists in the Middle East. Traditionally, secular Arab nationalism viewed radical Islam, with its emphasis on pan-Islamism, as an ideological rival. But the Iraq war has muted that rivalry and, in the process, accentuated the polarization between a Muslim 'us' and a Western 'them.'[50]

The process whereby this occurs seems now to be recognized by the states involved in pushing for war. In late July of 2003, a British report detailed how Muslims may be more receptive to the activities and politics of al Qaeda than they were prior to the war.[51] How damaging this will be to the war against terrorism is unclear. Muslim dissatisfaction with the West has risen and fallen with numerous political events over the past century. However, realists are right to point out how such a convergence of antipathy toward the United States could harm U.S. interests at home and abroad.

Finally, the fifth concern raised by realists argues that while a military victory seems certain, the complexities of rebuilding Iraq will prove too great for the United States – leading it into a long and arduous role as *occupying force*. Iraq's integrity may not hold; an independent Kurdistan in the north may divide the country in two. Elsewhere, rivalries among competing tribes and tensions between the Sunni and Shi'ite populations may undermine U.S. efforts to build a 'democratic' state.

Perhaps even more dangerous than these somewhat centralized political scenarios, a decentralized and highly disruptive guerrilla campaign to rid Iraq of 'Western imperial occupiers' might follow a short military victory, bringing

---

49 Such an argument was put forth by the former chief of CIA counterterrorism, Vincent Cannistraro, 'Terror's Undiminished Threat,' *Foreign Policy* 137 (July/August 2003), p. 69.

50 Husain Haqqani, 'Islam's Weakened Moderates,' *Foreign Policy* 137 (July/August 2003), p. 61.

51 Ben Russell, 'Conflict 'May Have Driven Muslims Into Arms of al-Qa'ida,' *The Independent*, 1 August 2003.

150 *Creating Insecurity*

fundamentalists, nationalists, common criminals, and Saddam loyalists into an unplanned and uncoordinated affiliation against the United States and its coalition partners. If this occurred, the United States would be vulnerable. The military capabilities harnessed in a traditional campaign against opposing forces would remain unmatched. But, these capabilities would be of little use against random grenade attacks, car bombs, and sniper shootings.

It was this final 'cautious paranoid' scenario that appeared to be the new Iraqi reality in the months after hostilities ended. By the end of July 2003, more U.S. soldiers had been killed in Iraq than in the previous Gulf War. Attacks on U.S. military personnel were occurring each day, killing an average of one U.S. soldier ever other day.

As Jessica Tuchman Mathews would write, '[the] U.S. plan assumed that Iraq's government could be removed with minimal disruption to the country's ability to function and that the United States would be welcomed with open arms. Best-case planning is bad enough; this plan was heavily weighted with wishful thinking.'[52] While not an avowed realist, Tuchman Mathews articulates the view of the 'cautious paranoid.' Realists insist that states plan for the worst probable case when venturing into an uncertain policy. The fact that the United States did not plan for such a likely contingency represents a failure on the part of the state to fulfill it obligation to act in the best interest of its citizens. Having planned for and outlined a war of *liberation*, the United States created a situation where heightened insecurity was the result.

In the end, the weight of the realist interpretation of the threat Iraq posed and the potential for increased insecurity if a war ensued rests on a profound need to mitigate rather than transcend instances of insecurity. *Balancing, deterrence*, and *containment* point toward the same policy goal – the minimization of threat within a state-centric, material understanding of security. These strategies are central in the realist assessment of the Iraqi issue. None of these policy tools attempt to transcend the insecurity posed. But, an occupation does. For realists like Mearsheimer and Walt, the strategic rationale for the war remained absent from the positions expressed by U.S. policy makers.[53] A rationale, however, for why the United States has acted against the regime in Baghdad is precisely what political constructivists seek to examine in their interpretation of the ideational moments of insecurity present in the run up to the war.

A Political Constructivist Interpretation of U.S. Policy

Unlike the realist interpretation that sought to counter the state understanding of the material threat posed by Iraq with a detailed theoretical and historical review of the policies being considered, political constructivists return to those first questions

---

52 Jessica Tuchman Mathews, 'Now for the Hard Part,' *Foreign Policy* 137 (July/August 2003), p. 51.

53 Mearsheimer and Walt, p. 59.

Creating Insecurity IV: Regime Change, WMD, and the Invasion of Iraq 151

and ask how it came to be that Saddam Hussein could be considered a imminent threat in the first place. An ideational interpretation of the securitization process uncovers hidden variables that a state or realist view does not consider. In many ways, a political constructivist interpretation of this issue looks quite similar to the interpretation of the BMD debate. The discussion in chapter five looked to how U.S. identity reflects back on itself (often through a nativist lens) in a need to protect its own identity by defending against an Other. The sanctity of the United States as a unique physical/moral space required a vigilant return to a sense of invulnerability. Such a reading of the BMD issue provides insight into the rationale behind regime change in Iraq as well. But, the political constructivist interpretation in this chapter argues that U.S. identity increasingly shapes its interests abroad. A national identity based on some notion of lone superpower status and often tinged with considerations of empire has expanded the national understanding of what happens to be in the interests of the United States.

Amitav Ghosh offers a cogent assessment of the inclusion of empire into the American identity in the years after the Cold War.

> The idea of empire, once so effectively used by Ronald Reagan to discredit the Soviet Union, has recently undergone a strange rehabilitation in the United States. This process, which started some years ago, has accelerated markedly since September 11. References to empire are no longer deployed ironically or in a tone of warning; the idea has become respectable enough that the New York Times ran an article describing the enthusiasm it now evokes in certain circles. It is of some significance that these circles are not easily identified as being located on either the right or the left. If there are some on the right who celebrate the projection of U.S. power, there are others on the left who believe that the world can only benefit from an ever-increasing U.S. engagement and intervention abroad.[54]

Situating this emerging notion of empire into a theoretical discussion of world politics, Ronnie Lipschutz argues that the terrorist attacks on the United States, the crusade against evil personified in the figure of Saddam Hussein, and the unilateralist approach to foreign policy pursued by the Bush Administration have substantially changed America's interpretation of its place in the world. Rather than seeking empire through neo-liberal globalization, the United States now pursues a more direct form. '[The] response of the United States has been to transform a system of global discipline based on the appearance of self-regulated behaviour toward one more dependent on the overt display, deployment and employment of military force and police power to keep populations and individuals in line.'[55] The result for Lipschutz is an *imperium* – a 'universalized social space, governed by the United States.'[56] Such a reading of the current international

---

54 Amitav Ghosh, 'Imperial Temptation,' *The Nation* 274 (27 May 2002), p. 24.
55 Ronnie D. Lipschutz, 'The Clash of Governmentalities: The Fall of the UN Republic and America's Reach for Empire,' *Contemporary Security Policy* 23 (December 2002), p. 215.
56 Ibid.

152   *Creating Insecurity*

environment follows the writings by Hardt and Negri, Foucault, and Dean.[57] Global governmentality, or the management of citizens around the world, emanates from Washington, DC (the center of instrumental power) which holds this imperium (made up of states, institutions, economic and social entities) together.[58] 'Actors are socialized to behave according to certain tenets of "normality" and "propriety", and thereby produce and reproduce both their identities *and* the "normal" conditions under which such behaviour takes place.'[59] This understanding of social relations is true not only for those outside the instrumental center of power, but it also disciplines the actions and behaviors of those wielding power at the center. This Orwellian turn is a necessary and often mis-understood point in an analysis of empire.[60] An exposé in the popular newsmagazine *Newsweek* underscored how many in the Bush Administration have been socialized to perceive of themselves as valiant warriors protecting the United States from evil doers.[61] Normality functions to define the identities at the center as well as at the boundaries.

Both at the center and beyond, '[deviance] is permitted, up to a point, but it is also actively policed and disciplined in order to reinforce concepts and practices of normality.'[62] This conception of governmentality and power allows us to recognize how the terrorist attacks have changed the policies emanating from the center. Under normal periods of international relations, '[power] is... not exercised in an overt or quantifiable form... governmentality relies, at most, [in] the display, rather than the exercise, of coercive power.'[63] Further, '[order] is maintained through the self-disciplining of behaviour, on the one hand, and the policing function of surveillance and law, on the other. Together, these constrain practices within a "zone of stability" or "normality". Power is manifest through the discourses that

---

57 Michael Hardt and Antonio Negri, *Empire* (Cambridge, MA: Harvard University Press, 2000); Michel Foucault, *Power/Knowledge* (New York: Pantheon Books, 1980); and Mitchell Dean, *Governmentality – Power and Rule in Modern Society* (London: Sage Publishing, 1999).

58 Lipschutz, p. 218.

59 Ibid, p. 219.

60 Amitav Ghosh puts the point nicely, 'George Orwell and many other observers of imperialism have pointed out, empires imprison their rulers as well as their subjects. In today's America, where people are increasingly disinclined to venture beyond the borders, this has already come to pass.' Amitav Ghosh, 'The Anglophone Empire,' *The New Yorker* 79 (7 April 2003), p. 46.

61 Evan Thomas, 'The 12 Year Itch,' *Newsweek* (31 March 2003), p. 54. Similar attributes can be seen in the knee-jerk jingoism after 11 September. As 'freedom fries' replaced 'french fries' at all venues served by the House of Representatives as well as various restaurant chains throughout the country and right-wing radio talk show hosts demanded a boycott against French and German products, imperial moments in the new world order emerged. See, Hugh Rawson, 'The Road to Freedom Fries,' *American Heritage* 54 (June/July 2003), p. 12.

62 Lipschutz, p. 219.

63 Ibid.

Creating Insecurity IV: Regime Change, WMD, and the Invasion of Iraq 153

naturalize normality, and which are hegemonic and products of power.'[64] However, when this 'zone of stability' or 'normality' is disrupted, as happened on 11 September 2001, 'more instrumental forms of power – force and coercion – become manifest.'[65] As Lipschutz argues, '[the] attacks on New York and Washington, DC disrupted the governmental regime associated with neo-liberal normality in a way that had not happened before. Only then was instrumental power deployed by the United States, against Afghanistan, as more embedded forms of power and discipline failed to constrain organizations such as Al Qaeda.'[66]

The subsequent war on Iraq can be viewed as a continuation of this disciplining effect. It is important to recognize that the concept of power being used by political constructivists goes beyond the material definition of capabilities recognized by realists. The many faces of power being discussed here locate hidden forms of ideational power existing within the fabric of social relations.[67] And, with the war on Iraq it is possible to recognize how power can discipline the identities of the center as well. The Bush Administration's identity in the aftermath of the campaign in Afghanistan tilted further toward a unilateralist understanding of practice in world politics and an instrumental understanding of power. This is best seen in the *National Security Strategy* of the United States. The claim that the United States will act preemptively as a matter of doctrine is a result of a self-disciplining that sees military force as the only true guarantor of national security. Reliance on multilateral institutions, carrots as well as sticks, and the cumbersome practices of containment and deterrence are not only unnecessary, they represent practices perceived to be outside the norm of a superpower at the helm of imperium. President Bush's speech at West Point underscores the new discourse. 'We must take the battle to the enemy, disrupt his plans and confront the worst threats before they emerge. In the world we have entered the only path to safety is the path of action.'[68] As Hugh Gusterson notes, '[all] discourses, especially government discourses, have something to hide.'[69] The imperial discourse in this case hides the ideational sources of insecurity from those that perpetuate it. By confronting the 'enemy' on a battlefield and insisting that [military] action is the only 'path' to safety, reliance on a material (instrumental) appreciation of security avoids the moments of insecurity that develop from antagonistic and hyper identity performances.

---

64 Ibid. Such a reading finds much in common with Michel Foucault, *Discipline and Punish: The Birth of the Prison* (New York: Vintage Books, 1977).

65 Ibid.

66 Ibid.

67 Consider the work of Michael Mann, *The Sources of Social Power* (Cambridge, UK: Cambridge University Press, 1986).

68 Cited in Record, p. 7.

69 Hugh Gusterson, 'Tall Tales and Deceptive Discourses,' *Bulletin of the Atomic Scientists* 57 (November/December 2001), p. 68.

154   *Creating Insecurity*

The question that remains for the political constructivist is whether there is an emancipatory moment in the imperial discourse. Is it possible to conceive of a reflexive change in identity that could redefine interests and bring them closer to the interests of identities beyond the boundaries of the United States? Can counter-discourses develop that 'originate from below and eventually gain enough credibility' to counter and even become co-opted by the center of power?[70] Only by locating such emancipatory moments is it possible to overcome cultural forms of insecurity that exist beyond the material concerns that animate state and realist alike.

Toward a Balanced Critique of the U.S. Invasion of Iraq

We are left with a need to bring both sides of the security calculus together. Realists offer a critique of state policy that demonstrates that a deeper understanding of material security would warn against a policy of war. Political constructivists offer a reading of ideational insecurity that demonstrates how the state comes to perceive itself as insecure in the first place. In keeping with the focus of this book, *both* readings are necessary if a comprehensive analysis of state security concerns is to be written.

The 'cautious paranoia' present in realist interpretations of world politics highlights the negative consequences of policy options being considered. In the case of war with Iraq, the stated policy of demanding regime change/removing the threat of WMD is viewed by realists as both unnecessary and potential dangerous. Employing traditional techniques like rational actor logic and an assessment of capabilities, realists compel the state to recognize that absolute security can never be guaranteed. Security is always a relative concept and the state must seek the mitigation of specific insecurities rather than their transcendence. This is why containment and deterrence play a central role in realist thought. And, it is not surprising that realists would return to these ideas in an assessment of the Iraqi threat. Mearsheimer and Walt as well as Betts challenge the state to recognize these points. Arriving at a similar understanding of 'threat', realists are in a good position to explain *how* insecurities might be rectified. Yet, these writers are at a loss to explain *why* the state has come to view Iraq as a threat. Indeed, a common theme of bewilderment seems to run through realist analyses of the war on Iraq.

This inability to explain why the state would seek war without a compelling strategic rationale might best be explained by recourse to a political constructivist interpretation. Eschewing a material understanding of security, it is possible to locate hidden sources of insecurity in the cultural milieu. Developments in world politics throughout the 1990s suggested that a dominant American view as Cold War victor, sole superpower, and moral/political leader was beginning to take hold in the cultural domain. As policy makers, on both the center and the right,

---

70 Such a moment is argued for in a similar reading of the current attempt to push for disarmament. See, Gusterson, p. 65.

internalized this image of the United States, imperial identities became transfixed. In the aftermath of the terrorist attacks and the subsequent neo-conservative revival in the Bush Administration, this imperial identity took on a more instrumental understanding of power. No longer would the United States be limited by the concerns of international society. Wars of preemption could and should replace policies that would not seek transcendence of threat.

If this interpretation of U.S. policy makers' identities is correct, it demonstrates how a material threat as minimal as Saddam Hussein could become a growing and imminent threat in the eyes of the state. For the political constructivist, a strategic rationale need not be present in the minds of state policy makers in order for a strategic threat to be *real*. The process of securitization plays equally well with ideational moments of insecurity as it does with material moments. But, the approach taken by political constructivists does not end merely with the analysis of insecurity. The critique is highly political and meant as a form of security mitigation in its own right. By pointing to the identities of key actors and how these identities are implicated in the construction of insecurity, the securitizing effect is questioned. Once the state interpretation is suspected of being incapable of offering enhanced security, the realist interpretation re-emerges.

By recognizing both realist and political constructivist critiques as necessary for an analysis of U.S. policy toward Iraq, this chapter offers a balanced challenge to the rationale(s) offered by the state. It highlights the need to recognize both a negative and a positive vision of international politics. Much like the applications above that challenge the state on matters like unilateral BMD development, the drug war, and globalization, this issue requires the analyst to incorporate a varied perspective on security into a broader, more comprehensive critique.

Chapter 9

Conclusion

This project has endeavored to bring together two seemingly contradictory approaches to the study of security. To date, the discipline has yet to provide a comprehensive analysis of the multiple sources of insecurity that confronts states and a means to overcome them. Because the study of security bridges the divide between theory and policy, it is imperative that a concept of security emerge that is both philosophically coherent and policy relevant.

The multiple sources of insecurity that influence the behavior of states require analysis if more pacific (and secure) relations are to be had. Both realism and political constructivism offer necessary but incomplete understandings of these sources of insecurity. When realism and political constructivism are treated as more or less complete approaches to the study of security, the conclusions reached and policies offered are potentially harmful to the state and its citizens. Security, like Janus himself, is two-faced. When Romans placed Janus on the faces of their coins, they reminded each other of the need to cautiously look in all directions before acting. Security theorists must learn to do the same before undertaking an analysis of state policy. Both a material and an ideational consideration of the sources of insecurity are required if a state is to succeed in formulating appropriate national security strategies.

While realism necessarily demonstrates the potential dangers that could befall a state in anarchy, it cannot be considered a complete rendition of international relations. Realism provides a study of security with a proper understanding of the *material* threats that influence state behavior. Their studies are rich in detail, offering the state an appropriate theoretical lens through which to view threats and assess capabilities. But, realism is unable to account for the *ideational* sources of insecurity that also threaten the state. If realism is treated as a comprehensive approach to security management, the state can only achieve a sub-optimal level of security. In order for the precepts and principles of realism to be useful to policy makers and security analysts, realism must be conceptualized a valuable rhetorical tool to influence the policy maker. In this way, realists are the 'cautious paranoids' at the security table. Re-conceptualizing realism as a rhetorical device – what Donnelly has termed an 'orienting set of insights' or a 'philosophical orientation'[1] – it emerges as a negative disposition requiring the attention of the

---

1 Jack Donnelly, *Realism and International Relations* (Cambridge: Cambridge University Press, 2000), p. 194. See, also, pp. 75-77.

Conclusion 157

policy maker. Its principles become warnings and cautionary tales to be considered in the construction and evaluation of national security policies. Moreover, because these warnings and cautionary tales develop out of a brought theoretical discourse, they are grounded in a sophisticated logical argument. Unlike the state assessment of material threats, realists do not sell or hype their negative vision of material threats.

In this work, it has been necessary to place realism within a broader constructivist epistemology in order to understand how it serves to challenge state policy at one end of the international relations spectrum. The governing laws common to previous studies grounded in positivism become strategic constraints within the pages above. As well, 'the need for caution...' no longer becomes 'confused with the invariance or inevitability of that which demands caution.'[2] Most importantly, realism comes to be seen as part of a larger security critique.

Similarly, studies employing political constructivism cannot be considered complete renditions of national security issues. Their emphasis on identity and culture, and their alternative forms of analysis, provide a necessary understanding of ideational threats and an emancipatory moment for changing state securitization. However, these reflexive critiques do not demonstrate an understanding of the role that material threats play in national security matters or the negative consequences of ignoring those material threats. Their alternative analytic focus often rejects the traditional state 'security dilemma' and its corresponding policy needs. The consistent deconstruction of identity performances and cultural givens may provide an opportunity for the emergence of a more democratic ethos, but the state is often marginalized in the process. Such an occurrence does not fulfill the requirements of a security framework that seeks theoretical rigor *and* policy relevance. It is a necessary (but insufficient) component of a more comprehensive understanding of security. The potentially positive political vision that emerges from political constructivism balances the negative vision provided by realism and suggests an opportunity to overcome culturally constructed threats.

These rhetorical approaches become complementary tools in the analysis of security rather than contradictory paradigms. Each approach offers a partial understanding of insecurity. At each instance, the other approach is necessary in order to balance the security analysis being offered. In this way, the discipline of Security Studies is offered a more comprehensive means to understanding this 'essentially contested concept.'[3] Previous approaches, whether realist or constructivist, have placed ontological and epistemological barriers on the concept of security. Seeking to remain relevant to the policy community, realists espousing a materialist ontology and state-centric bias reduced threats to existential dangers accessible to an empiricist epistemology. In response, constructivists challenged

---

2 Ibid., p. 193.
3 Barry Buzan uses W.B. Gallie's term in his assessment of security. See, Barry Buzan, *People, States & Fear: An Agenda for International Security Studies in the Post-Cold War Era*, 2nd edition (Boulder, CO: Lynne Rienner Publishers, 1991), p. 7.

158 *Creating Insecurity*

realism by deconstructing academic texts and policy statements to uncover hidden discourses and expose traditional efforts as discursively constituted and ultimately malleable. If realism demonstrated the importance of power in the national security calculus, constructivists demonstrated its 'necessary' (re)production by actors involved in multiple speech-acts. If realists argued that a specific (material) condition – tanks, bombs, hostile protests, etc. – was an existential threat, constructivists claimed an a priori establishment of these physical 'things' in security terms.

The result for the study of security was compelling. A schism in the field separated those pursuing a traditional (state-centric and policy relevant) approach from those pursuing an investigative critique.[4] Realists could claim to participate in the 'real world' while constructivists could claim to be intellectually and morally distinguished. But, what has been the cost to the field of Security Studies and the policies of the state?

Ultimately, an investigation of the sources of insecurity must attempt to manage the crises of human existence. Security is a necessary component to the construction of the good life. In an international environment largely defined by the presence of states, security policies must be understandable to those states. Policies must be designed that manage the security needs of all the relevant states in the system. This is not a new challenge. It returns the discussion of security to the works of earlier realists. Balancing the negative vision of realism with something positive engaged Carr, Herz, and others. In this way, these scholars could 'insist on keeping 'realist' insights in dialectical tension with higher human aspirations and possibilities.'[5] The challenge of this project has been to find a framework wherein this dialectical tension can move the study of security forward. Arnold Wolfers's conclusion that 'the ideal security policy is one that would lead to a distribution of values so satisfactory to all nations that the intention to attack and with it the problem of security would be minimized,'[6] challenges students of security to more completely understand the sources of insecurity. And this means something more than arguing over the concept of security. It means analyzing, critiquing, and challenging power. It means recognizing that security analysts are political agents involved in a political process. When done well, both realism and political constructivism resist the Thrasymachian statements and policy orientations of policy makers. What I have attempted to demonstrate, however, is that when they are viewed as components of a larger project, they provide a much more comprehensive and devastating critique of state action. In today's world, the

---

4   This is an extension of David Campbell's discussion in *Writing Security*. See, David Campbell, *Writing Security: United States Foreign Policy and the Politics of Identity*, revised edition (Minneapolis, MN: University of Minnesota Press, 1998), p. 226.

5   Donnelly, p. 193.

6   Arnold Wolfers, 'National Security as an Ambiguous Symbol,' in *Discord and Collaboration: Essays on International Politics* (Baltimore, MD: The Johns Hopkins Press, 1962), p. 161.

Conclusion

159

investigation of security that balances the negative with the positive, the realist with the constructivist, is a possibility. It can be achieved by investigating issues through the lens of the 'cautious paranoid' while simultaneously investigating the same issues through the lens of the political constructivist. Both offer something valuable to a more robust understanding of security and both are required if we are to achieve a more secure future.

I applied this theoretical approach, seeking to balance realism and constructivism, to four pressing security issues that currently animate U.S. security discourse. The discussions concerning unilateral BMD deployment, the drug war in Colombia, globalization and protests from below, and the decision to go to war in Iraq suggest that a more robust analysis of each issue – balancing the concerns of realists and political constructivists – can improve our understanding of the security problem and present a stronger critique of the official state policy. Such findings are important because, as has been discussed above, the state represents the most powerful international actor in the system and maintaining the state as the central focus of security studies commits this approach to a policy relevant critique. As the study of security bridges both theoretical inquiry and state policy considerations, this work has attempted to remain firmly attuned to the world-view of the state. To reiterate, if the concept of security is to resonate, then it must be applicable to the political units capable of producing system-wide effects because of their policies.

Because the United States represents the most powerful actor in international relations, it is important to examine how its security policies are created and transformed. As chapters five through eight suggest, the United States has, paradoxically, created insecurity while attempting to manage its security concerns. A balanced approach combining material and ideational issues offers a more rigorous test for policies designed to enhance national security. By combining realist and political constructivist positions on any given issue, analysts and policy makers are required to contemplate the requirements of two very different political visions.

Such an undertaking is far from complete. Additional studies might employ a similar approach in order to investigate other issues designated 'security' topics by relevant actors. The official American position towards non-nuclear rogues (Cuba, Libya, Syria, and possibly Venezuela) suggests a need to balance concern for their material capabilities with an understanding of the U.S. construction of these states as *antagonistic actors*. This requires that the security analyst look both to the material interests and the ideational identities of the United States. In addition, American policy in the Middle East requires a thoroughgoing analysis employing a more comprehensive approach to security. A realist critique of state policy in the Middle East (one which measures the material capabilities of the states in the region and demonstrates how regional balance of power issues influence state behavior) could be complemented by a political constructivist interpretation of U.S. self/other constructs. Such a study could demonstrate how the works of Edward

160 *Creating Insecurity*

Said, Noam Chomsky, and David Campbell,[7] might be supplemented by a realist discussion of U.S. interests in the region. As the applications to this approach have suggested, an investigation of this matter might bring about a more coherent policy package that offers the United States an opportunity to promote and encourage a more democratic ethos at home and abroad.

If this is deemed successful in demonstrating how the United States creates insecurity by not fully understanding its security environment, it might also be used to investigate security considerations for other states in the world. Regional hegemons, as well as minor powers, might benefit from a more comprehensive understanding of their relative power capabilities *and* their identity performances. A balanced understanding of the sources of insecurity provides a deeper critique of the security problematique that emerges.

Such an approach might prove valuable to states in the Middle East. For example, the Israeli need for military defense might be examined in light of the Palestinian need for basic, ontological security. The existential conditions for most Palestinians resemble the conditions present in South African townships during Apartheid[8] or the conditions of peasant communities in rural Colombia today.[9] A robust study involving Israel and its neighbors might improve the regional security environment by balancing realist and political constructivist interpretations. It would challenge Israel to recognize how Palestinian ontological security is a prerequisite for Israeli national security. Similarly, it would challenge Palestinians to recognize the security needs of Israel as fundamentally important to their own security environment.

In other regions, a study employing this discussion may prove useful as well. The security situation between India and Pakistan continues to deteriorate. Since both sides have refused to engage in a consistent and meaningful political dialogue, deciding instead to propagate a military understanding of their security interests, their separate understandings of the situation remains dangerously incomplete. The framework developed here provides a way for these states to investigate both the material and cultural sources of their shared insecurity.

---

7   See, for instance, Edward Said, *Orientalism* (New York: Pantheon Books, 1978); Edward Said and Christopher Hitchens, *Blaming the Victims: Spurious Scholarship and the Palestinian Question* (London: Verso Books, 1988); Noam Chomsky, *The Fateful Triangle: The United States, Israel, and the Palestinians* (Boston, MA: South End Press, 1983); and David Campbell, *Politics Without Principle: Sovereignty, Ethics, and the Narratives of the Gulf War* (Boulder, CO: Lynne Rienner Publishers, 1993).

8   See, for example, Fred T. Hendricks, *The Pillars of Apartheid: Land Tenure, Rural Planning, and the Chieftancy* (Uppsala, Sweden: Academiae Ubsaliensus, 1990); and David M. Smith, *Apartheid in South Africa* (Cambridge: Cambridge University Press, 1990).

9   A recent discussion of the plight of Colombia's indigenous communities is Garry M. Leech, 'No Sympathy for Either Side: Indigenous Communities Try to Survive,' *NACLA Report on the Americas* 35 (May/June 2002), pp. 53-54.

Conclusion 161

Perhaps Simon Dalby is most accurate, contending that the current debate in the field finds scholars 'contesting an essential concept.'[10] Security is, indeed, an essential concept. Without security, humans are unable to search for, obtain, or even imagine the good life. Dalby summarizes the issue convincingly:

> *security* is a crucial term, both in the political lexicon of state policy makers and among academics in the field of international relations. Precisely because of the salience of security, the current debates about reformulating it provide, when read as political discourse in need of analysis rather than as a series of solutions to problems, a very interesting way to come to grips with what is at stake in current debates around world politics and the constitution of the post-Cold War political order.[11]

The challenge for scholars is to conceptualize security in such a way that human beings are brought back in. The state, to be sure, is the primary guarantor of security in the world today. This requires recognition of where the theorist sits in relation to the state and what the theorist can do in resisting unsatisfactory claims of state *securitization*. By recognizing the Janus-like quality of security, scholars can come to understand the need to balance material threats with those constructed through repetitive identity performances.

---

10 Simon Dalby, 'Contesting an Essential Concept: Reading the Dilemmas in Contemporary Security Discourse,' in *Critical Security Studies*, Keith Krause and Michael C. Williams, eds. (Minneapolis, MN: University of Minnesota Press, 1997), pp. 3-31.

11 Ibid., p. 5.

Bibliography

Aburish, Saïd K. *Saddam Hussein: The Politics of Revenge*. New York: Bloomsbury Publishing, 2000.

Adams, Benson D. *Ballistic Missile Defense*. New York: American Elsevier Publishing Company, 1971.

Agrawal, Subhash. 'NMD: India's Curious Response.' *Far East Economic Review* 14 June 2001: 34.

Archibugi, Daniele; Held, David; and Köhler, Martin. *Re-imagining Political Community: Studies in Cosmopolitan Democracy*. Stanford, CA: Stanford University Press, 1998.

Arfi, Badredine. 'Ethnic Fear: The Social Construction of Security.' *Security Studies* 8 (Autumn 1998): 151-203.

Art, Robert J. 'American Foreign Policy and the Fungibility of Force.' *Security Studies* 5 (Summer 1996): 7-42.

Bagley, Bruce Michael. 'Colombia and the War on Drugs.' *Foreign Affairs* 67 (Fall 1988): 70-92.

_____. 'Dateline Drug Wars: Colombia: The Wrong Strategy.' *Foreign Policy* 77 (Winter 1989-90): 154-171.

_____. 'The New Hundred Years War? U.S. National Security and the War on Drugs in Latin America.' *Journal of InterAmerican Studies and World Affairs* 30 (Spring 1988): 161-182.

Bagley, Bruce Michael, and Tokatlian, Juan G. 'Explaining the Failure of U.S.-Latin American Drug Policies.' In *The United States and Latin America in the 1990s: Beyond the Cold War*, pp. 214-234. Edited by Jonathan Hartlyn, Lars Schoultz, and Augusto Varas. Chapel Hill, NC: The University of North Carolina Press, 1992.

Bahgat, Gawdat. 'The Iraqi Quagmire: What is Next?' *Contemporary Security Policy* 23 (August 2002): 135-148.

Barkawi, Tarak, and Laffey, Mark. *Democracy, Liberalism, and War: Rethinking the Democratic Peace Debate*. Boulder, CO: Lynne Rienner Publishers, 2001.

Bartelson, Jens. *A Genealogy of Sovereignty*. Cambridge: Cambridge University Press, 1995.

Ben-Ze'ev, Aaron. 'Is There a Problem in Explaining Cognitive Process?' In *Rethinking Knowledge: Reflections Across the Disciplines*, pp. 41-56. Edited by Robert F. Goodman and Walter R. Fisher. Albany, NY: State University of New York Press, 1995.

Berlin, Isaiah. 'Two Concepts of Liberty.' In *Liberalism and its Critics*, pp. 15-36. Edited by Michael Sandel. New York: New York University Press, 1984.

Betts, Richard K. 'Heavenly Gains or Earthly Losses?: Toward a Balance Sheet for Strategic Defense.' In *The Strategic Defense Initiative: Shield or Snare?* Edited by Harold Brown. Boulder, CO: Westview Press and The Johns Hopkins Policy Institute, School of Advanced International Studies, 1987; reprint ed. Washington, DC: The Brookings Institute, 1988.

_____. 'Suicide From Fear of Death? (Possible War Between the U.S. and Iraq).' *Foreign Affairs* 82 (January/February 2003): 34-43.

Bienefeld, Manfred. 'Capitalism and the Nation State in the Dog Days of the Twentieth Century.' *Socialist Register* (1994): 94-129.

Bibliography

Booth, Ken. 'Security and Self: Reflections of a Fallen Realist.' *Critical Security Studies*, pp. 83-119. Edited by Keith Krause and Michael C. Williams. Minneapolis, MN: University of Minnesota Press, 1997.

Bowen, Wyn Q. 'Missile Defence and the Transatlantic Security Relationship.' *International Affairs* 77, 3 (2001): 485-507.

Boyd, Graham. 'The New Drug War is the New Jim Crow.' *NACLA: Report on the Americas* 35 (July/August 2001): 18-22.

Brooke, James. 'Greenlanders Wary of a New Role in U.S. Defenses.' *New York Times* 18 September 2000: A6.

Brown, Harold. *Thinking About National Security: Defense and Foreign Policy in a Dangerous World*. Boulder, CO: Westview Press, 1983.

Brown, Seyom. *The Causes and Prevention of War*. 2nd ed. New York: St. Martin's Press, 1994.

Buzan, Barry. *People, States & Fear: An Agenda For International Security Studies in the Post-Cold War Era*. 2nd edition. Boulder, CO: Lynne Rienner Publishers, 1991.

————. 'From International System to International Society: Structural Realism and Regime Theory Meet the English School.' *International Organization* 47 (Summer 1993): 327-351.

Buzan, Barry; Jones, Charles; and Little, Richard. *The Logic of Anarchy: Neorealism to Structural Realism*. New York: Columbia University Press, 1993.

Buzan, Barry; Wæver, Ole; and de Wilde, Jaap. *Security: A New Framework for Analysis*. Boulder, CO: Lynne Rienner Publishers, 1998.

Campbell, David. *Politics Without Principle: Sovereignty, Ethics, and the Narratives of the Gulf War*. Boulder, CO: Lynne Rienner Publishers, 1993.

————. 'Violent Performances: Identity, Sovereignty, Responsibility.' *The Return of Culture and Identity in IR Theory*, pp. 163-180. Edited by Yosef Lapid and Friedrich Kratochwil. Boulder, CO: Lynne Rienner Publishers, 1996.

————. *Writing Security: United States Foreign Policy and the Politics of Identity*. Revised edition. Minneapolis, MN: University of Minnesota Press, 1998.

Cannistraro, Vincent. 'Terror's Undiminished Threat.' *Foreign Policy* 137 (July/August 2003): 69.

Carr, Craig L. 'Fairness and Political Obligation.' *Social Theory and Practice* 28 (January 2002): 1-28.

Carr, Craig L., and Scott, Gary L. 'The Libyan Raid: A Strategic Consequentialist Perspective.' *Crossroads* 31 (1990): 37-47.

Carr, Edward Hallett. *The Twenty Years' Crisis, 1919-1939: An Introduction to the Study of International Relations*. 2nd ed. New York: Harper and Row, Publishers, 1964.

Chafetz, Glenn; Spirtas, Michael; and Frankel, Benjamin. 'Introduction: Tracing the Influence of Identity on Foreign Policy.' *Security Studies* 8 (Winter 1998/9 – Spring 1999): vii-xxii.

Chernick, Marc. 'Elusive Peace.' *NACLA Report on the Americas* 34 (September/October 2000): 32-37.

Chomsky, Noam. *The Fateful Triangle: The United States, Israel, and the Palestinians*. Boston, MA: South End Press, 1983.

Clark, Grenville, and Sohn, Louis B. *World Peace through World Law*. Cambridge, MA: Harvard University Press, 1960.

Clark, Ian. *Globalization and International Relations Theory*. Oxford: Oxford University Press, 1999.

Cooper, Marc. 'Plan Colombia: Wrong Issue, Wrong Enemy, Wrong Country.' *The Nation* 272, 11 (March 19, 2001): 11-18.

164 *Creating Insecurity*

Copeland, Dale C. 'The Constructivist Challenge to Structural Realism: A Review Essay.' *International Security* 25 (Fall 2000): 187-212.

Cordesman, Anthony H. *Strategic Threats and National Missile Defenses: Defending the U.S. Homeland.* Westport, CT: Praeger Publishers, 2002.

Cox, Robert W. 'Social Forces, States and World Orders: Beyond International Relations Theory.' In *Neorealism and Its Critics*, pp. 204-254. Edited by Robert O. Keohane. New York: Columbia University Press, 1986.

Crandall, Russell. 'Clinton, Bush and Plan Colombia.' *Survival: The IISS Quarterly* 44 (Spring 2002): 159-172.

Crandall, Russell. *Driven by Drugs: US Policy Toward Colombia.* Boulder, CO: Lynne Rienner Publishers, 2002.

Cumings, Bruce. 'War, Security, and Democracy in East Asia.' In *Democracy, Liberalism, and War: Rethinking the Democratic Peace Debate*, pp. 129-152. Edited by Tarak Barkawi and Mark Laffey. Boulder, CO: Lynne Rienner Publishers, 2001.

Dalby, Simon. 'Contesting an Essential Concept: Reading the Dilemmas in Contemporary Security Discourse.' In *Critical Security Studies*, pp. 3-31. Edited by Keith Krause and Michael C. Williams. Minneapolis, MN: University of Minnesota Press, 1997.

Danaher, Kevin. *Democratizing the Global Economy: the Battle against the World Bank and International Monetary Fund.* Monroe, ME: Common Courage Press, 2001.

Dean, Mitchell. *Governmentality – Power and Rule in Modern Society.* London: Sage Publishing, 1999.

DeMartino, George. *Global Economy, Global Justice: Theoretical Objections and Policy Alternatives to Neoliberalism.* London: Routledge Press, 2000.

Der Derian, James. 'The Value of Security: Hobbes, Marx, Nietzsche, and Baudrillard.' In *On Security*, pp. 24-45. Edited by Ronnie Lipschutz. New York: Columbia University Press, 1995.

Deudney, Daniel H. 'Political Fission: State Structure, Civil Society, and Nuclear Security Politics in the United States.' In *On Security*, pp. 87-123. Edited by Ronnie Lipschutz. New York: Columbia University Press, 1995.

_____. 'Regrounding Realism: Anarchy, Security, and Changing Material Contexts.' *Security Studies* 10 (Autumn 2000): 1-42.

Deutch, John; Brown, Harold; and White, John P. 'National Missile Defense: Is There Another Way?' *Foreign Policy* (Summer 2000): 91-100.

Donnelly, Jack. *Realism and International Relations.* Cambridge: Cambridge University Press, 2000.

Donohue, George L. *Star Wars: A Case Study of Marginal Cost Analysis and Weapon System Technology.* Santa Monica, CA: RAND, 1994.

Doyle, Michael W. 'Liberalism and World Politics.' *American Political Science Review* 80 (December 1986): 1151-1169.

Drell, Sidney; Farley, Philip J.; and Holloway, David. 'Preserving the ABM Treaty: A Critique of the Reagan Strategic Defense Initiative.' In *The Star Wars Controversy*, pp. 57-97. Edited by Steven E. Miller and Stephen Van Evera. Princeton, NJ: Princeton University Press, 1986.

'Drugs, Latin America, and the United States.' *The Economist* 7 February 1998: 35-36.

Dryzek, John. *Democracy in Capitalist Times.* Oxford: Oxford University Press, 1996.

Elkins, David. *Beyond Sovereignty.* Toronto, Canada: University of Toronto Press, 1995.

Elman, Colin. 'Horses for Courses: Why *Not* Neorealist Theories of Foreign Policy?' *Security Studies* 6 (Autumn 1996): 7-53.

Farer, Tom. *Transnational Crime in the Americas: An Inter-American Dialogue Book.* New York: Routledge, 1999.

Bibliography 165

Farouk-Sluglett, Marion, and Slugett, Peter. *Iraq Since 1958: From Revolution to Dictatorship*. Revised ed. London: I.B. Tauris Publishers, 2001.

Ferguson, Yale H., and Mansbach, Richard W. *The Elusive Quest: Theory and International Politics*. Columbia, SC: University of South Carolina Press, 1988.

————. 'The Past as Prelude to the Future?: Identities and Loyalties in Global Politics.' In *The Return of Culture and Identity in IR Theory*, pp. 21-44. Edited by Yosef Lapid and Friedrich Kratochwil. Boulder, CO: Lynne Rienner Publishers, 1996.

Fierke, Karin M. 'Critical Methodology and Constructivism.' In *Constructing International Relations: The Next Generation*, pp. 115-135. Edited by Karin M. Fierke and Knud Erik Jorgensen. Armonk, NY: M.E. Sharpe, 2001.

Fierke, Karin M., and Jorgensen, Knud Erik. *Constructing International Relations: The Next Generation*. Armonk, NY: M.E. Sharpe, 2001.

Finnemore, Martha. *National Interests in International Society*. Ithaca, NY: Cornell University Press, 1996.

Foucault, Michel. *Discipline and Punish: The Birth of the Prison*. New York: Vintage Books, 1977.

————. *Power/Knowledge*. New York: Pantheon Books, 1980.

Frederking, Brian. *Resolving Security Dilemmas: A Constructivist Explanation of the INF Treaty*. Aldershot, UK: Ashgate Publishing, 2000.

Friedman, Thomas L. 'The Rumsfeld Defense.' Editorial. *New York Times* 13 July 2001, sec. 1, p. A21.

Fuller, Steve. 'The Reflexive Politics of Constructivism.' *History of the Human Sciences* 7, 1 (1994): 87-93.

Gaddis, John Lewis. 'International Relations and the End of the Cold War.' *International Security* 17 (Winter 1992/93): 5-58.

Galbraith, James K. 'Missile Defense: A Deadly Danger.' *Dissent* (Summer 2001): 5-7.

Gamarra, Eduardo. 'Bolivia.' In *International Handbook on Drug Control*, pp. 101-119. Edited By Scott B. MacDonald and Bruce Zagaris. Westport, CT: Greenwood Press, 1992.

Garfinkel, Harold. *Studies in Ethnomethodology*. Newark, NJ: Prentice Hall, 1967.

George, Jim. *Discourses of Global Politics: A Critical (Re)Introduction to International Relations*. Boulder, CO: Lynne Rienner Publishers, 1993.

Ghosh, Amitav. 'The Anglophone Empire.' *New Yorker* 7 April 2003: 46.

————. 'Imperial Temptation.' *The Nation* 27 May 2002: 24.

Giddens, Anthony. *Sociology*. Cambridge: Cambridge University Press, 1989.

Gilbert, Alan. *Democratic Individuality*. Cambridge: Cambridge University Press, 1990.

————. *Must Global Politics Constrain Democracy?: Great-Power Realism, Democratic Peace, and Democratic Internationalism*. Princeton, NJ: Princeton University Press, 1999.

Glaser, Charles L. 'Do We Want the Missile Defenses We Can Build?' In *The Star Wars Controversy*, pp. 98-130. Edited by Steven E. Miller and Stephen Van Evera. Princeton, NJ: Princeton University Press, 1986.

————. 'Realists as Optimists: Cooperation as Self-Help.' *International Security* 19 (Winter 1994/95): 50-90.

————. 'Why Even Good Defenses May Be Bad.' In *The Star Wars Controversy*, pp. 25-56. Edited by Steven E. Miller and Stephen Van Evera. Princeton, NJ: Princeton University Press, 1986.

Glaser, Charles L., and Fetter, Steve. 'National Missile Defense and the Future of U.S. Nuclear Weapons Policy.' *International Security* 26 (Summer 2001): 40-92.

166 *Creating Insecurity*

Godson, Roy. 'Intelligence and National Security.' In *Security Studies for the 1990s*, pp. 211-235. Edited by Richard Shultz, Roy Godson, and Ted Greenwood. Washington, DC: Brassey's, 1993.

Goldfischer, David. *The Best Defense: Policy Alternatives for U.S. Nuclear Security from the 1950s to the 1990s*. Ithaca, NY: Cornell University Press, 1993.

Goldman, Emily O. 'Thinking About Strategy Absent the Enemy.' *Security Studies* 4 (Autumn 1994): 40-85.

Gordon, Michael R. 'Serving Notice of a New U.S., Poised to Hit First and Alone.' *New York Times* 27 January 2003, sec. A: 1.

Gordon, Michael R., and Miller, Judith. 'U.S. Says Hussein Intensifies Quest for A-Bomb Parts.' *New York Times* 8 September 2002, sec. A: 1.

Gordon, Philip H. 'Bush, Missile Defence and the Atlantic Alliance.' *Survival* 43 (Spring 2001): 17-36.

Green, Duncan. *Silent Revolution: The Rise of Market Economies in Latin America*. London: Cassell LAB, 1995.

Grieco, Joseph M. 'Anarchy and the Limits of Cooperation: A Realist Critique of the Newest Liberal Institutionalism.' In *Controversies in International Relations Theory: Realism and the Neoliberal Challenge*, pp. 151-171. Edited by Charles W. Kegley, Jr. New York: St. Martin's Press, 1995.

Griffith, Ivelaw L. *The Political Economy of Drugs in the Caribbean*. New York: St. Martin's Press, 2000.

Gusterson, Hugh. 'Tall Tales and Deceptive Discourses.' *Bulletin of Atomic Scientists* 57 (November/December 2001): 65-68.

Guzzini, Stefano. 'A Reconstruction of Constructivism in International Relations.' *European Journal of International Relations* 6, 2 (2000): 147-182.

Haqqani, Husain. 'Islam's Weakened Moderates.' *Foreign Policy* 137 (July/August 2003): 61-63.

_____. 'The Ripple Effect: Turkey, Pakistan, and Indonesia.' *Foreign Policy* 137 (July/August 2003): 62.

Hardt, Michael, and Negri, Antonio. *Empire*. Cambridge: Cambridge University Press, 2000.

Hendricks, Fred T. *The Pillars of Apartheid: Land Tenure, Rural Planning, and the Chieftancy*. Uppsala, Sweden: Academiae Ubsaliensus, 1990.

Herz, John H. 'Idealist Internationalism and the Security Dilemma.' *World Politics* 2 (January 1950): 157-180.

_____. *Political Realism and Political Liberalism*. Chicago: University of Chicago Press, 1951.

Hirst, Paul. From *Statism to Pluralism: Democracy, Civil Society, and Global Politics*. London: UCL Press, 1997.

Hitchens, Christopher. 'Farewell to the Helmsman.' *Foreign Policy Magazine* (September/October 2001): 68-71.

Hodgson, Martin. 'The Coca Leaf War.' *The Bulletin of the Atomic Scientists* 56 (May/June 2000): 36-45.

Hoge, Warren. 'Blair Says Iraqis Could Launch Chemical Warheads in Minutes.' *New York Times* 25 September 2002, sec. A: 1.

Hollis, Martin, and Smith, Steve. *Explaining and Understanding International Relations*. Oxford: Clarendon Press, 1990.

Holsti, Kalevi J. *The State, War, and the State of War*. Cambridge: Cambridge University Press, 1996.

Bibliography

Hopf, Ted. 'The Promise of Constructivism in International Relations Theory.' *International Security* 23 (Summer 1998): 171-200.

Hurrell, Andrew. 'Security and Inequality.' In *Inequality, Globalization, and World Politics*, pp. 248-271. Edited by Andrew Hurrell and Ngaire Woods. Oxford: Oxford University Press, 1999.

Huth, Paul K. 'Reputations and Deterrence: A Theoretical and Empirical Assessment.' *Security Studies* 7 (Autumn 1997): 72-99.

Huxley, Thomas H. *Evolution and Ethics and Other Essays*. New York: Appleton, 1896.

Huysmans, Jef. 'Security! What Do You Mean?: From Concept to Thick Signifier.' *European Journal of International Relations* 4, 2 (1998): 226-255.

Ikenberry, G. John. *After Victory: Institutions, Strategic Restraint, and the Rebuilding of Order After Major Wars*. Princeton: Princeton University Press, 2001.

'Intelligence and Iraq: The War Isn't Over for Tony.' *The Economist* 12 July 2003: 49.

'Iraq, Niger, and Uranium: Spies Fall Out.' *The Economist* 12 July 2003: 50.

Ivanov, Igor. 'The Missile-Defense Mistake: Undermining Strategic Stability and the ABM Treaty.' *Foreign Affairs* 79 (September/October 2000): 15-20.

Jackson, Robert H. *Quasi-states: Sovereignty, International Relations and the Third World*. Cambridge University Press, 1990.

_____. 'The Security Dilemma in Africa.' In *The Insecurity Dilemma: National Security of Third World States*, pp. 75-97. Edited by Brian L. Job. Boulder, CO: Lynne Rienner, Publishers, 1992.

Jentleson, Bruce W. *American Foreign Policy: The Dynamics of Choice in the 21st Century.* New York: W. W. Norton & Company, 2000.

Jepperson, Ronald L.; Wendt, Alexander; and Katzenstein, Peter J. 'Norms, Identity, and Culture in National Security.' In *The Culture of National Security*, pp. 33-75. Edited by Peter J. Katzenstein. New York: Columbia University Press, 1996.

Job, Brian L. 'The Insecurity Dilemma: National, Regime, and State Insecurities in the Third World.' in *The Insecurity Dilemma: National Security of Third World States*. Boulder, CO: Lynne Rienner Publishers, 1992.

Johnson, Chalmers. *Blowback: The Costs and Consequences of American Empire*. New York: Henry Holt and Company, 2000.

Johnston, David, and Van Natta, Don. 'U.S. Focuses on Iraqi Links to Group Allied to Al Qaeda.' *New York Times* 30 January 2003, sec. A: 9.

Jordan, Amos A., and Taylor, William J. *American National Security: Policy and Process*. Revised ed. Baltimore, MD: The Johns Hopkins University Press, 1984.

Jorgensen, Knud Erik. 'Four Levels and a Discipline.' In *Constructing International Relations: The Next Generation*, pp. 36-53. Edited by Karin M. Fierke and Knud Erik Jorgensen. Armonk, NY: M.E. Sharpe, 2001.

Katzenstein, Peter J. *The Culture of National Security: Norms and Identity in World Politics*. New York: Columbia University Press, 1996.

_____. 'Introduction: Alternative Perspectives on National Security.' In *The Culture of National Security*, pp. 1-32. Edited by Peter J. Katzenstein. New York: Columbia University Press, 1996.

Keck, Margaret, and Sikkink, Kathryn. *Activists Beyond Borders: Advocacy Networks in International Politics*. Ithaca, NY: Cornell University Press, 1998.

Kegley, Charles W. *Controversies in International Relations: Realism and the Neoliberal Challenge*. New York: St. Martin's Press, 1995.

Kennan, George F. *American Diplomacy*, expanded edition. Chicago: University of Chicago Press, 1984.

_____. 'From World War to Cold War.' *American Heritage* 46 (December 1995): 42-58.

168   *Creating Insecurity*

_____. *Realities of American Foreign Policy*. Princeton: Princeton University Press, 1954.

Keohane, Robert O. *Neorealism and Its Critics*. New York: Columbia University Press, 1986.

Keohane, Robert O., and Nye, Joseph S. *Power and Interdependence: World Politics in Transition*. Boston: Little, Brown, 1977.

Klare, Michael T. 'Permanent Preeminence: U.S. Strategic Policy for the 21st Century.' *NACLA Report on the Americas* 34 (November/December 2000): 8-15.

_____. 'The Two-War Strategy.' *The Nation* 257, 10 (1993): 347-351.

Knobel, Dale T. *'America for the Americans' The Nativist Movement in the United States*. New York: Twayne Publishers, 1996.

Kowert, Paul. 'National Identity: Inside and Outside.' *Security Studies* 8 (Winter 1998/9 – Spring 1999): 1-34.

_____. 'Toward a Constructivist Theory of Foreign Policy.' In *Foreign Policy in a Constructed World*, pp. 266-287. Edited by Vendulka Kulbalkova. Armonk, NY: M.E.Sharpe, 2001.

Kowert, Paul, and Legro, Jeffrey. 'Norms, Identity, and Their Limits: A Theoretical Reprise.' In *The Culture of National Security*, pp. 451-497. Edited by Peter J. Katzenstein. New York: Columbia University Press, 1996.

Kratochwil, Friedrich. 'Citizenship: On the Border of Order.' In *The Return of Culture and Identity in IR Theory*, pp. 181-197. Edited by Yosef Lapid and Friedrich Kratochwil. Boulder, CO: Lynne Rienner Publishers, 1996.

Krause, Keith, and Williams, Michael C. *Critical Security Studies*. Minneapolis, MN: University of Minnesota Press, 1997.

Krepon, Michael. 'Moving Away from MAD.' *Survival* 43 (Summer 2001): 81-95.

Kryzanek, Michael J. *Leaders, Leadership, and U.S. Policy in Latin America*. Boulder, CO: Westview Press, 1992.

Kubalkova, Vendulka; Onuf, Nicholas; and Kowert, Paul. *International Relations in a Constructed World*. Armonk, New York: M.E. Sharpe, 1998.

Kubalkova, Vendulka, and Pettman, Ralph. *Foreign Policy in a Constructed World*. Armonk, NY: M.E. Sharpe, 2001.

Laclau, Ernesto, and Mouffe, Chantal. *Hegemony and Socialist Strategy: Towards a Radical Democratic Politics*. Translated by Winston Moore and Paul Cammack. London: Verso Books, 1985.

Lake David A. 'Ulysses's Triumph: American Power and the New World Order.' *Security Studies* 8 (Summer 1999): 44-78.

Landler, Mark, and Cowell, Alan. 'Powell, in Europe, Nearly Dismisses UN's Iraq Report.' *New York Times* 27 January 2003, sec. A: 1.

Lapid, Yosef. 'Culture's Ship: Returns and Departures in International Relations Theory.' In *The Return of Culture and Identity in IR Theory*, pp. 3-20. Edited by Yosef Lapid and Friedrich Kratochwil. Boulder, CO: Lynne Rienner Publishers, 1996.

_____. 'The Third Debate: On the Prospects of International Theory in a Post-Postivist Era.' *International Studies Quarterly* 33 (1989): 235-254.

Lapid, Yosef, and Kratochwil, Friedrich. *The Return of Culture and Identity in IR Theory*. Boulder, CO: Lynne Rienner Publishers, 1996.

Layne, Christopher. 'Kant or Cant: The Myth of the Democratic Peace.' *International Security* 19 (Fall 1994): 5-49.

Lazare, Daniel. 'A Battle Against Reason, Democracy and Drugs: The Drug War Deciphered.' *NACLA Report on the Americas* 35 (July/August 2001): 13-18.

Leech, Garry M. 'No Sympathy for Either Side: Indigenous Communities Try to Survive.' *NACLA Report on the Americas* 35 (May/June 2002): 53-54.

Legro, Jeffrey W., and Moravcsik, Andrew. 'Faux Realism: Spin Versus Substance in the Bush Foreign-Policy Doctrine.' *Foreign Policy* 125 (July/August 2001): 80-82.

LeoGrande, William M., and Sharpe, Kenneth E. 'Two Wars or One? Drugs, Guerrillas, and Colombia's New Violencia.' *World Policy Journal* 17 (Fall 2000): 1-11.

Levine, Robert A. 'Deterrence and the ABM: Retreading the Old Calculus.' *World Policy Journal* (Fall 2001): 23-31.

Lewis, George; Gronlund, Lisbeth; and Wright, David. 'National Missile Defense: An Indefensible System.' *Foreign Policy* (Winter 1999-2000): 120-137.

Lindsay, James M., and O'Hanlon, Michael E. *Defending America: The Case for Limited National Missile Defense.* Washington, DC: Brookings Institution Press, 2001.

Lippmann, Walter. *The Cold War.* New York: Harper and Brothers Press, 1947.

Lipschutz, Ronnie. 'The Clash of Governmentalities: The Fall of the UN Republic and America's Reach for Empire.' *Contemporary Security Policy* 23 (December 2002): 214-231.

_____. *On Security.* New York: Columbia University Press, 1995.

Lynn-Jones, Sean M. 'Offense-Defense Theory and Its Critics.' *Security Studies* 4 (Summer 1995): 660-91.

Mabry, Donald. *The Latin American Narcotics Trade and U.S. National Security.* New York: Greenwood Press, 1989.

MacDonald, Scott B. 'Colombia.' In *International Handbook on Drug Control.* Westport, CT: Greenwood Press, 1992.

MacDonald, Scott B. and Zagaris, Bruce. *International Handbook on Drug Control.* Westport, CT: Greenwood Press, 1992.

Macpherson, C.B. *Democratic Theory: Essays in Retrieval.* Oxford: Oxford University Press, 1973.

McSherry, J. Patrice. 'Preserving Hegemony: National Security Doctrine in the Post-Cold War Era.' *NACLA Report of the Americas* 34 (November/December 2000): 26-34.

McSweeney, Bill. *Security, Identity and Interests: A Sociology of International Relations.* Cambridge: Cambridge University Press, 1999.

Mann, Michael. *The Sources of Social Power.* Cambridge: Cambridge University Press, 1986.

Martin, Hans-Peter, and Schumann, Harald. *The Global Trap: Globalization and the Assault on Democracy and Prosperity.* London: Zed Books, 1996.

Mattern, Janice Bially. 'The Power Politics of Identity.' *European Journal of International Relations* 7, 3 (2001): 349-397.

Mearsheimer, John J. 'The False Promise of International Institutions.' *International Security* 19 (Winter 1994/95): 5-49.

_____. *The Tragedy of Great Power Politics.* New York: WW Norton and Company, 2001.

Mearsheimer, John J., and Walt, Stephen M. 'An Unnecessary War.' *Foreign Policy* 134 (January/February 2003): 51-59.

Menon, Anand. *France, NATO and the Limits of Independence 1981-97: The Politics of Ambivalence.* New York: St. Martin's Press, 2000.

Mercer, Jonathan. 'Anarchy and Identity.' *International Organization* 49 (Spring 1995): 229-252.

Michaels, Walter Benn. *Our America: Nativism, Modernism and Pluralism.* Durham, NC: Duke University Press, 1995.

170 *Creating Insecurity*

Miller, Steven E. 'The Flawed Case for Missile Defence.' *Survival* 43 (Autumn 2001): 95-110.

Miller, Steven E., and Van Evera, Stephen. *The Star Wars Controversy*. Princeton, NJ: Princeton University Press, 1986.

Milliken, Jennifer. 'Discourse Study: Brining Rigor to Critical Theory.' In *Constructing International Relations: The Next Generation*, pp. 136-159. Edited by Karin M. Fierke and Knud Erik Jorgensen. Armonk, NY: M.E. Sharpe, 2001.

Molano, Alfredo. 'The Evolution of the FARC.' *NACLA Report on the Americas* 34 (September/October 2000): 23-31.

Morgenthau, Hans J. 'Another "Great Debate": The National Interest of the United States.' *American Political Science Review* 46 (December 1952): 961-988.

_____. 'The Mainsprings of American Foreign Policy: The National Interest vs. Moral Abstractions.' *American Political Science Review* 44 (December 1950): 833-854.

_____. *Politics Among Nations: The Struggle for Power and Peace.* 5th ed. New York: Alfred A. Knopf, 1972.

_____. *Politics in the Twentieth Century: The Impasse of American Foreign Policy.* Vol. 2. Chicago: University of Chicago Press, 1962.

_____. *Truth and Power: Essays of a Decade 1960-1970.* New York: Praeger Publishers, 1970.

Muppidi, Himadeep. 'State Identity and Interstate Practices: The Limits of Democratic Peace in South Asia.' In *Democracy, Liberalism, and War: Rethinking the Democratic Peace Debate*, pp. 45-66. Edited by Tarak Barkawi and Mark Laffey. Boulder, CO: Lynne Rienner Publishers, 2001.

Nader, Ralph, and Wallach, Lori. 'GATT, NAFTA, and the Subversion of the Democratic Process.' In *The Case Against the Global Economy*, pp. 92-107. Edited by Jerry Mander and Edward Goldsmith. San Francisco, CA: Sierra Club Books, 1996.

Neufeld, Mark. 'Reflexivity and International Relations Theory.' *Millennium: Journal of International Studies* 22 (Spring 1993): 54-61.

Newhouse, John. 'The Missile Defense Debate.' *Foreign Affairs* 80 (July/August 2001): 97-109.

Nye, Joseph S., Jr. *Understanding International Conflicts: An Introduction to Theory and History.* New York: Addison Wesley Longman, 2000.

Onuf, Nicholas G. 'Constructivism: A User's Manual.' In *International Relations in a Constructed World*, pp. 58-78. Edited by Vendulka Kubalkova, Nicholas Onuf, and Paul Kowert. Armonk, NY: M.E. Sharpe, 1998.

_____. 'The Politics of Constructivism.' In *Constructing International Relations: The Next Generation*, pp. 236-254. Edited by Karin M. Fierke and Knud Erik Jorgensen. Armonk, NY: M.E. Sharpe, 2001.

_____. *World of Our Making: Rules and Rule in Social Theory and International Relations.* Columbia, SC: University of South Carolina Press, 1989.

Pagedas, Constantine A. *Anglo-American Strategic Relations and the French Problem 1960-1963.* London: Frank Cass Publishers, 2000.

Pardo, Rafael. 'Colombia's Two-Front War.' *Foreign Affairs* 79 (July/August 2000): 64-73.

Perl, Raphael F. *Drugs and Foreign Policy: A Critical Review.* Boulder, CO: Westview Press, 1994.

Pettman, Ralph. 'Commonsense Constructivism and Foreign Policy: A Critique of Rule-Oriented Constructivism.' In *Foreign Policy in a Constructed World*, pp. 249-265. Edited by Vendulka Kubalkova. Armonk, NY: M.E. Sharpe, 2001.

_____. *Commonsense Constructivism or the Making of World Affairs.* Armonk, NY: M.E. Sharpe, 2000.

Bibliography

171

Pitkin, Hanna Fenichel. *Wittgenstein and Justice: On the Significance of Ludwig Wittgenstein for Social and Political Thought.* Berkeley, CA: University of California Press, 1972.

Poku, Nana, and Graham, David T. *Redefining Security: Population Movements and National Security.* Westport, CT: Praeger Publishers, 1998.

Porter, Gareth, and Brown, Janet Welsh. *Global Environmental Politics.* 2nd ed. Boulder CO: Westview Press, 1996.

Potter, Jonathan. *Representing Reality: Discourse, Rhetoric, and Social Construction.* London: Sage Publications, 1996.

Powell, Robert. 'Anarchy in International Relations Theory: The Neorealist-Neoliberal Debate.' *International Organization* 48 (Spring 1994): 313-44.

Pozzetta, George E. *Nativism, Discrimination, and Images of Immigrants.* New York: Garland Publishers, 1991.

Pressler, Larry. *Star Wars: The Strategic Defense Initiative Debates in Congress.* Westport, CT: Praeger Publishers, 1986.

Price, Richard, and Reus-Smit, Christian. 'Dangerous Liaisons? Critical International Theory and Constructivism.' *European Journal of International Relations* 4, 3 (1998): 259-294.

Purdum, Todd S. 'The Brains Behind Bush's War Policy.' *New York Times* 1 February 2003, sec. B: 9.

Rawson, Hugh. 'The Road to Freedom Fries.' *American Heritage* 54 (June/July 2003): 12.

Record, Jeffrey. 'The Bush Doctrine and the War with Iraq.' *Parameters* 4 (Spring 2003): 4-21.

Remmer, Karen L. 'Does Democracy Promote Interstate Cooperation?: Lessons from the Mercosur Region.' *International Studies Quarterly* 42 (March 1998): 25-52.

Richani, Nazih. 'The Paramilitary Connection.' *NACLA Report on the Americas* 34 (September/October 2000): 38-41.

_____. *Systems of Violence: The Political Economy of War and Peace in Colombia.* Albany, NY: State University of New York Press, 2002.

Risen, James, and Sanger, David E. 'After the War: CIA Uproar, New Details Emerge on Uranium Claim and Bush's Speech.' *New York Times* 18 July 2003, sec. A: 1.

Robinson, William I. 'Polyarchy: Coercion's New Face in Latin America.' *NACLA Report of the Americas* 34 (November/December 2000): 42-48.

_____. *Promoting Polyarchy: Globalization, US Intervention, and Hegemony.* Cambridge: Cambridge University Press, 1996.

Rosenau, Pauline. 'Once Again Into the Fray: International Relations Confronts the Humanities.' *Millennium: Journal of International Studies* 19 (Spring 1990): 83-110.

Rosenthal, Joel H. *Righteous Realists: Political Realism, Responsible Power, and American Culture in the Nuclear Age.* Baton Rouge, LA: Louisiana State University Press, 1991.

Ruggie, John Gerard. 'The Past as Prologue?: Interests, Identity, and Foreign Policy.' *International Security* 21 (Spring 1997): 89-126.

_____. 'What Makes the World Hold Together? Neo-Utilitarianism and the Social Constructivist Challenge.' *International Organization* 52 (Autumn 1998): 855-885.

Rummel, R. J. 'Libertarianism and International Violence.' *Journal of Conflict Resolution* 27 (March 1983): 27-71.

Rupert, Mark. 'Democracy, Peace, What's Not to Love?' In *Democracy, Liberalism, and War: Rethinking the Democratic Peace Debate,* pp. 153-172. Edited by Tarak Barkawi and Mark Laffey. Boulder, CO: Lynne Rienner Publishers, 2001.

_____. *Ideologies of Globalization: Contending Visions of a New World Order.* London: Routledge Press, 2000.

172 *Creating Insecurity*

_____. *Producing Hegemony: The Politics of Mass Production and American Global Power*. Cambridge: Cambridge University Press, 1995.

Russell, Ben. 'Conflict 'May Have Driven Muslims Into Arms of al-Qa'ida.' *The Independent* 1 August 2003.

Russett, Bruce M. *No Clear and Present Danger: A Skeptical View of the U.S. Entry into World War II*. New York: Harper & Row, Publishers, 1972.

_____. *The Prisoners of Insecurity: Nuclear Deterrence, The Arms Race, and Arms Control*. San Francisco: W.H. Freeman and Company, 1983.

_____. *What Price Vigilance?: The Burden of National Defense*. New Haven, CT: Yale University Press, 1970.

Russett, Bruce M., and Antholis, William. 'Do Democracies Fight Each Other?: Evidence from the Peloponnesian War.' *Journal of Peace Research* 4 (1992): 415-434.

Russett, Bruce M., et al. 'The Democratic Peace.' *International Security* 19 (Spring 1995): 164-184.

Said, Edward. *Orientalism*. New York: Pantheon Books, 1978.

Said, Edward, and Hitchens, Christopher. *Blaming the Victims: Spurious Scholarship and the Palestinian Question*. London: Verso Books, 1988.

Schmitt, Eric. 'Cheney Asserts No Responsible Leader Could Have Ignored Danger from Iraq.' *New York Times* 25 January 2003, sec. A: 10.

Schweller, Randall L., and Wohlforth, William C. 'Power Test: Evaluating Realism in Response to the End of the Cold War.' *Security Studies* 9 (Spring 2000): 60-107.

Sciolino, Elaine. 'France and Germany Consider Possible Roles in Postwar Iraq.' *New York Times* 29 July 2003: sec. A: 10.

Scott, Gary L., and Carr, Craig L. 'Are States Moral Agents?' *Social Theory and Practice* 12 (Spring 1986): 75-102.

Scowcroft, Brent. 'Don't Attack Iraq.' Editorial. *New York Times* 15 August 2002: sec. A: 16.

Shifter, Michael. 'The United States and Colombia: Partners in Ambiguity.' *Current History* 99 (February 2000): 51-55.

Smith, David. *Apartheid in South Africa*. Cambridge: Cambridge University Press, 1990.

Smith, Steve. 'Foreign Policy is What States Make of it: Social Construction and International Relations Theory.' In *Foreign Policy in a Constructed World*. Edited by Vendulka Kubalkova and Ralph Pettman. Armonk, NY: M.E. Sharpe, 2001.

Sprout, Harold, and Sprout, Margaret. *Toward a Politics of the Planet Earth*. New York: Van Norstrand Reinhold Company, 1971.

Tate, Winifred. 'Repeating Past Mistakes.' *NACLA Report on the Americas* 34 (September/October 2000): 16-19.

'The Government, the BBC and WMD: What Did You Do In the War, Alastair?' *The Economist* 5 July 2003: 47.

Thomas, Evan. 'The 12 Year Itch.' *Newsweek* 31 March 2003: 54-65.

Thoumi, Francisco E. 'The Impact of the Illegal Drug Industry on Colombia.' In *Transnational Crime in the Americas: An Inter-American Dialogue Book*, pp. 117-142. Edited by Tom Farer. London: Routledge, 1999.

Tokatlian, Juan G. 'Colombian Catastrophe.' *The World Today* 56 (January 2000): 13-16.

_____. 'National Security and Drugs: Their Impact on Colombian-U.S. Relations.' *Journal of InterAmerican Studies and World Affairs* 30 (Spring 1988): 133-160.

Tritten, James J. 'America Promises to Come Back: the President's New National Security Strategy.' *Security Studies* 1 (Winter 1991): 173-234.

Tuchman Mathews, Jessica. 'Now for the Hard Part.' *Foreign Policy* 137 (July/August 2003): 51.

Bibliography

173

_____. 'Redefining Security.' *Foreign Affairs* 68 (Spring 1982): 162-177.

Ullman, Richard. 'Redefining Security.' *International Security* 8 (Summer 1983): 129-153.

United States Department of State. *A Democratic Vision of Security*. By Elliott Abrams. Current Policy No. 844. Washington, DC: Government Printing Office, 1986.

_____. *An End to Tyranny in Latin America*, By Elliott Abrams. Current Policy No. 777. Washington, DC: Government Printing Office, 1986.

_____. *U.S. Interests and Resource Needs in Latin America and the Caribbean*, By Elliott Abrams. Current Policy No. 932. Washington, DC: Government Printing Office, 1987.

Van Evera, Stephen. 'American Intervention in the Third World: Less Would Be Better.' *Security Studies* 1 (Autumn 1991): 1-24.

_____. 'Preface.' In *The Star Wars Controversy: An International Security Reader*, pp. ix-xxi. Edited by Steven E. Miller and Stephen Van Evera. Princeton, NJ: Princeton University Press, 1986.

Vargas Meza, Ricardo. 'Biowarfare in Colombia?' *NACLA Report on the Americas* 34 (September/October 2000): 20-22.

_____. *The Revolutionary Armed Forces of Colombia (FARC) and the Illicit Drug Trade*. Cochabamba, Bolivia: Accion Andina, June 1999.

Vasquez, John, ed. *Classics of International Relations*. Englewood Cliffs, NJ: Prentice-Hall, 1986.

Vasquez, Laura. 'Peru.' In *International Handbook on Drug Control*. Westport, CT: Greenwood Press, 1992.

Wæver, Ole. 'Securitization and Desecuritization.' In *On Security*, pp. 46-86. Edited by Ronnie Lipschutz. New York: Columbia University Press, 1995.

von der Walde, Erma, and Burbano, Carmen. 'Violence in Colombia: A Timeline.' *NACLA: Report on the Americas* 35 (July/August 2001): 24-25.

Walker, R.B.J. *Inside/Outside: International Relations as Political Theory*. Cambridge: Cambridge University Press, 1993.

Walker III, William O. 'A Reprise for "Nation Building": Low Intensity Conflict Spreads in the Andes.' *NACLA Report on the Americas* 35 (July/August 2001): 23-28.

Walt, Stephen. 'International Relations: One World, Many theories.' *Foreign Policy* 110 (Spring 1998): 29-46.

Waltz, Kenneth N. 'International Politics is Not Foreign Policy.' *Security Studies* 6 (Autumn 1996): 54-57.

_____. *Man, the State and War: A Theoretical Analysis*. New York: Columbia University Press, 1959.

_____. 'Reflections on Theory of International Politics: A Response to My Critics.' In *Neorealism and Its Critics*, pp. 322-345. Edited by Robert O. Keohane. New York: Columbia University Press, 1986.

_____. 'Structural Realism After the Cold War.' *International Security* 25 (Summer 2000): 5-41.

_____. *Theory of International Politics*. New York: Random House, 1979.

Weldes, Jutta; Laffey, Mark; Gusterson, Hugh; and Duvall, Raymond. *Cultures of Insecurity: States, Communities, and the Production of Danger*. Minneapolis, MN: University of Minnesota, 1999.

Wendt, Alexander. 'The Agent-Structure Problem in International Relations Theory.' *International Organization* 41 (Summer 1987): 335-370.

_____. 'Anarchy Is What States Make Of It: The Social Construction of Power Politics.' *International Organization* 46 (Spring 1992): 391-425.

174 *Creating Insecurity*

_____. 'Collective Identity Formation and the International State.' *The American Political Science Review* 88 (June 1994): 384-396.

_____. 'Identity and Structural Change in International Politics.' In *The Return of Culture and Identity in IR Theory*, pp. 47-64. Edited by Yosef Lapid and Friedrich Kratochwil. Boulder, CO: Lynne Rienner Publishers, 1996.

_____. *Social Theory of International Relations*. Cambridge: Cambridge University Press, 1999.

Williams, Michael C. 'Identity and the Politics of Security.' *European Journal of International Relations* 4, 2 (1998): 204-225.

Winch, Peter. *The Idea of a Social Science*. London: Routledge Books, 1958.

Wirtz, James J., and Larsen, Jeffrey A. *Rockets' Red Glare: Missile Defenses and the Future of World Politics*. Boulder, CO: Westview Press, 2001.

Wittgenstein, Ludwig. *Tractatus Logico-Philosophicus*. Translated by D.G. Pears and B.F. McGuiness. London: Routledge and Kegan Paul, 1961.

Wolfers, Arnold. 'National Security as an Ambiguous Symbol.' in *Discord and Collaboration: Essays on International Politics*. Baltimore, MD: The Johns Hopkins Press, 1962.

Woodward, Bob. *Bush at War*. New York: Simon and Schuster, 2002.

Yanarella, Ernest J. *The Missile Defense Controversy: Strategy, Technology, and Politics, 1955-1972*. Lexington, KY: The University Press of Kentucky, 1977.

Youngers, Coletta. 'Cocaine Madness: Counternarcotics and Militarization in the Andes.' *NACLA Report on the Americas* 34 (November/December 2000): 16-23.

Zacher, Mark W. and Matthew, Richard A. 'Liberal International Theory: Common Threads, Divergent Strands.' In *Controversies in International Relations Theory: Realism and the Neoliberal Challenge*, pp. 107-150. Edited by Charles W. Kegley, Jr. New York: St. Martin's Press, 1995.

Zehfuss, Maja. 'Constructivism and Identity: A Dangerous Liaison.' *European Journal of International Relations* 7, 3 (2001): 315-348.

_____. 'Constructivism in International Relations: Wendt, Onuf, and Kratochwil.' In *Constructing International Relations: The Next Generation*, pp. 54-75. Edited by Karin Fierke and Knud Erik Jorgensen. Armonk, NY: M.E. Sharpe, 2001.

Index

ABM (anti-ballistic missile) 69, 72, 73, 77, 79
ABM Treaty 73-75, 77, 82, 86, 91
Abrams, E. 107, 113
African-American males 115-116, 119
aluminum tubes 140-141
American exceptionalism 87-88
anarchy 2, 6, 12-13, 15, 19-20, 23, 25-26, 34, 38, 78, 109, 126, 139, 156
Andean Drug Strategy 104
Anderson, O. 145
AUC (Self-Defense Units of Columbia) 104, 107
Axis of Evil 84, 92

balance of power 4, 12-13, 16-17, 20, 26, 40, 78-80, 87, 122, 148, 150, 159
balloon effect 102, 104
Betts, R. 79, 144-146, 154
bipolarity 78-79, 87
Blitzkrieg 6
blowback 142, 148
BMD (ballistic missile defense)
 3+3 program 76
 Aegis Destroyer 77
 Galosh ABM 72
 National Missile Defense Act 76
 NIKE-ZEUS 70-71, 73
 SAFEGUARD 73-75, 90
 SENTINEL 73, 75
Bolivia 103-104
Bush, G. W. 68, 77, 80, 85, 94, 138,140
 and BMD (ballistic missile defense) 68, 77, 80, 85, 95
 on drug policy 114
 and imperium 151, 155
 on terrorism 139, 153
 views on Hussein, S. 137, 142
Bush, G. H. W. 75, 104-105
Buzan, B. 10, 17-20, 22, 25, 38-40, 45-46, 48, 51-53

Campbell, D. 28, 31, 41, 43-45, 59, 63-65, 67, 89, 106, 160
Carr, E. H. 4, 23, 158
Castaño, C. 104
cautious paranoia 25, 49, 55, 65, 69, 77, 80-81, 108-109, 137, 142, 145, 150, 154, 156, 159
Cheney, R. 138, 140
China 17, 68, 76-77, 80-82, 84
civil liberties 116, 121
Clear and Present Danger 112
Clinton, W. 76, 105
 3+3 program 76
 and *National Missile Defense Act* 76
 Rumsfeld Commission and 76
Cold War 115, 117-118, 159-160
Colombia 8, 98-107, 111-112, 115, 117-118
 AUC (Self-Defense Units of Columbia) 104, 107
 and drugs in Andean region 98, 100-102, 105, 109,111-112, 114
 as failed state 105
 FARC (Revolutionary Armed Forces of Columbia) 101, 104, 107-108, 113
 Independent Republics in 100-101
 La Violencia and 100
 MTT (military training team) 101
 National Front 100
 Plan Colombia 105-107
 Rojas Pinilla and 100
 and U.S. military assistance 99-100, 105-106
common good 9, 110, 125-128, 131-134, 136
constructivism
 commonsense 59
 epistemological 8, 41, 48-50, 52-53, 58, 65, 67
 Miami group of 59
 neo-liberal 33, 44,45

político 8-9, 37, 39, 49-51, 53, 57, 59-69, 86-90, 92-98, 112, 116-117, 119-121, 125, 128, 131, 134, 136-138, 150-151, 153-160
post-structural 44-45, 49
and reflection 5, 29, 45-46, 49-50, 59-61, 63, 66-67, 89, 95, 117, 119, 151
containment 10, 63, 137, 139-140, 142-145, 150, 153-154
Copeland, D. 42
cultural constructs 4-5, 53, 64, 67, 89
culture 2, 3, 5-6, 29, 36-37, 41-44, 48, 50, 57, 62, 87-90, 98, 112, 114, 116, 118,157

Defense Planning Guidance 138
democracy
deliberative 9, 123-124, 127, 132-136
and democratic ethos 30, 45
and governance 125, 128, 130, 133, 136
lite 133
as oligarchy with parliamentary forms 131, 136
and popular rule 129-131, 133
procedural 120-121, 123-125, 130-136
democratic internationalism 73, 134
democratic peace 9, 120-126, 128-133, 135-136
deterrence 23, 32, 70-71, 73-75, 77-79, 81, 85, 87-88, 90-91, 93, 96, 98, 137, 139-140, 142-145, 150, 153-154
domestic/foreign 30
Donnelly, J. 23, 25, 126, 156
Doyle, M. 122, 128-129, 131
drug war 8, 67,97-98, 102, 105, 107-108, 110-114, 117, 119-120, 137, 155, 159
drugs
coca production 103-105, 107-108, 118-119
cocaine 100, 102-106, 108, 11, 115
marijuana 101-103
and narcoguerilla 113
and narcotrafficking 104, 110, 112-114, 116

Egypt 147
Eisenhower, D. 100-101
embedded liberalism 121
empiricism 3-6, 27, 54-55
epistemology
constructivist 38, 48, 53, 55-56, 66, 80, 128, 130, 157
empiricist 41, 51, 54, 109, 157
Europe 17, 49, 75, 80-81, 92, 94, 105, 125
Evil Empire 88

FARC (Revolutionary Armed Forces of Columbia) 101, 104, 107-108, 113
fear 11-12, 14, 33, 64, 75
Ferguson, Y. 26, 54, 56-57
Finnemore, M. 43, 90
foreign policy 11-12, 14-17, 21, 27-29, 49, 59, 61, 63-64, 78, 82, 87, 98-99, 121-122, 151
Fortress America 87-88

GATT 121, 124
Gilbert, A. 110, 115, 125-126, 131-132, 134
Glaser, C. 23, 25, 80-83, 85
globalization
economic 9, 120-122, 127, 134-135
from above 120, 123-124, 126-128, 133-136
from below 136
neo-liberal 151
Gulf War 63, 144, 150
Guzzini, S. 52

hegemony 7, 16-17, 61, 67, 91-92, 94, 106, 113, 122, 132, 136, 138, 142-143, 148, 153, 160
Herz, J. 4, 10, 12-16, 22-23, 25, 65, 158
Hitler, A. 24, 49
human intelligence 148
human nature 3, 23
Hussein, S. 9, 137-148, 150-151, 155

ICBM (intercontinental ballistic missile) 70-73, 75-77, 81, 83-85, 87, 90
idealism 3, 14, 24-25, 49, 55, 64
ideational sources of insecurity 61, 98, 118, 153, 156

identity 3, 5-6, 8, 28-31, 33-37, 41, 43-45, 48, 61-67, 69, 87, 89-92, 94-97, 106, 112-113, 151, 153-155, 157
identity performance 9, 28, 30, 50, 53, 57, 61-67, 86, 90, 112, 116-117, 119, 138, 153, 157, 160-161
IMF (International Monetary Fund) 121, 125
imperium 151-153
   and discourses 152-154
   normality of 152-153
   zone of stability in 152-153
insecurity dilemma 19
inside/outside 30
intermestic issues 98, 106
IR (International Relations) theory 16, 53, 57, 117
Iran 76, 84, 131, 142-144, 147
Iraq 9, 67, 84, 137-151, 153-155
   Kurds 142, 147
   liberation of 144, 150
   Shi'ite population 142-143, 147, 149
   Sunni population 147, 149
Israel 142, 144, 146-147, 160

Jackson, R. 21, 105
Jepperson, R. 35-37
Jordan 147

Kant, I. 121, 128-131
Katzenstein, P. 35-37, 45
Kellogg-Briand Pact 24
Kennan, G. 4, 23, 47

language 5-6, 8-9, 26-27, 34, 39, 42, 46, 48, 51-53, 71, 92, 107-108, 110, 112, 120
legalism 23
legitimacy 17, 39, 108, 122, 139, 148

MAD (mutually assured destruction) 71-72, 74, 78, 87, 91
manifest destiny 87
Mansbach, R. 26, 54, 56-57
material capabilities 16, 36, 38, 50, 53, 55-57, 65-67, 84, 86-87, 89, 96-97, 159
materialism 55, 64
McCaffrey, B. 107

McSweeney, B. 31-35, 41, 43-45, 63, 96, 118
MDAP (Mutual Defense Assistance Pact) 99-100
Mearsheimer, J. 22-23, 25, 58, 143-145, 150, 154
Miami Vice 112
military force 31, 36, 151, 153
Miller, S. 76, 78-79, 81-82, 84-86, 94
missiles
   de-alerting 93
   ICBM (intercontinental ballistic missile) 70-73, 75-77, 81, 83-85, 87, 90
   Nunn-Lugar initiative and 95
   al Samoud 147
   Scud 144, 147
Morgenthau, H. 4, 10-14, 16, 22-25, 74, 96, 108

national interest 10-12, 14, 87, 91-92, 94, 96, 100, 108-110, 123-124
National Missile Defense Act 76
National Security Strategy 139-140, 153
nativism 115-117, 151
NATO (North Atlantic Treaty Organization) 17, 72, 80-81, 92
neo-conservative 138, 148, 155
neoliberalism 36, 57-58
NIKE-ZEUS 70-71, 73
NMD (national missile defense) 69, 81-83, 85, 88, 96
North Korea 76, 84, 96-97
NSC-68 99

obligation 21, 25, 65, 113, 126, 136, 150
ontology 31, 41, 45, 51, 54, 97, 109, 157
Onuf, N. 51, 59

Palestinians 147, 160
Panama Canal 99
Peru 103-104
Pettman, R. 43, 59
physical capabilities 18-19
politico/strategic logic 110
positivism 41, 43-44, 48, 53-54, 56, 59, 128-129, 157
power
   of aggression 15, 25
   functional limitation of 109, 117

178 *Creating Insecurity*

of resistance 15, 25
pre-emption 137, 139-140, 142

quasi-war 109

racism 117, 119
Reagan, R. 75, 79, 88, 91, 94, 102, 105, 107, 113, 122, 143
realism
   as general theory 4, 7, 10, 16, 25, 46, 54, 56, 65,
   neorealism 16, 33-34, 36-38, 43, 45, 51, 54
   new 85, 94
   sophisticated 95, 111, 119-121, 125-127, 135-136
   structural 17, 128
realist liberalism 13-14, 64
reasonably decent polities 2, 7
regime change 9, 67, 92, 137, 140, 142, 145-146, 151, 154
rhetorical devices 5, 7, 10, 25, 46, 49-50, 54, 65, 119, 156
Rumsfeld, D. 143
   Rumsfeld Commission 76, 84
Rupert, M. 122, 131-132, 135-136
Russia 17, 68, 76-77, 80-82, 84, 93, 95, 141

SAFEGUARD 73-76, 90
Schumpeter-Dahl Axis 129
scientific theory 15, 54
SDI (Strategic Defense Initiative) 74-75, 79, 88, 91
Seattle 123, 125
securitization 38-40, 46, 48-49, 51, 52-53, 56, 114, 142, 151, 155, 157, 161
security
   democratic 120-121, 123, 130, 134, 136-137
   economic 123, 127
   as essentially contested concept 157
   human 1-2, 32, 36
   individual 1, 5-6, 20, 66
   international 3, 9, 19, 38, 50, 121
   Janus-faced notion of 156, 161
   ontological 32, 66, 118, 160
   as referent 1, 11, 13, 19-20, 31, 38, 60

security dilemma 12-15, 19, 23, 39-40, 64, 66, 77, 157
Security Studies 2-4, 7-8, 10, 26, 126, 157-158
   and schism 3, 6, 158
self-help 16, 25, 66, 93
SENTINEL 73, 75, 76
Smith, S. 58
social science 29, 33, 41, 44, 52, 59
SOUTHCOM 107, 113
speech-acts 7, 29, 42, 46, 48-49, 51-52, 56, 60, 158
Stalin, J. 24, 146
Star Wars 74-75
survival 13-14, 16, 25, 33, 118, 139, 145
Syria 142, 146-147, 159

terrorism 65-67, 92, 107-108, 137-138, 148-149
   11 September 2001 1, 6, 21, 61, 65-66, 108, 137-138, 148, 151-153, 155
   al Qaeda 139, 141, 146, 149, 153
   terrorists 55, 61-62, 67, 108, 139-140, 142, 146, 148-149
Traffic 112
Turkey 142, 147-148

unipolar system 16, 75, 80
UNSCOM (U.N. Special Commission) 144
uranium and Niger 140, 149

V-2 rocket 70
Venezuela 100, 159
vulnerability 18, 38, 72, 83

Wendt, A. 20, 35-37, 43-44
West Point 139, 153
Wittgenstein, L. 5, 27, 42
WMD (weapons of mass destruction) 9, 85, 95, 137, 139-142, 145-147, 154
Wolfers, A. 10, 14-17, 19, 22-23, 25, 64-65, 67, 158
Wolfowitz, P. 78, 138-139
World Bank 121, 125
WTO (World Trade Organization) 123-125

Zeitgeist 25, 56